Illuminated Books of the Middle Ages and Renaissance

cum uenerit inclari
patris sui cum ange
lis scis;
Et dicebat illis Amen
dico uobis quia sunt
quidam hic stantib;
qui non gustabunt
morte donec uide
ant regnum di ueni
ens inuirtute Et
post dies sex assumit
ihs petru et iacobum
et iohanne et ducit
illos in monte ex
celsum seorsu solus
et transfiguratus
est coram ipsis Et
uestimenta eius fac
ta sunt splendentia
candida nimis uelut
nix qualia fullo super
terram non potest
candida facere Et
apparuit illis helias cu
moyse et erant loquen
tes cum ihu Et respon
dens petrus ait ihu
Rabi bonum est nos
hic esse Et faciamus
tria tabernacula

tibi unu et moysi unu
et heliae unu Non eni
sciebat quid diceret
Erant enim timore ex
territi Et facta est
nubes obumbrans eos
et uenit uox de nube
dicens hic est filius
meus carissimus au
dite illum Et statim
circumspicientes ne
minem amplius uide
runt nisi ihm tantu
secum Et descenden
tib; illis de monte
praecepit illis ne cui
quae uidissent nar
rarent nisi cum fili
us hominis a mortuis
resurrexerit;
Et uerbum continue
runt apud se conqui
rentes quid esset
cum a mortuis re
surrexerit;
Et interrogabant eu
dicentes Quid ergo
dicunt pharisaei et
scribae quia heliam
oporteat uenire

THE WALTERS ART GALLERY

ILLUMINATED BOOKS
OF THE
MIDDLE AGES *and* RENAISSANCE

AN EXHIBITION HELD AT

THE BALTIMORE MUSEUM OF ART

January 27 - March 13

Organized by

THE WALTERS ART GALLERY

In cooperation with

THE BALTIMORE MUSEUM OF ART

Baltimore, 1949

Published by the Trustees of the Walters Art Gallery

COPYRIGHT 1949
BY
THE WALTERS ART GALLERY
BALTIMORE
MARYLAND

PRINTED BY
THE JOHN D. LUCAS PRINTING COMPANY
BALTIMORE, MARYLAND

LIST OF LENDERS

Art Institute of Chicago
Boston Public Library
Cleveland Museum of Art
Heinrich Eisemann, London
Mrs. William Emerson, Cambridge, Mass.
Fogg Art Museum, Harvard University
Howard L. Goodhart, New York City
Mr. and Mrs. Nelson Gutman, Baltimore
Harvard College Library
Mr. and Mrs. Philip Hofer, Rockport, Maine
H. P. Kraus, New York City
Robert Lehman, New York City
Library of Congress
National Gallery of Art
New York Public Library
Free Library of Philadelphia
Philadelphia Museum of Art
Pierpont Morgan Library
Princeton University Library
William K. Richardson, Boston
Carleton R. Richmond, Milton, Mass.
C. L. Ricketts Scriptorium, Chicago
The Rosenbach Company, New York City
Lessing J. Rosenwald, Jenkintown, Pa.
Trinity College, Hartford
Dimitri Tselos, New York City
Walters Art Gallery
Wellesley College Library
Yale University Library

ILLUMINATED BOOKS OF THE MIDDLE AGES AND RENAISSANCE

ADDENDA AND CORRIGENDA TO THE CATALOGUE

p. xi. paragraph 2 line 8: for "monagrammized", read "monogrammized".

2a, p. 2   Title should read: LEAF FROM A GRADUAL.
The leaf is the relic of a book similar to the famous purple Gradual in the Cathedral Treasury at Monza (cf. Dom R. J. Herbert, ed., *Antiphonale Missarum Sextuplex*, Brussels, 1935, pp. 18, 20, 22, 64, 66, 68).

4, p. 3   line 3 of Bibliography: for "1928" read "1938".

18, p. 9   line 8 of main text: for "1250" read "1150".

21, p. 10   line 5 of main text: for "Mejeanes" read "Méjanes".

25, p. 12   This Psalter includes a commentary on the Psalms.

29, p. 13   This manuscript is the basis of an edition, now in press, of Pseudo-Philo's *Liber antiquitatum biblicarum*, prepared by Prof. Guido Kisch, which will form vol. X of the *Publications in Medieval Studies* of the University of Notre Dame.

33, p. 15   last line of main text should read: "although certain elements relate this leaf to the Franconian style, particularly to that of the school associated with Würzburg."

41, p. 18   line 1 of main text: for "third quarter", read "second quarter".

57, p. 23   for "Lavagnia" read "Lavagna".

60, p. 24   line 2 of main text: for "Seigns" read "Seans".

62, p. 25   line 3 of Bibliography: for "p. 235" read "p. 23".

68, p. 27   line 2 of main text: for "no. 127" read "no. 66".

80, p. 31   for Pl. XXXV read Pl. XXXVI, where 88 should be numbered 80.

88, p. 33   Title line, for "ca. 1420-25" read "1415-20".
line 2 of main text: read "and for the duc de Berry".
Pl. XXXVI should read Pl. XXXV, where 80 should be numbered 88.

163, p. 60   title line read: Italy (Siena), ca. 1345.

164, p. 60   line 3 of main text: St. Alle is an Italianization of St. Eloi, the French form of St. Eligius, the patron saint of goldsmiths.

189, p. 69   last line of main text: for "Eudoxios" read "Eudoxos".

228, p. 83   last line of main text: omit "Duke of Bavaria".

Pl. XXXII nos. 67 and 68 should be interchanged.

FOREWORD

IT WAS NOT realized how great were the accumulations of medieval and renaissance manuscripts in this country until 1935, when the late Seymour De Ricci and his colleague, W. J. Wilson, published the first of the two massive volumes of the *Census of Medieval and Renaissance Manuscripts in the United States and Canada*—soon supplemented by an Index volume. The usefulness of this great achievement, even with the limitations and imperfections which are inevitable in such an undertaking, is too well known to scholars in the field to require comment. The 15,000 or so items listed by this work in the collections of nearly 500 American libraries demonstrate the unsuspected proportions of the migration of manuscript material to this country, almost entirely the result of the activities of American private collectors of the nineteenth and twentieth centuries.

For those concerned with the illuminated book—the historians of art—only a relatively small proportion of this vast accumulation of texts is pertinent. The necessary limitations of the *Census* prevented any more specific guide to the artistic interest of the books than a mere mention of the number of miniatures. Therefore, even with the *Census* as an aid, the general scope of our national resources in fine illuminated manuscripts is not too well known, except to a very small handful of the most adventurous scholars.

The outstanding exception to this generalization is, of course, the Pierpont Morgan Library, whose preeminence among all American collections in this field will probably always remain unchallenged. Its resources are well known to specialists and are available for research under conditions more nearly ideal than in any library in the world. The general public of New York has also had ample opportunity to enjoy these illuminated manuscripts through the distinguished series of exhibitions of the last fifteen years, commencing with the unforgettable display of the chief Morgan treasures at the New York Public Library in 1933-34. For the casual visitor, the New York Public Library itself regularly keeps a selection of its own distinguished Spencer Collection on exhibit. But in most regions outside New York the opportunities for the general public to see fine examples of medieval illumination are very few indeed.

Until recently, no serious efforts were made to represent medieval illumination in American art museums, so that it might appear in its rightful and important position in relation to the history of art. Henry Walters was a pioneer when he developed a collection of nearly 800 illuminated manuscripts as an integral part of the art gallery that he bequeathed to the City of Baltimore. The Cleveland Museum of Art during the past twenty years has been forming a collection, largely of single miniatures, selected with admirable discrimination as a complement to its painting collection. Most recently the National Gallery of Art, through Lessing J. Rosenwald's generosity, has commenced to build up a group of miniatures with a similar intention. Toledo Museum for long has paid tribute to the arts of calligraphy and book-making with a collection of single leaves. Lately certain other art museums, such as those of Boston, Philadelphia and Chicago, for example, have been enabled to add a few specimens of illumination or, occasionally, actual illuminated volumes to their exhibitions. But in general, the American public is unaware of this important and particularly delightful aspect of our artistic heritage, hidden carefully as it is in the treasure rooms of research libraries or in private collections.

It was primarily with a view to widening the public experience in this field that the present exhibition was undertaken. In the course of organizing the event, however, it soon became clear that the display would provide an unprecedented opportunity for specialists as well. No comprehensive loan exhibition of the best available examples of illuminated manuscripts has ever been undertaken before in this country. With the exception of the Pierpont Morgan Library, which for long has made exceedingly generous loans to important exhibitions in various fields, nearly every institution contacted had never loaned manuscripts before. A very few—Henry E. Huntington Library and John Carter Brown Library, for example—are actually prevented by their charters from lending, and so are unrepresented here. But, in a general way, it may be considered that this exhibition presents for the first time a survey of the best achievements of American collecting in this field during the past two hundred years. The Pierpont Morgan Library can, of course, be said to be represented only by a token of its riches, despite the fact that it has sent twenty of its greatest manuscripts in a loan probably unprecedented in generosity, even for this institution.

From the point of view of the history of American collecting, the earliest manuscript in the show is the unpretentious but suitably edifying gothic *Speculum Humanae Salvationis* (no. 139) which Elihu Yale in 1714 gave to the infant college later named after him. As far as can be determined now, this is the first illuminated manuscript to enter an American library. The first illuminated manuscript to become part of a Baltimore collection appears to be a little fifteenth-century Book of Hours of the "Boucicault" atelier that one of our earliest American art collectors, Robert Gilmor II, bought in Charleston in 1807, and which is now in the Library of Congress (no. 92). The acquisition of fine manuscripts of the earlier Middle Ages started in this country with a rush of enthusiasm in the last decade or so of the nineteenth century, when the great age of American book collecting got under way. The honor of being the first really important early medieval manuscript to lead all the others to these shores probably belongs to Ms. 1 in the Manuscript Division of the New York Public Library, which was purchased by John Jacob Astor in 1884 (no. 9).

For the rest, specialists who visit the exhibition will see many familiar masterpieces, and some others completely new to them, either because of having been relatively inaccessible or because they are recent acquisitions. For, while American collecting is no longer as lavish as in the first three decades of the century, it is still active. Many manuscripts in this show do not figure in the De Ricci *Census*. As this is written, an announcement is being distributed of the Supplement to the *Census*, which is even now in preparation.

A word of explanation is in order concerning the field of the exhibition. Oriental manuscripts are not included, since they are best understood separately. Byzantine and Armenian manuscripts have been omitted because all the distinguished ones available were brought together in Baltimore only two years ago, as a part of the Exhibition of Early Christian and Byzantine Art.

Exhibition catalogues always must be prepared under difficulties and pressures understood only by those who have attempted such tasks—and this one is no exception. Familiarity with the actual manuscripts, and access to them, extent and dependability of information, even availability of photographs varied greatly in respect to the various items. Mindful of the insufficiency of De Ricci in regard to artistic analysis, an effort has been made to describe to some extent the nature and quality of the illuminations, for these books are being presented primarily as works of art. In desiring to make this something more informative than a mere check-list, we have by the same motion laid ourselves open to the inadequacies and errors that attend such an attempt, when undertaken in advance of the exhibit. However, we hope that the catalogue will serve a useful purpose even after the close of the exhibition, and that its very deficiencies will serve to point up the unstudied problems that await the leisurely scholar.

Such an exhibition as this is composed as much of the efforts of people who made it possible as it is of the objects displayed. First expression of obligation must be to the Trustees of the Walters Art Gallery and the Trustees of the Baltimore Museum of Art, for their support of this cooperative undertaking of the two art museums of Baltimore. To Adelyn D. Breeskin, Director of the Baltimore Museum of Art, and to Edward S. King, Administrator of the Walters Art Gallery, I am indebted for unfailing help, advice, patience and sympathy of every kind. The work on the show has involved the labor of the staff of both institutions in innumerable ways, from the curators to the carpenter shops. My greatest thanks must go to Dr. Gertrude Rosenthal, general Curator of the Baltimore Museum, for her invaluable and loyal assistance, without which this catalogue would have been impossible. Also to Margaret Powell and Mabel Kaji of the same museum who created the installations, to Winifred Kennedy, Registrar of the Walters Art Gallery and Jean C. Bodenstein of the Baltimore Museum of Art, for shouldering the tremendous mass of details attendant upon registration, insurance and similar vital administrative matters, to Marvin C. Ross, Curator of Medieval and Renaissance Decorative Arts, and to John C. Kirby, Assistant to the Administrator of the Walters Art Gallery, for invaluable help with arrangements; to Lynn D. Poole, Director of Public Relations of the Johns Hopkins University, and James W. Foster, Jr., Executive Assistant of the Baltimore Museum of Art, for the exacting task of handling the publicity; and last, but far from least, to my own indefatigable assistants, Mrs. Thomas Butterbaugh and Mrs. Richard Mottu.

To the lenders we are all under the greatest debt, and to the several Boards and Committees of the institutions, which made possible the loans. The names of these lenders are listed elsewhere in this catalogue and I cannot single one out above another—except perhaps to call attention to those who contributed the largest groups of material, aside from the Walters Art Gallery, and whose generosity and interest in the undertaking are the very fabric which made the exhibition feasible: the Pierpont Morgan Library, the New York Public Library and Princeton University, among the institutions, and among the private collectors, Mr. and Mrs. Philip Hofer. To the last named I am deeply indebted for the most generous help and friendly encouragement possible, and for a personal activity on behalf of the exhibition without which a number of the most important private loans would not have been available to me. To Karl Kup of the Spencer Collection and Robert Hill of the Manuscript Division of the New York Public Library I owe gratitude for friendliness, help and much expenditure of time, as well as to Dr. Paul North Rice, Chief of the Reference Department of the same great institution. Unquestionably my greatest debt, and that of the visitor to the exhibition, must be to Belle da Costa Greene, who made the consummation of the loan of the Morgan manuscripts a chief concern during the final months before her recent retirement from the Directorship of the Pierpont Morgan Library, and who is, in fact, responsible for the actual presence in this country of all but three of the magnificent Morgan manuscripts displayed.

The assembling of the exhibition laid great burdens on the librarians and curators of the several institutions, all of whom should be listed by name. I can only signal here those for whom I realize the task was particularly demanding: Director Frederick B. Adams, Jr., and Miss Meta Harrsen of the Pierpont Morgan Library, Miss Elizabeth Mongan, Curator of Prints of the National Gallery of Art, Dr. William Jackson, Librarian of the Houghton Library of Harvard, Dr. Jakob Rosenberg of the Fogg Museum of Art, Dr. Zoltan Haraszti, Keeper of Rare Books of the Boston Public Library, Dr. Julian Boyd, Librarian of Princeton University, and Mrs. Marvin Dixon, Miss Julie Hudson and Miss Frances Jones, all of Princeton, Dr. Luther Evans, Librarian of Congress, and Mr. Frederick Goff, Chief of the Rare Book Division of that library, Dr. Frederick H. Price, Librarian, and Dr. John Powell, Assistant Librarian, both of the Philadelphia Free Library, Mr. Carl Zigrosser, Curator of Prints of the Philadelphia Museum of Art, Mr. William Milliken, Director, and Miss Helen Foote, Assistant Curator of

Decorative Arts, of the Cleveland Museum of Art, Dr. Oswald Goetz of the Chicago Art Institute, Miss Hannah D. French, Research Librarian of Wellesley College, Professor George Heard Hamilton of Yale, Dr. James T. Babb, Librarian, and Miss Marjorie Wynne, Librarian of the Rare Book Room at Yale.

I cannot conclude this list of those to whom I am indebted without expressing my appreciation of Mr. Benjamin Meeks, Jr. and The John D. Lucas Printing Company and also of the Publicity Engravers Inc., whose wholehearted cooperation made it possible to produce this catalogue under exceptional handicaps of time.

The reproductions are published by courtesy of the respective owners. The photographs of the Walters manuscripts, as well as of certain others, were made by Sherley B. Hobbs, Photographer of the Walters Art Gallery. The color-plate used as frontispiece has been generously loaned by the Pierpont Morgan Library.

DOROTHY MINER

NOTE: S. De Ricci and W. J. Wilson, *Census of Medieval and Renaissance Manuscripts in the United States and Canada*, New York, 1935-1940, 3 vols., is referred to throughout the Catalogue as 'De Ricci'.

NOTE TO THE GENERAL VISITOR

Generally speaking, books do not lend themselves ideally to public exhibition, for their mission is a personal one. They are designed by their very nature and physical construction to address the reader privately and as his mood dictates. Even in this present day of mechanical production and vast editions and of large public libraries, this is still the great charm, the unfailing solace, the real power of the book. It is for this reason, too, that the possession of fine books, the collection of rare volumes, is by far the most absorbing and the most passionate of all forms of collecting. The delight of the book collector in his treasures, his shameless boasting as he shows them to his colleagues, his unending personal joy, not only in poring over text and picture, but just in turning the pages, stroking the bindings, weighing the volumes in his hand—these obsessions have been extolled or ridiculed—as the case may be—ever since the days of Seneca and Lucian.

This exhibition is an attempt to share with the general public some of the rarest delights that have ever come to book-lovers. It is true that for such a display a few of the pleasures must be sacrificed. Even books that have been in daily use for a thousand years would deteriorate rapidly under the appreciative but uninformed thumbing of a crowd. So the visitor must be content to imagine the soft touch of the vellum, ranging from velvety suede to silken smoothness. He must imagine the endless diversity as the leaves are turned: in the earliest manuscripts, the succession of majestic pages of superb script lit here and there with gold—or sometimes even written entirely in the burnished metal, the great ornamental pages which initiate the text with monagrammized words of the most inconceivable intricacy and ingenuity, the illustrations monumental enough in concept to be the designs for frescos. In the gothic manuscripts he would find an intricacy of another kind. In addition to the gracious illustration of the main story, he would discover a thousand whimsical diversions, unconnected with the text, and addressed to himself alone—fantastic line-endings, monsters and grotesques, humorous figures playing in the margins, a world-full of incidents: children at their games, women at their work, nobles at their pleasures. So abundant would be the decorations that they could not be seen all at once. Each day when the book was handled some new surprise would be discovered—and there would be enough to last for years—a lifetime of refreshing pleasure in a single book. The renaissance volumes he would find more sober. As he turned the pages they would present to his eye the clarity and balance and serenity which befitted the book-room of an intellectual. In these days libraries were bigger and books easier to come by than in the Middle Ages. Each volume was expected to yield its pleasures only sporadically. And so, despite the individual beauty of their vellum and illumination and calligraphy, the general nature of these renaissance books is closer to the character of fine books of today.

Thus, with the help of his imagination, the visitor will realize that the pages displayed are but a pause in the fluttering of storied leaves. He will remember that these same leaves have been turned by generation after generation of book collectors, of ladies at their diversion, of scholars at their studies, of monks at their devotions. And before anyone of these touched hand to the pages, they were spread out as flat sheets of softly dressed vellum on the work tables of the monastery atelier, or, for the later ones, in the studio of some duly enrolled members of the Guild of St. Luke, patron of artists. And there the painstaking labor upon the book began: the careful ruling off of the leaves to guide the writing and to preserve a regular format throughout; the copying out of the text in a fine, even hand, by men who spent their lives forming fair letters; the insertion of the rubrics and the ornamental initial letters; the sketching in rough outline of the pictures, usually adapted from those of older books—honored for the authority bestowed by age—or else from the series of model-pictures in use in the studio. The chief painter and his assistants might well work together on the project, especially in the larger studios— this was true both in the monasteries and in the later gothic guild ateliers. The work was well systematized. The outlines of the drawing would be clarified, the gold leaf laid and burnished carefully, the flat ground-colors painted in. And then would come the final important task of building up the form, defining the crisp patterns and lines of the stylized early works or, in the case of the products of the later gothic times and of the renaissance, developing the modelling and perfecting the delicate surface finish. And then the book was ready to be gathered and sewed by the binder, and encased in stout wood boards to protect it from injury, and covered with leather or textile or even gold and silver (if the books were for altar use); and these all had to be worked with designs.

So all of this should suggest to those who look at this exhibition that the personal quality that makes all books dear, even the cheapest reprints—the personal privacy of the reading and owning of even such a book—is multiplied a thousand times in these handsome handwrought books of the past. From the day when some monk started to polish the surface of the calf skin a thousand years ago, to make a soft white surface for the scribe, every element of these volumes represents personal care and earnest labor and art, a still living portion of the minds and hearts of folk long dead. We do not know their names, generally—occasionally we do. Their motives were variations of a single aim: to create a fine and beautiful thing that would give lasting pleasure. The earlier books were done to please God, to embellish the altar table with their glowing gold and purple. The gothic books, as often as not, were done to please a lady; and the finest products of the fifteenth and sixteenth centuries were created to please the bibliophiles. So the laymen coming to see these books need be prepared with no more learning nor serious purpose than this—to be ready to share a delight with a host of others of today and of a thousand years ago, since it was for this that these superbly illuminated books were created.

Of course, there are many other facets to their interest, too, and one may concentrate on these according to his information and inclination. These books reflect the channels through which the thought and learning of ancient times have reached our own. They reflect the changing emphasis and preoccupations of life during succeeding eras, from the chaotic Europe of Charlemagne's day to the sixteenth century, when our own more immediate tastes and institutions were in the process of formation. One will find enshrined in the luxurious presentation reserved for things of value, not only some texts now unfamiliar and disused, but the Bible, the Magna Charta, Caesar, Cicero, Vergil, Chaucer and others which are still giants in our heritage. One will find the small, quaint beginnings of science, a field whose development has been the major accomplishment of modern times. But all these elements of interest would be present, often more diversely, in manuscripts undistinguished for their beauty—the work-a-day books of past students. The luxurious, richly embellished volumes exhibited here, have another and particular value for our times. They preserve for us the history of painting for a thousand years after the fall of the Roman Empire. If it were not for the finely executed illustrations in these books, painted by the best artistic skill of their day, we would know very little indeed of the development of painting north of the Alps before the advent of the Renaissance. The painted altarpieces of wood and the frescoed walls have disintegrated or fallen prey to violent destruction. Mere scattered fragments remain. It is only through the generally excellent preservation of the book illustrations that we can reconstruct the story of how European painting developed: its evolution out of the fusion of the ancient classical tradition with the dynamic decorative arts of the indigenous cultures, such as that of the Celts, and of the migratory cultures of the sixth and seventh centuries.

D. M.

ILLUMINATED BOOKS

CATALOGUE

1. PSALTER   Southern England (Canterbury ?), 8th cent.

    M. 776. In Latin with Anglo-Saxon and Latin glosses. Insular majuscule script with half-uncial characteristics. 88 vellum leaves, 12 x 9 inches. Ornamental initials to each Psalm; ornamental first line to four of the Psalms. Binding: 18th century calf. Ex-colls.: City of Lincoln (16th-17th century); Sir Richard Ellys of Nocton, Lincolnshire; Marquess of Lothian, Blickling Hall, Norfolk (Sale, New York, Jan. 27, 1932, no. 1).

Written about the middle of the eighth century in a fine, even, insular script, with characteristic initial ornament of lacertine and interlace motives. The rich black of the ornamented letters is relieved by outlines of red dots and particolored fillings of lavender, orange and green, with a few touches of powder-gold.

The text is that of Jerome's earlier version, known as the Roman Psalter, with some Gallican readings. Only two other eighth-century examples survive. A particularly interesting feature of the present example is the insertion of occasional Anglo-Saxon glosses.

    BIBLIOGRAPHY: R. Morris, ed., *The Blickling Homilies of the Tenth Century,* Early English Text Society, pt. II, 1876, vol. 63, pp. 251-263 (for the Anglo-Saxon glosses of the Blickling Psalter); New Palaeographical Society, London, Series I, London, 1903, pls. 231-2; E. H. Zimmermann, *Vorkarolingische Miniaturen,* Berlin, 1916, *Text,* p. 120; p. 273; vol. III, pl. 251; The Pierpont Morgan Library, *Review of the Activities and Acquisitions . . . 1930 through 1935,* New York, 1937, pp. 15-16, 92; idem, *The Bible,* New York, 1947, no. 12, pl. III.

LENT BY THE PIERPONT MORGAN LIBRARY.   PL. I

2. THE FOUR GOSPELS   North France, early 9th cent.

    M. 23. In Latin. Gold uncial script in double columns. 144 vellum leaves, 14½ x 10½ inches. Binding: English 18th century red morocco. Ex-colls.: King Henry VIII of England, ca. 1528; Bibliotheca Palmeriana, Chelsea (1747); Duke of Hamilton, ms. 167; Hamilton Palace Library, no. 251 (Sale, London, 1889, no. 1); Theodore Irwin, Oswego, New York.

This codex, written throughout in burnished gold uncial letters upon leaves dyed purple, relies for its splendor solely upon the sumptuousness of its materials and the magnificence of its script and ample format. The pages range in shade from royal purple to tones of blue and of rose-lavender, the opposing pages always being carefully matched in color.

The manuscript has been attributed to various regions of origin, but recent scholarship inclines to locate it in the north of France, and early in the ninth century.

    BIBLIOGRAPHY: Belle da Costa Greene and Meta P. Harrsen, *Exhibition of Illuminated Manuscripts . . . ,* New York, 1934, no. 4; De Ricci, II, p. 1369, no. 23, both listing the extensive previous literature; The Pierpont Morgan Library, *Illustrated Catalogue of an Exhibition held on the Occasion of the New York World's Fair,* New York, 1940, no. 1; idem, *The Bible,* New York, 1947, no. 17, colored plate.

LENT BY THE PIERPONT MORGAN LIBRARY.   FRONTISPIECE

2a. LEAF FROM A LECTIONARY OF THE GOSPELS
Germany, 9th cent.

In Latin. Gold uncials and silver rustic capitals, in 2 cols. Single vellum leaf, 11¼ x 7⅝ inches. Formerly in Trier: Chapter Library.

A fragment of a luxurious manuscript similar to no. 2 of this catalogue. It was preserved together with another leaf from the same lectionary, now in Berlin, as a cover lining of a twelfth-century manuscript in the Chapter Library at Trier (ms. 142).

BIBLIOGRAPHY: G. Swarzenski in *Städel-Jahrbuch*, VII-VIII (1932), p. 278; William M. Milliken in *Bulletin of the Cleveland Museum of Art*, XXI (1934), p. 37.

LENT BY THE CLEVELAND MUSEUM OF ART.

3. THE FOUR GOSPELS
France (Tours), 9th cent.

M. 191. In Latin. Caroline minuscule script. 238 vellum leaves, 11 x 7⅝ inches. Ornamented Canon Tables and illuminated headbands. Binding: English 19th century maroon morocco. Ex-colls.: Bernhardus de Gutonibus (ca. 1400); Earl of Ashburnham (Appendix, no. 10); H. Yates Thompson (Sale, London, May 14, 1902, no. 14).

Begun in the monastery of St. Martin at Tours, shortly after the death of Abbot Alcuin (804) and completed during the incumbency of Abbot Fridugisus (807-34), when the ornamental Canon Tables are believed to have been executed. The text is the revised version established at St. Martin's, and generally attributed to the activity there of the great English scholar, Alcuin of York, who became Abbot in 796. He is credited also with furnishing the stimulus which made Tours the most important intellectual and artistic center of the first half of the ninth century.

BIBLIOGRAPHY: E. K. Rand, *A Survey of the Manuscripts of Tours*, Cambridge, Mass., 1929, I, pp. 110-111, no. 35, pls. XLVIII-XLIX; W. Köhler, *Die Karolingischen Miniaturen*, I, *Die Schule von Tours*, Berlin, 1930, pl. 30, pp. 94, 161-162, 379, note 1; Belle da Costa Greene and Meta P. Harrsen, *Exhibition of Illuminated Manuscripts . . .*, New York, 1934, no. 5, fig. 2; De Ricci, II, p. 1402, no. 191, with previous literature; The Pierpont Morgan Library, *The Bible*, New York, 1947, no. 14.

LENT BY THE PIERPONT MORGAN LIBRARY.

4. THE FOUR GOSPELS
France (Reims), 9th cent.

M. 728. In Latin. Gold minuscule script. 188 vellum leaves, 12½ x 10 inches. 4 full-page miniatures; 4 ornamental introductory pages; ornamented Canon Tables. Binding: 18th century French red morocco with arms of Abbey of St. Remi. Ex-colls.: Abbey of St. Remi, Reims; J. L. Bourdillon (cat. 1830, pp. 2-3, no. 4); Robert S. Holford; Sir George Holford.

This manuscript, certainly the most monumental example of Carolingian painting in this country, was executed in the diocese of Reims during the period of Archbishop Hincmar (845-882). The four Evangelist portraits are based closely on late classical models, but the modelling in light and shade, which merely gives solidity to ancient painting, is here handled in a tensely dynamic manner. The paint is built up thickly, with sharp contrasts of light and shade, and the colors are sultry rather than gay. The Canon Tables are ornamented with a more fluid and impressionistic version of this characteristic Reims style, the vivacious poses and rapid technique giving great liveliness to the classical satyrs and other creatures that clamber over the pediments and columns. The ornamental introductory pages show large golden strapwork initials and archaic capitals, mostly on backgrounds of purple. Silver also is used in the ornament. The entire text of the Gospels is finely written in minuscules of burnished gold.

BIBLIOGRAPHY: Burlington Fine Arts Club, *Exhibition of Illuminated Manuscripts*, London, 1908, pp. 6-7, no. 13, pl. 19; F. M. Carey, *The Scriptorium of Reims in Classical and Medieval Studies in Honor of E. K. Rand*, New York [1928], p. 57, pl. 1; The Pierpont Morgan Library, *Review of the Growth, Development . . . 1924-1929*, New York, 1930, pp. 16-17, pls. I-II; Belle da Costa Greene and Meta P. Harrsen, *Exhibition of Illuminated Manuscripts* . . ., New York, 1934, no. 6, fig. 1, pl. 3; De Ricci, II, pp. 1489-90, no. 728, with other literature; Worcester Art Museum, *The Dark Ages*, Worcester, 1937, no. 27, ill.; The Pierpont Morgan Library, *Illustrated Catalogue of an Exhibition held on the Occasion of the New York World's Fair*, New York, 1940, no. 2; idem, *The Bible*, New York, 1947, no. 15.

LENT BY THE PIERPONT MORGAN LIBRARY. PL. III

5. THE FOUR GOSPELS Northeast France, 9th cent.

M. 640. In Latin. Caroline minuscule script. 195 vellum leaves, 9⅛ x 7⅞ inches. 2 full-page miniatures and 4 ornamented initial pages. Binding: 15th century leather over boards. Ex-colls.: Earl of Ashburnham (Appendix, no. 11); H. Yates Thompson (Sale, London, 1919, no. 24).

This book was executed in the second half of the ninth century in an atelier strongly influenced by the artists of Reims. Its miniatures are so close in style to those of the Loisel Gospels, in the Bibliothèque Nationale, Paris, as to suggest that they may be the work of the same artist. The Loisel Gospels have liturgical indications pointing to Beauvais.

The spirited Evangelist portraits, only two of which have been completed, are drawn with brown outline, with washes of light brown brushed in to intensify the modelling. Dull gold picks out the halo, footstool, lectern, etc. The transition to a linear technique, as seen here, was a natural development of the dynamic style represented by the Reims Gospels (no. 4).

BIBLIOGRAPHY: Belle da Costa Greene and Meta P. Harrsen, *Exhibition of Illuminated Manuscripts* . . ., New York, 1934, p. vii, p. 5, no. 9, p. 73, pl. 8; De Ricci, II, p. 1476, no. 640, with other literature; The Pierpont Morgan Library, *The Bible*, New York, 1947, no. 16.

LENT BY THE PIERPONT MORGAN LIBRARY. PL. II.

6. THE FOUR GOSPELS Northeast France, early 10th cent.

W. 4. In Latin. Minuscule script. 215 vellum leaves, 7 x 4¾ inches. 4 miniatures; ornamented Canon Tables. Binding: modern violet velvet.

Executed about 900 A.D. in the region of the Meuse, in a center much influenced by the script and painting style of Reims. No gold is used in the manuscript. The Evangelist portraits retain in their composition, coloring and other details a strong reflection of late antique prototypes, but the modelling of these has been translated into whirling lines of emotional expression.

BIBLIOGRAPHY: Walters Art Gallery, *Handbook of the Collection*, Baltimore, 1936, p. 96, ill.; De Ricci, I, p. 767, no. 62.

COLLECTION OF THE WALTERS ART GALLERY. PL. II

7. THE FOUR GOSPELS   Northern France, late 10th cent.

    W. 3. In Latin. Caroline minuscules. 148 vellum leaves, 12¼ x 7 inches. 1 drawing; 4 ornamented initial pages; 12 ornamented Canon Tables. Binding: Italian 18th century morocco.

The ornament of this manuscript, which was produced in a provincial atelier in the north of France, betrays influences from several of the great Carolingian schools, particularly that of Tours. Like most of the provincial works of the period, it depends upon a few colors: orange, yellow ochre, lavender, light green, and a dull blue. An unusual feature of this book is the employment of the Signs of the Zodiac as subjects for the tympani of the twelve arches of the Canon Tables.

COLLECTION OF THE WALTERS ART GALLERY.   PL. IV

8. THE FOUR GOSPELS   Germany (Westphalia), 10th cent.

    M. 755. In Latin. Minuscule script in double columns. 201 vellum leaves, 13¾ x 10 inches. 16 decorated Canon Tables; 17 ornamented introductory pages to the Gospels. Binding: 16th century German pigskin over boards. Ex-colls.: Friederich Boyesen of Quedlinburg (1763); Count Christian Ernst zu Stolberg-Wernigerode (1691-1771); the Princely Library at Wernigerode near Quedlinburg until 1929.

The best known example of a small group of luxurious manuscripts executed somewhere in the general region of the Weser River in northern Germany, and sometimes attributed more precisely to the monastery of Corvey. A distinguishing characteristic of the group is the use of rich introductory pages with purple backgrounds delicately shaded or boldly patterned with foliage, birds and animals, suggestive of Byzantine textile designs. With these are combined exceptionally complex initials or even whole words in monogrammized form, the elements of the ornament showing the influence of the earlier Corbie and Franco-Saxon styles.

    BIBLIOGRAPHY: A. Haseloff in *Meisterwerke der Kunst aus Sachsen und Thüringen* (ed. by Doering and Voss), Magdeburg, 1905, pp. 89-90, pls. 102-104; The Pierpont Morgan Library, *Review of the Growth, Development and Activities . . . 1924-1929*, New York, 1930, pp. 16 ff.; Belle da Costa Greene and Meta P. Harrsen, *Exhibition of Illuminated Manuscripts . . .*, New York, 1934, p. 6, no. 11, pl. 10; De Ricci, II, pp. 1496 f., no. 755; the last two give previous literature; Worcester Art Museum, *The Dark Ages*, Worcester, 1937, no. 31.

LENT BY THE PIERPONT MORGAN LIBRARY.   PL. IV

9. LECTIONARY OF THE GOSPELS   Germany (Westphalia), 10th cent.

    Ms. 1. In Latin. Minuscule and occasional uncial script. 200 vellum leaves, 10 x 7⅛ inches. 6 full-page miniatures; numerous elaborate initial pages and ornamental passages; many purple pages written in gold. Binding: 19th century German half-leather. Ex-coll.: John Jacob Astor (acquired 1884).

This Lectionary, executed in the second half of the tenth century for a foundation dedicated to St. Michael, ranks as the foremost example of the "Weser group" of manuscripts described under the previous entry (no. 8). It is the only one of the group, now known, to contain illustrations as well as ornamental pages. The miniatures consist of four full-page portraits of the Evangelists, the symbols of the Evangelists combined on a single page in four compartments, and Christ in Glory. The painting style has exactly the same quality of rich surface decoration that appears in the ornamental initial pages. Although a slight modelling of the flesh is carried out with strokes of orange and highlights of pink and white, and the drapery lines are emphasized with gold, there is no preoccupation whatever with plasticity or spatial concepts. There is exceptionally prolific use of ornamental writing in gold in the form of complex monogram pages and decorative passages of capitals, as well as sections of text in gold uncials or minuscules. Many pages are written on backgrounds of purple, shading from pink-lavender to blue-purple, and frequently displaying behind the letters a shadowy patterning of foliate and other motives. There is in fact a marked predilection for purple in the color schemes throughout the manuscript, its chief foil being a green-blue suggesting the color of enamel, and very beautiful in effect.

This codex, acquired by John Jacob Astor in 1884, was probably the first important illuminated manuscript of the early Middle Ages to come to America.

BIBLIOGRAPHY: Hanns Swarzenski in *Zeitschrift für Bildende Kunst*, LXIII (1929-30), p. 194, 2 figs.; idem, *Vorgotische Miniaturen*, Königstein & Leipzig, 2nd ed., 1931, p. 5, fig. p. 16; De Ricci, II, p. 1315, no. 1; *Bulletin of the New York Public Library*, vol. 41 (1937), pp. 455-62.

LENT BY THE NEW YORK PUBLIC LIBRARY, MANUSCRIPT DIVISION.   PL. V

10. THE FOUR GOSPELS   Austria (Salzburg), early 11th cent.

    M. 781. In Latin. Minuscule script. 226 vellum leaves, 13½ x 10½ inches. 7 full-page and 16 smaller miniatures; 4 decorated introductory pages. Binding: old wooden boards. At St. Peter's, Salzburg (cod. a.X.6) until 1933.

The style of this luxuriously illustrated Gospels indicates that it was executed in Salzburg during the first decade of the eleventh century. An index of privileges added at the end in the twelfth century proves that at least as early as that the book belonged to the Benedictine Abbey of St. Peter's in Salzburg, where it remained until acquired by the Pierpont Morgan Library fifteen years ago, together with the Lectionary described under no. 11.

In addition to the Canon Tables, Evangelist portraits and rich *incipit* pages, the decoration of the manuscript consists of nineteen illustrations dispersed through the text. These are executed in pastel, somewhat chalky pigments upon backgrounds of gold or untarnished silver (doubtless alloyed with tin). There is no attempt at space or plasticity, but the composition, figure style, and schematized drapery are highly decorative in character, and achieve a monumentality of effect that is not unrelated to Reichenau productions, although without their dynamic qualities.

BIBLIOGRAPHY: Georg Swarzenski, *Die Salzburger Malerei*, Leipzig, 1913, pp. 30-41, pls. 9 and 11-19; Belle da Costa Greene and Meta P. Harrsen, *Exhibition of Illuminated Manuscripts . . .*, New York, 1934, no. 17, pl. 15, with other literature; The Pierpont Morgan Library, *Review of the Activities and Acquisitions . . . 1930 through 1935*, New York, 1937, pp. 17-18, 94-95, pl. I; De Ricci, II, p. 1503, no. 781; Boston Museum of Fine Arts, *Arts of the Middle Ages*, Boston, 1940, no. 16, ill.; The Pierpont Morgan Library, *Illustrated Catalogue of an Exhibition held on the Occasion of the New York World's Fair*, New York, 1940, no. 50; idem, *The Bible*, New York, 1947, no. 23, pl. IV.

LENT BY THE PIERPONT MORGAN LIBRARY.   PL. VI

11. LECTIONARY OF THE GOSPELS   Austria (Salzburg), 2nd half of 11th cent.

>   M. 780. In Latin. Minuscule script. 80 vellum leaves, 9⅝ x 7¼ inches. 19 miniatures; numerous illuminated initials. Binding: 13th century wooden boards. At St. Peter's, Salzburg (cod. a. VI. 55) until 1933.

Bertolt "the Custodian", who made this book in St. Peter's, Salzburg, during the second half of the eleventh century, signed his name at the end, with the statement that he offered it to St. Peter as a prayer in expiation of his sins. Presumably he also did a Gospel-book that is preserved at the Abbey of Admont (ms. 805) not far from Salzburg.

The paintings show more Byzantine characteristics in style and iconography than appear in the slightly earlier Salzburg manuscript described above (no. 10). The colors are similar, however, and present an effect of great lightness and beauty. The drapery, though still highly stylized, is developed as a rhythmic reflection of the form and movement of the figures, and heads are modelled after the Byzantine fashion by laying successive layers of lighter color upon a dark underpaint. Custos Bertolt survives in this work as a highly sensitive and accomplished artist.

> BIBLIOGRAPHY: Georg Swarzenski, *Die Regensburger Buchmalerei*, Leipzig, 1901, pp. 156-167; Belle da Costa Greene and Meta P. Harrsen, *Exhibition of Illuminated Manuscripts* . . ., New York, 1934, no. 18, pl. 16, with other literature; The Pierpont Morgan Library, *Review of the Activities and Acquisitions* . . . *1930 through 1935*, New York, 1937, pp. 18-19, 94, pl. II; De Ricci, II, p. 1503, no. 780; K. Löffler and J. Kirchner, *Lexikon des gesammten Buchwesens*, 1935-1937, vol. III, p. 189.

LENT BY THE PIERPONT MORGAN LIBRARY.   PL. VI

12. THE FOUR GOSPELS   Southern Germany (Reichenau), 11th cent.

>   W. 7. In Latin. Minuscule script. 202 vellum leaves, 9-1/16 x 6½ inches. 5 full-page miniatures; 4 ornamented introductory pages; 16 decorated Canon Tables. Binding: modern plain vellum. Ex-colls.: Sir Thomas Brooke, Huddersfield, Yorkshire; Rev. Ingham Brooke (Sale, London, March 7, 1913, no. 8, with 2 colored plates).

This manuscript was executed around 1040 A.D. at the great Benedictine monastery on the isle of Reichenau in Lake Constance. From this renowned scriptorium sumptuous volumes were ordered by prelates in other centers and by the Ottonian emperors, and extensively influenced other German schools of painting. The Reichenau artists during their great period—the decades immediately preceding and following the year 1000—produced works of marvellous richness and beauty, characterized by monumentality and a peculiarly psychological intensity.

The subsequent phase of the school, represented by the present example, shows a hardening of the style and a relaxation of the energy inherent in the earlier works. Nevertheless, it still preserves in its rich purple *incipit* pages and the gay, pastel hues of the paintings a reminiscence of the days of greatness.

An interesting feature of the Walters manuscript is a dedication page representing an abbot presenting the volume to an Apostle, doubtless St. Peter. The composition was copied in several other works related directly or indirectly to the late phases of the Reichenau school.

> BIBLIOGRAPHY: Dorothy Miner in *The Art Bulletin*, XVIII, 1936, pp. 168-185, 16 figs., where previous literature is cited; De Ricci, I, p. 767, no. 64, and II, p. 2289, additional notes; Walters Art Gallery, *Handbook of the Collection*, Baltimore, 1936, p. 97, ill.

COLLECTION OF THE WALTERS ART GALLERY.   PL. VII

13. SACRAMENTARY-MISSAL
Southern Italy, 11th cent.

W. 6. In Latin. Beneventan script with neumes. 232 vellum leaves, 7½ x 4¾ inches. 2 large illuminated initials and numerous smaller ones. Binding: modern green velvet.

The contents of this service-book indicate that it is transitional in form between the earlier Sacramentary and the full Missal. It was executed after 1054 in one of the dependencies of Monte Cassino, the script and ornament resembling that attributed to the Bari group by Dr. E. A. Lowe.

BIBLIOGRAPHY: De Ricci, I, p. 775, no. 112; Walters Art Gallery, *Handbook of the Collection*, Baltimore, 1936, p. 98, ill.; Boston Museum of Fine Arts, *Arts of the Middle Ages*, Boston, 1940, no. 30, ill.

COLLECTION OF THE WALTERS ART GALLERY.
PL. XII

14. BEATUS OF LIEBANA. COMMENTARY ON THE APOCALYPSE
Spain, early 10th cent.

M. 644. In Latin. Visigothic minuscule script. 300 vellum leaves, 15 x 11-1/16 inches. 62 full-page and 48 smaller miniatures. Binding: three-quarter morocco by M. Lahey. Ex-colls.: G. Libri (1847); Earl of Ashburnham (Appendix, no. 15); H. Yates Thompson (Sale, London, 1919, no. 21).

The Apocalypse commentary composed about the year 776 by the Spanish monk, Beatus, was illustrated with an extensive picture cycle that had considerable influence on medieval iconography. Although the prototypes for the illustrations were doubtless in a late classical style, the majority of the two dozen Beatus manuscripts surviving are strongly Mozarabic in appearance. The scenes are converted into almost abstract patterns of a highly decorative character, the stylized figures and banded backgrounds presenting a mosaic of rich and lively color, most skillfully handled.

The Pierpont Morgan manuscript, the earliest known of all the Beatus copies, has a colophon stating that it was illuminated in 926 A.D. by Maius or Magius at the order of Abbot Victor, for a monastery dedicated to St. Michael. (The date was formerly interpreted as 894). Maius worked in the monastery of San Salvador de Tavara, where he died in 968 while illuminating another copy of Beatus' commentaries, which is now preserved in the Archivo Histórico of Madrid. San Miguel de Camarzana, not far from Tavara, may have been the monastery for which the Morgan manuscript was commissioned.

BIBLIOGRAPHY: J. Dominguez Bordona, *Spanish Illumination*, Florence, 1930, p. 15, pls. 9, 10; H. A. Sanders, *Beati in Apocalipsim*, Rome, 1930, p. xii and frontispiece; W. Neuss, *Die Apokalypse des Hl. Johannes in der altspanischen und altchristlichen Bibelillustration*, Münster in W., 1931, I, pp. 9-16, 20, 56; II, figs. 9, 44, 53, 107, 115, 136, 194, 202; Belle da Costa Greene and Meta P. Harrsen, *Exhibition of Illuminated Manuscripts . . .*, New York, 1934, no. 15, pl. 14, with other literature; De Ricci, II, p. 1477, no. 644; Worcester Art Museum, *The Dark Ages*, Worcester, 1937, no. 28; The Pierpont Morgan Library, *Illustrated Catalogue of an Exhibition held on the Occasion of the New York World's Fair*, New York, 1940, no. 4.

LENT BY THE PIERPONT MORGAN LIBRARY.
PL. X

15. THE FOUR GOSPELS
Anglo-French, late 10th cent.

M. 827. In Latin. Franco-Saxon minuscule script. 128 vellum leaves, 14 x 10 inches. 4 full-page miniatures; 10 ornamented or purple pages; 14 decorated Canon Tables. Binding: original wooden boards, the upper cover with cavities for ornaments now lost, the lower covered with an ajouré copper plaque. Ex-coll.: Duke of Anhalt-Dessau.

This manuscript is a demonstration of the close artistic interchange existing at the end of the tenth century among the Franco-Saxon art of the region around Arras, the Anglo-Saxon style of England and the so-called "Channel-school", and the richly ornamental products of pure Saxon art. The book evidently was not carried through at one time or place. Dr. Hanns Swarzenski explains its inconsistent character by proposing that the codex was originally undertaken in a Franco-Saxon center, such as Arras, and the Evangelist portraits were drawn by an artist trained in English style, while much of the enrichment of blue and purple backgrounds was added after the year 1000 when the manuscript had been taken to some place in Saxony. It remained in this region until recently.

BIBLIOGRAPHY: A. Haseloff in *Meisterwerke der Kunst aus Sachsen und Thüringen* (ed. by Doering and Voss), Magdeburg, 1905, p. 91, pl. 108; O. Homburger, *Die Anfänge der Malerschule von Winchester im X. Jahrhundert*, Leipzig, 1912, p. 5; A. Boeckler, *Die Abendländischen Miniaturen*, Berlin, 1930, p. 60.

LENT BY THE PIERPONT MORGAN LIBRARY.   PL. VIII

16. THE FOUR GOSPELS   England (East Anglia), 11th cent.

M. 709. In Latin. Insular minuscule script. 154 vellum leaves, 11½ x 7½ inches. 5 full-page miniatures; 4 illuminated introductory pages. Binding: boards with English or Flemish 11th cent. gold reliefs of Christ in Majesty, 12th cent. German jewelled filigree frame. Ex-colls.: Countess Judith of Flanders (1032-1094); Benedictine monastery of Weingarten, until 1805; Frederick William of Orange-Nassau; Baron Thiébault; Thomas Coke, later Earl of Leicester (ms. 16).

The pictures, datable around 1040, are painted in what is generally considered characteristic Winchester style—a rapid calligraphic delineation, delicately tinted in rose, blue and yellow on uncolored grounds, and framed by borders of richly sprouting foliage banded with gold. However, a Psalter in the Bodleian Library (Douce 296), illuminated in a style very close indeed to this Gospel manuscript, has a calendar for Croyland, a monastery in East Anglia dependent on Peterborough.

This and another early English manuscript in the Pierpont Morgan Library (M. 708) were acquired by Countess Judith of Flanders during her sojourn in England, where she went in 1051 as the bride of Earl Tostig of Northumbria. After her second marriage in 1071, to Duke Welf IV of Bavaria, she became patroness of the Benedictine monastery of Weingarten in the diocese of Constance, and bequeathed her library to it in 1094. For over a hundred years the artistic production of the Weingarten scriptorium was based fundamentally on designs in the manuscripts donated by Judith.

BIBLIOGRAPHY: O. Homburger, *Die Anfänge der Malerschule von Winchester im X. Jahrhundert*, Leipzig, 1912, p. 67; Meta P. Harrsen in *Papers of the Bibliographical Society of America*, XXIV (1931), pp. 1-13; Belle da Costa Greene and Meta P. Harrsen, *Exhibition of Illuminated Manuscripts . . .*, New York, 1934, no. 19, pls. 17, 18, with other literature; The Pierpont Morgan Library, *Review of the Growth, Development and Activities . . . 1924-1929*, New York, 1930, pp. 20-23, pls. VII, VIII; De Ricci, II, p. 1485 f., no. 709; Boston Museum of Fine Arts, *Arts of the Middle Ages*, Boston, 1940, no. 13, ill.; The Pierpont Morgan Library, *Illustrated Catalogue of an Exhibition held on the Occasion of the New York World's Fair*, New York, 1940, no. 10; F. Wormald, in *Proceedings of the British Academy*, XXX (1944), pp. 4-5, pl. 2; The Pierpont Morgan Library, *The Bible*, New York, 1947, no. 19. Cf. F. Wormald, *English Kalendars before A.D. 1100*, London, 1934, no. 20.

LENT BY THE PIERPONT MORGAN LIBRARY.   PL. IX

17. SACRAMENTARY Northern France (Mont St. Michel), 2nd half of 11th cent.

> M. 641. In Latin. Minuscule script; neumes. 184 vellum leaves, 11¼ x 8¼ inches. 16 miniatures; 18 historiated or ornamented initials. Binding: modern red velvet. Ex-colls.: Earl of Ashburnham (Appendix, no. 43); H. Yates Thompson (Sale, London, 1919, no. 1).

Executed after 1067 in the island abbey of Mont St. Michel for use in a monastery in the diocese of Rouen, probably Fécamp. Several of the important pages employ royal purple grounds and burnished gold, but the characteristic pictures of the book are painted in flat, somewhat chalky colors, thinly applied. Light blue and lavender dominate, relieved by smaller areas of green and minium, all handled with extraordinary subtlety and decorative effect.

> BIBLIOGRAPHY: Belle da Costa Greene and Meta P. Harrsen, *Exhibition of Illuminated Manuscripts . . .*, New York, 1934, no. 22, fig. 3, pl. 22, with previous literature; De Ricci, II, p. 1476, no. 641; The Pierpont Morgan Library, *Illustrated Catalogue of an Exhibition held on the Occasion of the New York World's Fair*, New York, 1940, no. 12, color plate; Boston Museum of Fine Arts, *Arts of the Middle Ages*, Boston, 1940, no. 27.

LENT BY THE PIERPONT MORGAN LIBRARY. PL. XII

18. LEAF FROM A BIBLE England (Winchester), 12th cent.

> M. 619. In Latin. Single vellum leaf, 22½ x 15¼ inches. 1 full-page and 1 three-quarter-page miniature.

Illuminated on both sides with illustrations of the first and second Books of Samuel. The paintings on this leaf are to be ranked among the masterpieces of the twelfth century. The folio was executed for one of the fine Bibles of monumental size that were a feature of English manuscript production at this period. It has been conjectured that this leaf was prepared for the most celebrated of all these large Bibles, a work, originally in two volumes, now belonging to Winchester Cathedral and illuminated in St. Swithin's Priory, Winchester. The decoration of this Bible is by a number of artists, including the master of the Morgan leaf, who worked on it apparently over several decades from around 1250 onward, and even then left the project unfinished. Inasmuch as no other traces of another such ambitious Bible by these same artists have been found, it is now supposed that the Morgan leaf was prepared for the Winchester Bible, but never used, a hypothesis strengthened by certain textual peculiarities.

The artist of the Morgan leaf is a painter of great power and expressiveness, revealing some influence from the style of Byzantine painting. He is notable for the versatility of his rendering and the individuality with which he endows the faces and figures of his people, as contrasted with the more standardized types of his contemporary artists.

> BIBLIOGRAPHY: E. Millar, *English Illuminated Manuscripts from the Xth to the XIIIth Century*, (Paris, 1926), pp. 35, 85-86, pl. 48; Belle da Costa Greene and Meta P. Harrsen, *Exhibition of Illuminated Manuscripts. . . .*, New York, 1934, pp. 18-19, no. 32, pl. 32; De Ricci, II, p. 1473, no. 619; Winchester College Library, *Catalogue of an Exhibition*, Mar. 31—Apr. 8, 1936, pl. vii; Walter Oakeshott, *The Artists of the Winchester Bible*, London, (1945), pp. 12, 18-20.

LENT BY THE PIERPONT MORGAN LIBRARY. PL. XI

19. NEW TESTAMENT England (Canterbury?), 12th cent.

> W. 18. In Latin. Large insular script in 2 cols. 247 vellum leaves, 14½ x 10¾ inches. 26 illuminated initials. Binding: old, worn red velvet over boards.

A volume of impressive format, the bold dark brown script being relieved by large initials vigorously wrought of vines and beasts. Red, blue, green and yellow are employed, but no gold or silver. This appears to be part of a large Bible, doubtless always bound in two or more volumes, another section of which (Joshua, Judges, Ruth and Kings) is now in the British Museum, Royal ms. I C VII. The latter is attributed to the scriptorium of Christ Church, Canterbury, and was in the Royal Library as early as 1542.

BIBLIOGRAPHY: De Ricci, I, p. 766, no. 57. *Cf.* G. F. Warner and J. P. Gilson, *Catalogue of Western Manuscripts in the Old Royal and King's Collections*, British Museum, London, 1921, I, p. 14, IV, pl. 9.

COLLECTION OF THE WALTERS ART GALLERY.   PL. XIII

20. HAYMO OF HALBERSTADT, COMMENTARY ON ISAIAH   England, 12th cent.

Garrett ms. 73. In Latin. Insular book script in 2 cols. 168 vellum leaves, 15 x 6⅝ inches. 3 decorated initials. Binding: 17th century calf. Ex-colls.: Thomas Brudenell (1502-1586) of Deene, Northhamptonshire; Robert Garrett.

A characteristic English manuscript of the period, its large, handsome script well placed on the suede-like vellum. The ornamented initials are executed in delicate pen outline in brown ink, showing birds, animals and grotesques on grounds of light blue, green and lavender. The initial showing Isaiah is in the best English outline style of the period, and resembles the work of Bury St. Edmunds or St. Albans. There is some use of dull gold and of silver.

BIBLIOGRAPHY: De Ricci, I, p. 878, no. 73.

LENT BY PRINCETON UNIVERSITY LIBRARY, GARRETT COLLECTION.

21. THE FOUR GOSPELS   South France, ca. 1100

W. 17. In Latin. Minuscule script. 161 vellum leaves, 10⅝ x 8⅝ inches. 1 miniature and 3 ornamented initials. Binding: worn red velvet.

A manuscript of unusual style, preserving in its large, simple forms a reminiscence of Carolingian prototypes, and in its thick, flatly applied areas of bright red, blue and yellow a suggestion of Catalonian taste. The introductory pages of the Gospels are written in alternating lines of red and blue capitals, with numerous monogrammized contractions. A manuscript showing many similarities is in the Bibliothèque Mejeanes in Aix-en-Provence (ms. 7).

BIBLIOGRAPHY: De Ricci, I, p. 767, no. 65; Walters Art Gallery, *Handbook of the Collection*, Baltimore, 1936, p. 70; Boston Museum of Fine Arts, *Arts of the Middle Ages*, Boston, 1940, no. 28, ill.

COLLECTION OF THE WALTERS ART GALLERY.   PL. XIII

22. SACRAMENTARY FOR USE OF REIMS   Northern France, 12th cent.

W. 28. In Latin. Gothic script. 73 vellum leaves, 9 x 5½ inches. 2 full-page miniatures; two large ornamental initials. Binding: orange velvet over boards. Formerly in Reims Cathedral; Beauvais Cathedral Chapter Library (inventory, no. 26); Chateau de Troussures (Sale, Paris, June 9, 1909, no. 14, ill.).

Despite its fragmentary and disordered state, this manuscript preserves many unusual liturgical features, including an abridged coronation formula according to the Gallican rite. Although its text indicates that the Sacramentary was written for the use of Reims Cathedral, as Dr. Niver has shown, the miniatures do not correspond with Reims work, but suggest that the manuscript was executed in the region of Arras or Marchiennes. The paintings are somewhat archaic in style, being extremely delicate of outline, and light of color. Contrasting colors shot through the draperies to indicate folds and high lights produce an iridescent effect.

BIBLIOGRAPHY: H. Omont in *Memoires de l'Academie des Inscriptions et Belles Lettres*, XL (1916), p. 80; idem, in *Memoires de l'Institute National de France*, XL (1926), esp. pp. 60, no. 26 and p. 89; C. Niver in *Speculum*, X (1935), pp. 333-337, with 3 ill.; De Ricci, I, p. 775, no. 113; P. E. Schramm in *Archiv für Urkundenforschung*, XVI (1939), p. 282; H. Swarzenski in *Art Bulletin*, XXIV (1942), pp. 295 f.

COLLECTION OF THE WALTERS ART GALLERY.   PL. XIV

23. NEW TESTAMENT   North France, ca. 1200 A.D.

W. 67. In Latin. Gothic script in 2 cols. 78 vellum leaves, 17 x 12½ inches. 10 pages of ornamented Canon Tables; 8 historiated and 33 ornamented initials. Binding: modern red velvet over boards, with metal ornaments.

The illuminations are by several hands, the finest being responsible for a representation of St. James of impressive proto-gothic style. The Canon Tables, on the other hand, preserve archaic features reminiscent of early romanesque art.

BIBLIOGRAPHY: De Ricci, I, p. 766, no. 58.

COLLECTION OF THE WALTERS ART GALLERY.   PL. XIV

24. PSALTER   Germany (Helmarshausen), 12th cent.

W. 10. In Latin. Minuscule script. 125 vellum leaves, 4-7/16 x 2-9/16 inches. 3 full-page miniatures and 4 ornamented initial pages. Binding: modern red velvet. Ex-coll.: Petrus Grillinger, Canon of Salzburg (early 15th century).

This little Psalter was made in the Benedictine monastery of Helmarshausen near Paderborn, in Westphalia. The tiny format, very unusual at this epoch, can only be explained by supposing that the book was for the personal use of a lady, whose picture appears in the first miniature. The late Adolph Goldschmidt proposed that she might have been Gertrude, daughter of the Guelph Henry the Lion, who ordered from Helmarshausen around 1175 two other and more elaborate manuscripts which are now in the British Museum (Landsdowne ms. 381) and the collection of the Duke of Brunswick, respectively. Gertrude married first in 1166, and again in 1177, becoming eventually Queen of Denmark. Hanns Swarzenski considers that the style is earlier, pointing to the middle of the century, which would exclude Gertrude as the original owner. In this case, it is possible that the lady on the dedication page may be Gertrude's mother, Clementia of Zähringen, the first wife of Henry the Lion, whose marriage occurred in 1147.

BIBLIOGRAPHY: De Ricci, I, p. 768, no. 73; Adolph Goldschmidt in *The Journal of the Walters Art Gallery*, I (1938), pp. 19-23, with 8 ill.; Boston Museum of Fine Arts, *Arts of the Middle Ages*, Boston, 1940, no. 20; Hanns Swarzenski in *The Art Bulletin*, XXIV (1942), p. 296.

COLLECTION OF THE WALTERS ART GALLERY.   PL. XXI

25. PSALTER   Southern Germany, early 13th cent.

>   Ms. 20. In Latin. 288 vellum leaves, 14 x 10 inches. Historiated and ornamental initials. Binding: 19th century English brown morocco. Formerly at the Praemonstratensian monastery at Weissenau.

An inscription states that this Psalter was the donation of "Rudolfus plebanus de Lindaugia", or Lindau on the Lake of Constance. The style of the initials and especially the intense movement of the figures in the illuminations lead Hanns Swarzenski to see influence from Weingarten and to attribute this manuscript to the nearby monastery of Weissenau, where it was at least as early as the eighteenth century.

>   BIBLIOGRAPHY: E. F. Rothschild in *The University of Chicago Magazine*, XXII (Feb. 1930), p. 194; De Ricci, I, p. 621, no. 20; H. Swarzenski, *The Berthold Missal*, New York, 1943, pp. 61f., fig. 87.

LENT BY THE SCRIPTORIUM OF C. L. RICKETTS, CHICAGO.   PL. XX

26. FRONTISPIECE TO VITA GREGORII   Southern Germany (Weingarten), late 12th cent.

>   44.704. Single vellum leaf, 11¾ x 9⅛ inches. 2 full-page miniatures.

St. Gregory writing and, on the reverse, St. Gregory celebrating the Mass. This leaf, one of the few surviving examples of Weingarten illumination previous to the great period of Abbot Berthold (see nos. 31, 32), is probably the frontispiece of a lost codex of the Life of St. Gregory that, according to early accounts, was written by the monk Konradus during the time of Abbots Wernher and Meingoz (1181-1200). Dr. Hanns Swarzenski has pointed out certain details in the paintings on this leaf that reflect the use of Countess Judith's manuscripts as models (see no. 16).

>   BIBLIOGRAPHY: H. Swarzenski, *The Berthold Missal*, New York, 1943, p. 7, with full bibliography, pp. 15, 17, note 36, 25, 26, figs. 10, 11; M. R. Rogers and O. Goetz, *Handbook to the Lucy Maud Buckingham Collection*, Art Institute of Chicago, 1945, p. 64, no. 20, pls. XXIV, XXV.

LENT BY THE ART INSTITUTE OF CHICAGO.   PL. XVI

27. HONORIUS AUGUSTODUNENSIS. EXPOSITIO SUPER CANTICA CANTICORUM
                                                                                Austria, 12th cent.

>   W. 29. In Latin. Minuscule script. 150 vellum leaves, 10⅜ x 7⅛ inches. 3 half-page miniatures; 3 historiated and 5 ornamented initials. Binding: 12th century stamped deerskin over boards. Formerly in the Benedictine monastery of Seitenstetten, near Linz.

The author, usually called Honorius of Autun, was a monk and scholastic active in Germany in the first half of the twelfth century. His popularized theological writings seem to have been particularly influential in southern Germany and Austria, the region in which all the known examples of this text were executed. The Walters manuscript belongs to a group, all containing the same text and illustrations, and all to be dated between 1150 and 1175, which was copied very shortly after the original work was completed. In addition to the exposition on the *Cantica Canticorum*, the compilation includes the *Sigillum Sanctae Mariae* and *Neocosmus*.

The symbolic illustrations are executed with the polychrome pen-outlines and strongly colored backgrounds particularly developed at Salzburg during the romanesque period. No silver or gold is used.

BIBLIOGRAPHY: Jacques Rosenthal, *Bibliotheca Medii Aevi Manuscripta* (cat. 90), Munich [1928], no. 144, pp. 48-51, pl. VIII; De Ricci, I, p. 821, no. 387; Boston Museum of Fine Arts, *Arts of the Middle Ages*, Boston, 1940, no. 19, ill. Cf. J. A. Endres, *Das St. Jacobsportal im Regensburg*, Kempten, 1903, pp. 32-36; Georg Swarzenski, *Die Salzburger Malerei*, Leipzig, 1913, pp. 94-95. For binding: G. D. Hobson in *Transactions of the Bibliographical Society*, London, Sept. 1934.

COLLECTION OF THE WALTERS ART GALLERY.   PL. XVIII

28. GISELBERTUS AUTISSIODORENSIS. GLOSA IN THRENOS JEREMIAE
Austria, 12th cent.

W. 30. In Latin. Minuscule script. 53 vellum leaves, 10¼ x 7¼ inches. 3 miniatures; 5 pages of ornamented arcades; 2 historiated and 3 ornamented initials. Binding: early sheepskin over boards. Ex-colls.: during the 16th century, in Weyer (Austria); subsequently Benedictine monastery of Seitenstetten, near Linz.

Jeremiah's *Lament*, written in very large minuscules, is surrounded by the glosses composed by Giselbertus (Universalis) of Auxerre, who died in 1134. This manuscript, one of the earliest copies of Giselbert's work, preserves the original form of the text. The drawings in colored inks resemble the style of Admont, a monastery near the town of Weyer, where this book was in private hands in the sixteenth century, according to ownership inscriptions on the flyleaf.

BIBLIOGRAPHY: Jacques Rosenthal, *Bibliotheca Medii Aevi Manuscripta* (cat. 90), Munich [1928], no. 139, pp. 40-42, pl. VII; De Ricci, I, p. 821, no. 388; Boston Museum of Fine Arts, *Arts of the Middle Ages*, Boston, 1940, no. 18.

COLLECTION OF THE WALTERS ART GALLERY.   PL. XIX

29. PSEUDO-PHILO, DE BIBLICIS ANTIQUITATIBUS, ETC.
Austria, 12th cent.

In Latin. Minuscule script. 98 vellum leaves, 10⅝ x 7⅜ inches. 2 historiated initials. Binding: 14th century leather over boards. In Admont monastery until the 20th century (ms. 359).

This volume was listed in the inventory of the Benedictine monastery of Admont as early as 1370, and probably was executed there. It contains the earliest known Latin version of parts of the *Quaestiones in Genesim* and of the *De Vita Contempletiva* of Philo Judaeus, and it is considered the best manuscript of the earliest version of Pseudo-Philos' *Antiquitates Biblicae*. The latter is of interest as representing the survival into the Middle Ages of an unadulterated Jewish work of the first century A.D., which like the Fourth Book of Esdras and the Apocalypse of Baruch, was composed following the destruction of Jerusalem in 70 A.D. Both the Church Fathers and the later scholastics held Philo in esteem.

The manuscript is embellished with two interesting historiated initials in characteristic Austrian romanesque style.

BIBLIOGRAPHY: P. Buberl, *Die Illuminierten Handschriften in Steiermark*, I, (Band IV, *Beschreibendes Verzeichnis der illuminierten Handschriften in Osterreich*), Leipzig, 1911, p. 78, figs. 79, 80, p. 79, no. 60; De Ricci, II, p. 1679, no. 16, with additional bibliography.

LENT BY HOWARD L. GOODHART.   PL. XX

30. MISSAL FOR THE USE OF MELK   Austria, ca. 1200

    W. 33. In Latin. Minuscule script; neumes. 287 vellum leaves, 10⅞ x 6½ inches. 2 full-page miniatures; 6 historiated and 11 ornamented initials. Binding: Austrian 15th century boards covered with calfskin stamped with inscribed scrolls. Formerly in the Benedictine monastery of Seitenstetten (near Linz, Austria), cod. 127.

Executed for the use of a church in the diocese of Melk in upper Austria, this is a particularly notable example of the provincial outline style that is closely related to romanesque works of the school of Salzburg. The figures are finely drawn in red and lavender inks against flat backgrounds of light blue and green. The use of inscribed frames and partitions is characteristic. The volume contains the "summer part" of the Missal only.

The binding belongs to an interesting group of Austrian works, all datable between 1475 and 1480, which are ornamented with German poetical inscriptions impressed with movable type.

    BIBLIOGRAPHY: *Jahrbuch der K.K. Central Kommission*, Vienna, II (1857), p. 128; Georg Swarzenski, *Die Salzburger Malerei*, Leipzig, 1913, pp. 153, 165, pl. CXXI, figs. 406-407; Jacques Rosenthal, *Bibliotheca Medii Aevi Manuscripta* (cat. 90), Munich [1928], no. 167, pp. 88-90; De Ricci, I, p. 775, no. 115. Cf. E. P. Goldschmidt, *Gothic and Renaissance Bookbindings*, London, 1928, I, p. 45, no. 16, pl. IX.

COLLECTION OF THE WALTERS ART GALLERY.   PL. XVIII

31. THE BERTHOLD MISSAL   Germany (Weingarten), 13th cent.

    M. 710. In Latin. Large minuscule script. 165 vellum leaves, 11½ x 8 inches. 21 full-page and 7 smaller miniatures; 18 historiated and 70 ornamented initials. Binding: contemporary heavy oak boards; on the upper cover, elaborate 13th century silver gilt plaques with Virgin and Child enthroned, surrounded by saints and the figure of Abbot Berthold, all framed in jewelled filigree. In Weingarten Abbey until 1802. Ex-colls.: Frederick William of Orange-Nassau; Baron Thiébault; Thomas Coke, later first Earl of Leicester of Holkham (1818).

One of the chief monuments of German romanesque art, this Missal was commissioned early in the thirteenth century by Berthold, Abbot of the Benedictine Abbey of Weingarten from 1200 to 1232, who was active in enhancing his abbey with fine books and other artistic works. He has taken care to have himself depicted upon the jewelled cover among the worshippers of the Virgin.

The Missal is very richly illuminated, the chief miniatures being by an artist of exceptional brilliance and power. Both figures and ornament show great decorative splendor and a fondness for rotating dynamic movement which is attained both by linear play and by sharply patterned modelling. Particularly characteristic are the intense, almost menacing expressions and gestures of the people. Influences from Byzantine painting, as well as from Flemish and English romanesque art, are here fused with southern German traditions into a unique creative achievement. The extraordinarily rich use of gold and silver, as well as many ornamental motives, recall the productions of the goldsmith. This Missal, together with another that is by a follower of the Berthold Master and two English manuscripts presented in the eleventh century by Countess Judith (see no. 16 of this catalogue), remained in the Treasure of Weingarten Abbey until the secularization of the monastery in 1802. All four are still preserved together in the Pierpont Morgan Library. See also nos. 26 and 32.

    BIBLIOGRAPHY: Belle da Costa Greene and Meta P. Harrsen, *Exhibition of Illuminated Manuscripts . . .*, New York, 1934, pp. 31-32, no. 60, pl. 56; De Ricci, II, p. 1486, no. 710; Hanns Swarzenski, *The Berthold Missal*, New York, 1943, a complete study and facsimile, with full bibliography.

LENT BY THE PIERPONT MORGAN LIBRARY.   PL. XV

32. PROPHETAE MINORES Germany (Weingarten), early 13th cent.

In Latin. Large minuscule script in 2 cols. 146 vellum leaves, 17 x 12¼ inches. 9 large and 22 small historiated and illuminated initials. Binding: 16th century German stamped calf over boards. In Weingarten Abbey (ms. A 9 Fol.) until 1802. Ex-coll.: Baron Vernon (Sale, London, no. 68 and pl.).

This book was illuminated in the abbey of Weingarten by the Master of the "Berthold Missal" (see no. 31). Although not as rich in its pictorial scheme, its miniatures display the powerful and original conception, the dynamic drawing and plastic rendering that reach their apogee in the Missal. The almost unparalleled device of representing the Prophets seated upon the ground within the initials produces a compression of form which the artist deliberately enhances with strong movement of line and volume and with exciting contrasts of color. The result is an intensity of expression that is the very essence of the great visionaries of the Old Testament.

This work is mentioned in Abbot Berthold's catalogue of the books made at his order (to be found in the "Berthold Missal"), which cites two volumes containing the Twelve Minor Prophets and Lives of the Saints. When this book received its present binding in the sixteenth century, six of the Prophets were bound together with the Lives. The remaining Prophets at the same time were bound into another volume which, as Dr. Swarzenski has recognized, is now in the Public Library of Leningrad (ms. lat. F.V.1.133). The very large format and the enormous archaistic script are exceptional for these texts, but recall the great folio Bibles of the late eleventh and early twelfth centuries. It has been suggested that the New York and Leningrad manuscripts were commissioned by Berthold to replace missing parts of such an early Bible.

BIBLIOGRAPHY: De Ricci, II, p. 1335, no. 1, with previous literature; H. Swarzenski, *The Berthold Missal*, New York, 1943, pp. 20ff., 24, 32ff., 103ff., detailed description and full bibliography, pls. LIV-LIX.

LENT BY THE NEW YORK PUBLIC LIBRARY, SPENCER COLLECTION. PL. XV

33. LEAF FROM A PSALTER: PARADISE Germany (Thuringia), 13th cent.

Latin text on reverse. One vellum leaf, 9⅛ x 6⅛ inches. 1 full-page miniature. Ex-coll.: R. Forrer, Strassburg.

The patriarch, Abraham, clad in a yellowish-white tunic and tan mantle, sits enthroned, holding on his lap a small beardless figure with a cruciform nimbus, who gives apples to the Blessed of Paradise. The mandorla-shaped frame is intercepted by four roundels containing the symbolic figures of the Rivers of Paradise. The miniature probably represents Lazarus in "Abraham's bosom", referring to the story of the rich man and Lazarus in Luke, XVI, although the presence of the cruciform halo on Lazarus is unique. It perhaps is used to identify Lazarus as a manifestation of Christ.

This is one of three leaves, of which another is now in the Chicago Art Institute, that became separated from a Psalter formerly in the collection of the Duke of Arenberg, and supposed to have been completed before 1239. The hieratic dignity of the design, the angular stylization of the drapery and the intensity of expression are characteristic of Thuringian painting of the period, particularly of the school associated with Würzburg.

BIBLIOGRAPHY: R. Forrer in *Strassburger Post*, Sept. 20, 1904; Dusseldorf Exhibition Catalogue, 1904; R. Forrer, *Unedierte Federzeichnungen und Initialen des Mittelalters*, II, Strassburg, 1907, pl. IX; H. Swarzenski, *Die Lateinischen Illuminierten Handschriften des XIII. Jahrhunderts in den Ländern an Rhein, Main und Donau*, Berlin, 1936, text vol., pp. 79, 155, n. 2, 157, n. 3, 161, n. 2; E. Rosenthal in *The Pacific Art Review*, IV (1945-46), pp. 7-23, ill.

LENT BY THE NATIONAL GALLERY OF ART, ROSENWALD COLLECTION. PL. XVII

34. LEAF FROM A PSALTER   Germany (Augsburg), 13th cent.

One vellum leaf, 7-1/16 x 4-3/16 inches. 2 full-page miniatures. Ex-coll.: Victor Goldschmidt.

The Crucifixion and, on the reverse, the Three Marys at the Tomb. Two illuminated leaves from the same book belong to the Germanisches Museum and another to the Gewerbe Museum, both in Nuremberg. They may all have come from an incomplete Psalter now in Prague, ms. XIV E 3.

BIBLIOGRAPHY: H. Swarzenski, *Die Lateinischen Illuminierten Handschriften des XIII. Jahrhunderts in den Ländern an Rhein, Main und Donau*, Berlin, 1936, pl. 133, nos. 735-736. Cf. *Beilagen zum Anzeiger für Kunde der Deutschen Vorzeit*, 1881, p. 2, fig. 2, with ill.; Bredt, *Katalog der Mittelalterlichen Miniaturen des Germ. National Museum*, 1903, pp. 38, fig. 34, etc.

LENT BY THE NATIONAL GALLERY OF ART, ROSENWALD COLLECTION.

35. COSMOGRAPHY   France, 12th cent.

W. 73. In Latin. Gothic script. 9 vellum leaves, 10⅝ x 6¼ inches. 20 diagrams. Binding: modern French brown calf.

An unidentified text illustrated with colored diagrams of considerable decorative character, depicting eclipses, movements of the planets, the influences of the zodiacal signs, the winds, the elements and other matters of concern to the medieval astronomer.

BIBLIOGRAPHY: De Ricci, I, p. 826, no. 412.

COLLECTION OF THE WALTERS ART GALLERY.   PL. XX

36. LECTIONARY OF THE BIBLE   Northern Italy, 13th cent.

W. 152. In Latin. Gothic script in 2 cols. 164 vellum leaves, 14¼ x 9¾ inches. 128 miniatures. Binding: 19th century red velvet. Ex-colls.: Comte de Bastard; F. Spitzer (Sale, Paris, 1893, no. 3030).

This manuscript, which is but a fragment of a large and abundantly illustrated Lectionary, is said by an unconfirmed tradition to have been sent in 1267 or 1268 from Sicily to Conradinus of Hohenstauffen. It is ornamented in an extraordinary style, with large marginal figures placed upon irregularly shaped parti-colored grounds of rose and blue which are studded with discs of gold. The drawing of the figures and drapery is flat and romanesque, but the heads, greatly influenced by Byzantine types, are strongly modelled with flesh-tints brushed with vigorous, broken strokes over a dark greenish undercoat. The colors are strong and include sharp reds and yellows, as well as subdued lavender and dull rose. The peculiarly restless and decorative page layout cannot be compared with any other manuscript at present known, but the pictorial style is very close to the Epistolarium in Padua that was executed by Gaibana in 1259. Resemblance to other manuscripts and to frescos, as well as certain textual details, suggest the region of the Veneto or possibly Aquileia as the place where the manuscript may have originated.

BIBLIOGRAPHY: De Ricci, I, p. 764, no. 44, with previous bibliography; Boston Museum of Fine Arts, *Arts of the Middle Ages*, Boston, 1940, no. 33, ill. Cf. B. Katterbach, *Le miniature dell'Epistolario di Padova dell'anno 1259*. Città del Vaticano, 1932.

COLLECTION OF THE WALTERS ART GALLERY.   PL. XXIII

37. MINIATURE FROM AN ANTIPHONARY Italy (Tuscany ?), 13th cent.

   Single vellum leaf, 18½ x 14½ inches. 1 miniature. Said to be from a convent near Bologna. Ex-coll.: Arthur Sambon.

The Nativity is represented as occurring in a rocky cave. The Christ Child is being bathed by two women at the left, and appears again, lying in the manger beside the reclining Virgin, a double representation that is frequent in Byzantine painting. The entire composition, of monumental proportions, is exceptionally decorative in handling; its main features are accented and tied together by the inscribed red banderolles flaunted by the crowd of angels above and by the six Dominican monks praying in their cloister below.

LENT BY THE NATIONAL GALLERY OF ART, ROSENWALD COLLECTION.   PL. XXII

38. BIBLE Northern Italy, ca. 1300

   W. 151. In Latin. Gothic script in 2 cols. 558 vellum leaves, 11¼ x 8⅛ inches. 87 historiated initials; numerous drolleries. Binding: modern black morocco. Ex-colls.: Bentivoglio (15th cent.); H. Yates Thompson (Sale, London, 1919, no. 13).

A Bible probably executed in the region of Bologna around 1300 or slightly earlier. The well composed and decorative miniatures, initials and marginal ornaments are painted in flat tones of subdued blue, pink, green and grey, enlivened by an orange-red and gold. There is a predilection for Franciscan subjects. The arms of the Bentivoglio family of Bologna were inserted throughout the book in the fifteenth century.

   BIBLIOGRAPHY: De Ricci, I, p. 766, no. 56, with previous literature.

COLLECTION OF THE WALTERS ART GALLERY.

39. BIBLE Northern Italy, 13th cent.

   W. 122. In Latin. Gothic script in 2 cols. 442 vellum leaves, 9½ x 7 inches. 82 historiated and numerous ornamented initials. Binding: modern vellum.

Executed around 1275, by a group of artists whose figure style and modelling are based upon Byzantine traditions, but whose work has a light and gay effect because of the delicacy of their technique and color.

   BIBLIOGRAPHY: De Ricci, I, p. 765, no. 53.

COLLECTION OF THE WALTERS ART GALLERY.

40. GRATIAN, DECRETALS Italy (Bologna ?), ca. 1300

   Garrett ms. 97. In Latin. Written in 2 cols. with surrounding commentary and numerous annotations. 331 vellum leaves, 18¼ x 11⅞ inches. 37 miniatures. Binding: 19th century stamped calf. Ex-coll.: Robert Garrett.

This work, composed in northern Italy in the first half of the twelfth century, became the foundation of medieval Canon Law. The present copy is exceptional for the diversity and interest of the illustrations, which are unusually explicit in detail. Two principal hands can be distinguished.

Twenty-eight of the miniatures are in characteristic early Bologna style, flat and romanesque. The remainder are by a gifted artist greatly influenced by Byzantine painting, who works in a vivid, delicate style, employing light, clear colors and cold, sharp highlights to enhance the modelling.

BIBLIOGRAPHY: De Ricci, I, p. 884, no. 97.

LENT BY PRINCETON UNIVERSITY LIBRARY, GARRETT COLLECTION.

41. SCENES FROM THE BIBLE   England, 13th cent.

W. 106. French tituli. 24 vellum leaves, 5¼ x 3⅞ inches. 27 full-page miniatures. Binding: modern red velvet set with a 14th century French ivory plaque.

These miniatures were executed in the third quarter of the thirteenth century by W. de Brailes, an English artist, probably a monk, and one of only two thirteenth century English painters whose name can now be associated with definite works. Brailes was first discovered by Sir Sydney Cockerell, who was able to find six books or groups of leaves in his hand, including four instances of his signed self-portrait. The Walters leaves are not signed, but Brailes' somewhat humorous style is sufficiently individual to make the attribution to him perfectly certain. Such series of Bible illustrations were generally prefixed to Psalters in England during the thirteenth century. Dr. Hanns Swarzenski, who first recognized Brailes' hand in these miniatures, has proposed that they may possibly have formed part of the same manuscript as an incomplete prayer-book illuminated by Brailes in the collection of Mr. Dyson Perrins. Seven more full-page miniatures from our series were discovered by Mr. Eric Millar in the Georges Wildenstein collection in Paris. Of particular interest is the great range of scenes, including many episodes rarely depicted, which when considered together with earlier English works, must reflect a tradition going back to a very ancient lost cycle of Bible illustrations.

BIBLIOGRAPHY: De Ricci, I, p. 844, no. 500; Hanns Swarzenski, *Unknown Bible Pictures by W. de Brailes* in *Journal of the Walters Art Gallery*, I (1938), pp. 55-69, with complete illustration; E. Millar, *Additional Miniatures by W. de Brailes* in *Journal of the Walters Art Gallery*, II (1939), pp. 106-109, illus. (Wildenstein leaves). Cf. S. C. Cockerell, *The Work of W. de Brailes. An English Illuminator of the Thirteenth Century*. The Roxburghe Club. Cambridge, 1930; E. G. Millar, *English Illuminated Manuscripts from the Xth to the XIIIth Century*, Paris and Brussels, 1926, pp. 49-51.

COLLECTION OF THE WALTERS ART GALLERY.   PL. XXI

42. BIBLE   England, 13th cent.

Garrett ms. 28. In Latin. Gothic script. 458 vellum leaves, 9½ x 6¾ inches. Illuminated initials. Binding: 19th century English blue morocco. Ex-colls.: Robert Gilmor II (bought 1832); William Gilmor; T. Harrison Garrett; Robert Garrett.

Most of the initials are executed in red and blue with foliate rinceaux, pen flourishes, drolleries and figures of considerable imaginative quality. Particularly English is the recurring use of rather naturalistic foliage, such as strawberry leaves. The historiated initials often are shaped of contorted animals, reminiscent of the bestiaries, and are well executed on gold or delicately diapered backgrounds. This Bible was one of about a dozen manuscripts owned by Robert Gilmor II of Baltimore, one of the earliest American art collectors.

BIBLIOGRAPHY: De Ricci, I, p. 869, no. 28.

LENT BY PRINCETON UNIVERSITY LIBRARY, GARRETT COLLECTION.

43. BIBLE   France, 13th cent.

    W. 56. In Latin. Gothic script in 2 cols. 464 vellum leaves, 8⅜ x 5¾ inches. 64 historiated initials. Binding: modern purple velvet.

Executed about 1260 in a style similar to that of the Lewis Psalter (no. 52). The free vigorous movement of the figures, the flowing folds of the drapery and the coloring relate these minute scenes to the paintings of the larger book.

    BIBLIOGRAPHY: De Ricci, I, p. 766, no. 49.

COLLECTION OF THE WALTERS ART GALLERY.   PL. XXX

44. BIBLE   England ?, 13th cent.

    W. 59. In Latin. Gothic script in 2 cols. 523 vellum leaves, 10¼ x 6¾ inches. Numerous historiated and ornamented initials. Binding: 15th century Spanish stamped morocco over boards.

The drawing of the scenes in the initials is delicate and expressive in outline and has the sureness of works on a far larger scale.

    BIBLIOGRAPHY: De Ricci, I, p. 765, no. 50.

COLLECTION OF THE WALTERS ART GALLERY.

45. BIBLE   France, 13th cent.

    W. 51. In Latin. Gothic script in 2 cols. 525 vellum leaves, 5¾ x 3¾ inches. 2 full-page miniatures; 38 historiated and 37 ornamented initials. Binding: 18th century French morocco.

A characteristic example of the small, handy Bibles for personal use, finely written in minute script on tissue-thin vellum, that were produced in great numbers in Paris in the thirteenth century as a result of the impetus given to Biblical studies by the scholars of the Sorbonne. The initials in this example avoid the use of gold, but the scenes are vigorously designed and finely drawn.

    BIBLIOGRAPHY: De Ricci, I, p. 765, no. 46.

COLLECTION OF THE WALTERS ART GALLERY.

46. ILLUSTRATIONS FROM THE OLD TESTAMENT   France (Paris), ca. 1250

    M. 638. 43 vellum leaves, 15⅜ x 11¾ inches. 86 full-page illustrations. Binding: Oriental leather. Ex-colls.: Cardinal Bernard Maciejowski of Poland (16th century), presented 1604 to Shah Abbas the Great of Persia; Giovanni d'Athanasi (Sale, London, March 15, 1833, no. 201); Sir Thomas Phillipps, no. 8025.

It is considered probable that these remarkable leaves, containing 283 scenes by several artists of great ability, were originally prefixed to a large Psalter. Two other leaves from this manuscript are in the Bibliothèque Nationale in Paris, and another is in the possession of Sir Sydney Cockerell. The illustrations commence with the Creation and terminate with II *Samuel*, XX. Many episodes rarely represented are included, all presented with great richness of narrative detail. As customary at the time, the events are depicted as if of contemporary occurrence, so that the miniatures present us with a detailed picture-book of thirteenth century life. Particularly notable is the facile rendering of unusual and foreshortened poses, and the dignity and serenity with which the figures move through the complex narratives represented.

The book has travelled widely and bears witness to the diverse owners who have been fascinated by the pictures. The margins bear explanatory inscriptions in a fourteenth century Italian writing and also in Persian and in Hebrew. These last two sets of captions date from the early seventeenth century, when the book was presented to Shah Abbas the Great of Persia, who ordered the meaning of each picture to be transcribed for his benefit.

BIBLIOGRAPHY: S. C. Cockerell and M. R. James, *A Book of Old Testament Illustrations . . . in the Pierpont Morgan Library*, Cambridge, for the Roxburghe Club, 1927; Belle da Costa Greene and Meta P. Harrsen, *Exhibition of Illuminated Manuscripts. . . .*, New York, 1934, pp. 27-28, no. 53, pl. 49, with previous literature; De Ricci, II, p. 1475, no. 638.

LENT BY THE PIERPONT MORGAN LIBRARY.   PL. XXV

47. BIBLE HISTORIÉE ET VIES DES SAINTS — Northern France, ca. 1300

In French. Gothic script. 154 vellum leaves, 12¼ x 8¾ inches. 846 miniatures. Binding: 19th century English red morocco. Ex-colls.: John Perceval, fourth Earl of Egmont (Sale, London, July 14, 1834, p. 63, no. 1308); Robert S. Holford; Sir George Holford (Sale, London, July 29, 1929, no. 9, pl. VIII-IX).

The table of contents of this book states that it was "extracted from the histories of the Old and the New Testament" and that it recounts the lives and miracles of the Apostles, saints and martyrs, illustrated by 1034 figures and "explained in writing". Of these pictures 846 survive in the book at present, executed by several hands, the finest distinguished for the graceful and expressive character of the drawing. The color, as in many north French manuscripts of the period, tends to be somewhat dark and heavy in tone. The most frequent arrangement of the scenes is in the form of a column of illustrations on patterned backgrounds of great variety, paralleling a column of text.

BIBLIOGRAPHY: De Ricci, II, p. 1340, no. 22, with previous literature.

LENT BY THE NEW YORK PUBLIC LIBRARY, SPENCER COLLECTION.   PL. XXVIII

48. PSALTER AND HOURS — England (East Anglia), 13th cent.

W. 34. In Latin. Gothic script. 32 vellum leaves, 9¾ x 7 inches. 26 full-page miniatures; 11 historiated and numerous armorial initials. Binding: modern English limp vellum. Ex-colls.: John Baptist, third Lord Caryll (1716-1780); George Galway Mills (Sale, London, Feb. 24, 1800); Rev. David T. Powell (Sale, London, July 31, 1848, no. 642); Earl of Ashburnham (Appendix, no. 33); H. Yates Thompson (Sale, London, 1920, no. 34, pls.).

Executed in East Anglia between 1250 and 1260, by the fifteenth century this abundantly illuminated Psalter belonged to the nuns of Carrow Abbey near Norwich. Although the miniatures are not of great delicacy, they all are characterized by the gentle humor of English thirteenth-century painting, and the best of them, such as the Annunciation, are well designed. The gold backgrounds are especially rich. The initial at the beginning of the Psalms frames a number of scenes from the life of St. Olaf, an unusual subject.

BIBLIOGRAPHY: De Ricci, I, p. 771, no. 90, with previous literature; G. Haseloff, *Die Psalterillustration im 13. Jahrhundert*, n.p., 1938, p. 61.

COLLECTION OF THE WALTERS ART GALLERY.   PL. XXX

49. PSALTERFlanders, ca. 1300

    W. 85. In Latin. Gothic script. 116 vellum leaves, 2¾ x 2 inches. Numerous historiated initials and marginal drolleries. Binding: modern green velvet.

A tiny book, embellished on every page with historiated or ornamented initials and vigorous marginal grotesques.

    BIBLIOGRAPHY: De Ricci, I, p. 782, no. 160.

COLLECTION OF THE WALTERS ART GALLERY.PL. XXXI

50. PSALTERFlanders, ca. 1270

    W. 112. In Latin. Gothic script. 256 vellum leaves, 4¾ x 3-9/16 inches. 9 historiated initials and 12 calendar pictures. Binding: modern red velvet.

Although not elaborate in illumination, this Psalter has fine qualities of drawing.

    BIBLIOGRAPHY: De Ricci, I, p. 772, no. 92.

COLLECTION OF THE WALTERS ART GALLERY.

51. BOOK OF HOURSNorthern France (Thérouanne use), 1st half of 14th cent.

    W. 90. In Latin. Gothic script. 254 vellum leaves, 5¼ x 3¾ inches. 7 full-page miniatures; 24 historiated initials; numerous drolleries. Binding: 18th century French green morocco, in manner of Derôme le Jeune.

Executed for a lady of the region of Thérouanne in French Flanders, this little prayer book has, in addition to the main illumination, an abundance of ornamental borders peopled with marginal grotesques, which decorate nearly every page. The entry for Easter in the calendar would indicate that the manuscript was written either in 1323 or 1334.

    BIBLIOGRAPHY: De Ricci, I, p. 783, no. 168.

COLLECTION OF THE WALTERS ART GALLERY.PL. XXVIII

52. PSALTERNorthern France, ca. 1260

    Lewis ms. 185. In Latin. Gothic script. 191 vellum leaves, 9 x 6½ inches. 24 full-page miniatures; 24 small calendar illustrations; 1 large and numerous smaller historiated initials; numerous fantastic line-endings. Binding: 17th century French black morocco. Ex-colls.: Henry Gee Barnard, Cave Castle, Howden, Yorkshire; Clarence S. Bement; Robert Hoe (Sale, New York, 1912, II, no. 2507); John F. Lewis.

A manuscript of exceptional richness and beauty, which is a noteworthy example of the luxury books of the thirteenth century. Not only the abundance of the illumination, but the sustained quality that characterizes the workmanship throughout, the richness of the materials, fineness of the semi-transparent vellum, the meticulous finish of even the least of the illuminated initials, all suggest that this book was destined for an owner or an occasion of distinction. However, indications of original personal ownership are lacking. Certain saints in the calendar point to the region of Sens, but as yet no precise locality has been established. The main illustration consists of the forty-eight scenes from Christ's life contained in pairs of roundels on the preliminary pages. The roundels are set against patterned backgrounds alternately rose and blue, the spaces left by the curved shapes at midpoint and corners being filled by heraldic animals executed in liquid gold, thickly laid on, so as to suggest elements of goldsmith's work.

The scenes are composed with clarity and grace, the abundant drapery folds being modelled by succeeding washes of grey and even black over the basic color, which is always soft: rose, blue, grey, grey-blue, light green and a dull lavender. The general effect is luminous, but not brilliant.

BIBLIOGRAPHY: E. Wolf, 2nd, *A Descriptive Catalogue of the John Frederick Lewis Collection of European Manuscripts in the Free Library of Philadelphia*, Philadelphia, 1937, pp. 200-204, no. 185, frontispiece and pls. XXXIX-XLII; De Ricci, II, p. 2028, no. 21, both with previous literature.

LENT BY THE PHILADELPHIA FREE LIBRARY, JOHN FREDERICK LEWIS COLLECTION.   PL. XXVI

53. PSALTER AND CANTICLES — Northern France, 13th cent.

W. 44. In Latin. Gothic script. 207 vellum leaves, 6⅛ x 4 inches. 10 full-page miniatures and 10 historiated initials. Binding: modern brown velvet.

The somewhat attenuated figures are delicately outlined as to heads and hands, but the drapery is more heavily drawn and is modelled with grey shadows.

BIBLIOGRAPHY: De Ricci, I, p. 770, no. 80.

COLLECTION OF THE WALTERS ART GALLERY.

54. PSALTER AND HOURS — Northeastern France, end of 13th cent.

Widener ms. 9. In Latin. Gothic script. 241 vellum leaves, 7½ x 5¼ inches. 12 full-page miniatures; 24 calendar pictures; 20 historiated initials; numerous drolleries. Binding: late 16th century French morocco, fanfare. Early in possession of family of La Tour d'Auvergne. Ex-colls.: Count Max Mielzynski, Pawlowice Castle, Poland; Joseph Widener.

The main illustration consists of scenes from the life of Christ—in two registers on a series of preliminary leaves. The figures are drawn with considerable freedom of line and movement against very heavy burnished gold grounds.

BIBLIOGRAPHY: De Ricci, II, p. 2117, no. 9; G. Haseloff, *Die Psalterillustration im 13. Jahrhundert*, n.p., 1938, pp. 54 ff.

LENT BY THE PHILADELPHIA FREE LIBRARY, PRESENTED IN MEMORY OF JOSEPH E. WIDENER.
PL. XXVIII

55. BOOK OF HOURS — Flanders, late 13th cent.

W. 37. In Latin. Gothic script. 197 vellum leaves, 3⅝ x 2¾ inches. 14 full-page miniatures; 11 large and numerous small historiated initials; 24 calendar pictures; numerous marginal drolleries. Binding: 15th century wooden boards and stamped calf.

An example of the tiny prayer books that first became popular for personal use at the end of the thirteenth century and remained in favor until the early years of the sixteenth. On the flyleaves of this book are the ownership notes of the noble family of the Figinnes of Huy, who handed it down from generation to generation, commencing with Guillaume de Figinnes, lord of Boullion, who died in 1410.

BIBLIOGRAPHY: De Ricci, I, p. 782, no. 158.

COLLECTION OF THE WALTERS ART GALLERY.   PL. XXXI

56. BOOK OF HOURS   Northern France, late 13th cent.

W. 39. In Latin. Gothic script. 157 vellum leaves, 7⅞ x 2⅝ inches. 9 historiated initials and 12 calendar pictures; numerous drolleries. Binding: modern French morocco set with 14th century ivory plaque.

The calendar pictures are particularly well designed for a work on such a small scale of this period.

BIBLIOGRAPHY: De Ricci, I, p. 781, no. 156.

COLLECTION OF THE WALTERS ART GALLERY.   PL. XXXI

57. PSALTER   Northern France, ca. 1250

W. 45. In Latin. Gothic script. 291 vellum leaves, 7⅛ x 4¾ inches. 8 historiated initials and numerous marginal drolleries. Binding: early 16th century stamped calf by Vivianus da Varese of Genoa.

A book of Franciscan use that was executed for a member of the Fieschi family of the Genoese campagna (Lavagnia). The calendar records the birth in 1246 of Leonardo da Fieschi, son of Albert, Count of Lavagnia. There were many intermarriages of the Fieschi with French families during the fifteenth century, so this book may have come to Italy as the result of one of these weddings. The marginal drolleries are finely conceived and executed.

BIBLIOGRAPHY: De Ricci, I, pp. 771 f., no. 91.

COLLECTION OF THE WALTERS ART GALLERY.

58. PSALTER   Franco-Flemish, 13th cent.

M. 72. In Latin. Gothic script. 219 vellum leaves, 6¼ x 4½ inches. 16 full-page miniatures and 12 calendar illustrations. Binding: modern red morocco. Ex-colls.: Gerard de Damville, Bishop of Cambrai; A. Firmin-Didot (Sale, Paris, 1875, no. 5); Prince Liechtenstein; Richard Bennett.

This Psalter is one of a small group, related by a common illustrative scheme, which appears to have been produced in the region of St. Omer during the second half of the thirteenth century. The miniatures in this book are characterized by particular refinement of style, the figures appearing against the heavy burnished gold backgrounds with a charming elegance of pose and movement. Draperies fall with a gothic grace that has not yet become mannered. Accessories, reduced to the minimum essential for the narrative, are incorporated into the compositions as a subtle emphasis to the rhythm of the figures.

BIBLIOGRAPHY: Belle da Costa Greene and Meta P. Harrsen, *Exhibition of Illuminated Manuscripts....*, New York, 1934, p. 29, no. 55, pl. 51, with previous literature; De Ricci, II, p. 1379, no. 72; G. Haseloff, *Die Psalterillustration im 13. Jahrhundert*, n.p., 1938, pp. 68, 122-123.

LENT BY THE PIERPONT MORGAN LIBRARY.   PL. XXVII

59. PSALTER AND HOURS OF THE VIRGIN — France (Amiens ?), ca. 1275

M. 729. In Latin. Gothic script. 434 vellum leaves, 7⅛ x 5⅛ inches. 40 full-page miniatures; 66 historiated initials; numerous borders with armorial decoration; numerous drolleries. Binding: modern blue morocco. Ex-colls.: W. Y. Ottley (Sale, London, May 11, 1838, nos. 127 and 2440); Robert S. Holford; Sir George Holford.

Executed for Yolande, Vicomtesse de Soissons, wife of Bernard V, sire de Moreuil, showing her arms in the borders throughout. The abundant illustration includes many unusual subjects. Several artists executed the miniatures, the most skillful employing a style resembling that ascribed to "Maître Honoré" of Paris. The figures and drapery are drawn with a notable grace and sweetness of line, which has not yet become mannered or exaggerated. Dignity and a certain solidity is achieved by the lack of attenuation and by the light modelling. The scenes are represented either against heavy burnished gold or against delicately patterned color, and many of the frames are capped by the gabled gothic arcading that often characterizes manuscripts of this period from French Flanders.

BIBLIOGRAPHY: The Pierpont Morgan Library, *Review of the Growth, Development . . . 1924-1929*, New York, 1930, pp. 27-29, pl. XIV; Belle da Costa Greene and Meta P. Harrsen, *Exhibition of Illuminated Manuscripts. . . .*, New York, 1934, no. 57, pl. 52; De Ricci, II, p. 1490, no. 729, with previous literature.

LENT BY THE PIERPONT MORGAN LIBRARY.   PL. XXVII

60. BOOK OF HOURS — Northern France, ca. 1300

W. 98. In Latin and French. 121 vellum leaves, 6 x 4⅜ inches; incomplete and misbound. 5 large and 7 small historiated initials. Binding: modern maroon velvet.

This manuscript was executed for a lady who is depicted in several of the miniatures and whose motto "Seigns lignars" appears on one page. The imperfect state of the book renders liturgical localization difficult, but the representation of St. Honorine in one of the major initials suggests the region of Honfleur in Normandy, a localization that would accord well with the English influence to be seen in the paintings and ornament. The illustrations are finely drawn, and are, for the period, somewhat unusual in the completely flat and decorative handling of all elements of the composition, which contrasts with the realistically differentiated leaves in the ornamental sprays and borders. Six historiated initials are devoted to episodes in the finding of the True Cross by St. Helena, mother of Constantine.

BIBLIOGRAPHY: De Ricci, I, p. 784, no. 170.

COLLECTION OF THE WALTERS ART GALLERY.

61. BREVIARY FOR DIJON USE — France, end of 13th cent.

W. 109. In Latin. Gothic script in 2 cols. 411 vellum leaves, 7⅛ x 4¾ inches. 33 historiated initials; 8 ornamented initials; 41 partial borders with drolleries. Binding: modern rose velvet. Formerly belonged to monastery of St. Benigne de Dijon.

The initials and drolleries are executed in an exceptionally delicate and vivacious style. The book is prefaced by a Table of Easter dates from 1287 to 1500.

BIBLIOGRAPHY: De Ricci, I, p. 777, no. 131.

COLLECTION OF THE WALTERS ART GALLERY.

62. APOCALYPSE							England (St. Albans ?), ca. 1260

> M. 524. In Latin. Gothic script. 77 vellum leaves, 10¾ x 7⅝ inches. 42 full-page and 1 half-page illustration. Binding: modern morocco in 2 vols. Ex-coll.: Vicomte Blin de Bourdon.

An example of the Apocalypse picture-books that achieved a considerable vogue in France and England during the thirteenth century. The text in this case is confined to excerpts from the Book of Revelations, written in red and blue on the uncolored backgrounds of the miniatures or on banderolles held by the figures. A commentary, now bound separately, was added to this manuscript around 1400.

The rectangular miniatures, disposed two to a page, are tinted outline drawings of much grace. The translucent washes of light green, blue, rose and tan serve only to point up the lyric quality of the outlines, which trace compositions knit by gently undulating, continuous movement.

The manuscript is listed in the "first family" of the gothic Apocalypses, as classified by Delisle and Meyer. It is very close to the Bodleian ms. Auct. D. 4.17

> BIBLIOGRAPHY: Rohault de Fleury, *Les Saints de la messe*, VIII, Paris, 1899, pl. 54; L. Delisle and P. Meyer, *L'apocalypse en français au XIIIe siècle*, Paris, 1901, pp. LXXIII-LXXVII and CLV-CLXIV, pl.; Belle da Costa Greene and Meta P. Harrsen, *Exhibition of Illuminated Manuscripts...*, New York, 1934, p. 235, no. 44, pl. 41; M. R. James, *The Apocalypse in Art*, London, 1931, no. 3, p. 3; De Ricci, II, p. 1466, no. 524.

LENT BY THE PIERPONT MORGAN LIBRARY.					PL. XXIX

63. MISSAL FOR NOYON USE						Northern France, before 1250

> In Latin. Gothic script and music in 2 cols. 6 vellum leaves, 17 x 11 inches. 7 historiated and 6 ornamented initials.

These leaves, from a lost Missal of luxurious nature, are of particular interest because the illumination has been attributed to Villard de Honnecourt, the thirteenth century architect whose album of sketches is one of the most instructive relics of this period. The style of the paintings is indeed very close to his—especially in the combination of plasticity and of rhythmic linear grace, in the proportions of the slightly swaying figures, the character of the drapery with its curving loop-shaped folds, and the play of long skirts about the feet. Outright attribution of these paintings to Villard is no longer agreed to by scholars, as the conditions of collaboration in the medieval atelier usually make such definite assignments debatable, but the close connection with Villard's style is unquestioned. In any case, these leaves with their miniatures and the delicately rotating foliate initials populated by springing beasts are the very essence of French thirteenth-century painting in its "purest" and most refined phase.

> BIBLIOGRAPHY: Graf Vitzthum, *Fragment eines Missale von Noyon mit Miniaturen von Villard de Honnecourt* in *Beiträge zur Forschung; Studien und Mitteilungen aus dem Antiquariat Jacques Rosenthal*, Munich, 1 Folge, Heft IV/V, pp. 102-113, taf. XIV-XVI; H. R. Hahnloser, *Villard de Honnecourt*, Vienna, 1935, pp. 217-219, figs. 10, 17.

LENT BY PHILIP AND FRANCES HOFER.					PL. XXIV

64. ROMAN DE LANCELOT DU LAC   Northeast France, ca. 1300

 M. 805-6. In French. Gothic script in 3 cols. 2 vols. (originally in 1). 266 vellum leaves, 10¾ x 7½ inches. 39 miniatures. Binding: 19th century English pink morocco. Ex-colls.: Jehan de Brosse, Maréchal de France (d. 1433); Joseph Barrois; Earl of Ashburnham (ms. Barrois 36), (Sale, London, 1901, no. 537, pl.); C. Fairfax Murray; H. Yates Thompson (Sale, London, June, 1921, III, no. 69, pls. IX-XI); Cortlandt F. Bishop (Sale, New York, April 25, 1938, no. 1264).

This manuscript, containing the first two sections of the Romance of Lancelot, is considered the finest illuminated example of his legend. The long, rectangular miniatures extending across the page, are each divided into halves, the background at the left being of burnished gold, while the right is diapered in blue or pink. They are executed with exceptional charm, the graphic elegance and vivacious colors, as well as the over-refined figures with their rhythmic and delicate movements appearing to modern eyes as the very epitome of the age of chivalry.

 BIBLIOGRAPHY: De Ricci, II, pp. 1658-1659, nos. 20-22, with previous literature; *The Pierpont Morgan Library, Illustrated Catalogue of an Exhibition held on the Occasion of the New York World's Fair*, New York, 1940, p. 11, no. 27, pl. III, 2 color pls.; *The Pierpont Morgan Library, 1936-1940*, New York, 1941, pp. 46-48, pl. I, with literature; R. S. Loomis and L. H. Loomis, *Arthurian Legends in Medieval Art*, London & New York, 1938, pp. 98-101, figs. 250-253 and color pl.; M. R. Scherer, *About the Round Table*, New York, 1945, pp. 53-54, 56, ill.

LENT BY THE PIERPONT MORGAN LIBRARY.   PL. XXXII

65. DECRETALS OF GRATIAN   North France or England, ca. 1300

 W. 133. In Latin. Gothic book hand in 2 cols. with surrounding commentary. 344 vellum leaves, 17 x 12 inches. 35 historiated initials and 4 large illuminated initials. Binding: 19th century French morocco over boards. Ex-colls.: Astorga (Sale, 1870, no. 14); A. Firmin-Didot (Sale, Paris, 1879, no. 38); Prince Liechtenstein; William Morris (Sale, London, 1898, no. 558); L. W. Hodson of Compton Hall (Sale, London, 1906, no. 275).

Written in brown ink on even sheets of suede-like vellum. The miniatures are in a good style which suggests an origin in England or in a locality in northern France influenced by England. The commentary is that of Bartholomew of Brescia.

 BIBLIOGRAPHY: De Ricci, I, p. 825, no. 407.

COLLECTION OF THE WALTERS ART GALLERY.

66. MISSAL   Flanders, 1300

 W. 127. In Latin. Gothic script. 214 vellum leaves, 13½ x 9½ inches. 13 historiated initials. Binding: modern red velvet.

A handsome book of large script and decorative, well-executed initials, several of unusual iconography. The book is precisely dated not only by the entries for Palm Sunday, Good Friday and Easter in the calendar, but by the mention of the turning of the century, inscribed under March 18, in accordance with the Old Style Roman calendar.

 BIBLIOGRAPHY: De Ricci, I, p. 775, no. 116.

COLLECTION OF THE WALTERS ART GALLERY.

67. PSALTER   French Flanders (Arras), ca. 1310

> W. 115. In Latin. Gothic script with music. 222 vellum leaves, 5¾ x 4 inches. 8 historiated initials. Binding: 18th century French citron morocco.

A little Psalter of fine material and exceptional excellence of workmanship. The elegantly drawn figures are shown against diapered grounds of color and gold, or, in some cases, carefully tooled and burnished gold leaf. Each large initial, its form lightened by areas of interlace, sends forth a fine ivy border to surround the page.

The book, of Dominican use, was made for a member of the family of Phillipe d'Artois and his wife Marguerite of Arras, countess of Evreux.

> BIBLIOGRAPHY: De Ricci, I, p. 774, no. 105.

COLLECTION OF THE WALTERS ART GALLERY.   PL. XXXII

68. ALBERTUS MAGNUS. DE LAUDIBUS VIRGINIS   French Flanders, ca. 1300

> Ms. 19. In Latin. Gothic script. 503 vellum leaves, 11¾ x 8¼ inches. 12 historiated initials. Binding: 19th century calf. Ex-colls.: Margaret Rood Hazard; Caroline Hazard.

Illuminated in a delicate style very close indeed to that of no. 67. The allegorical miniatures in the initials also recall certain of the illustrations in a Flemish Missal, no. 127 in this catalogue, although more refined in execution. Some of the leaves of Book XII were added in Italy in the fifteenth century.

> BIBLIOGRAPHY: S. Der Nersessian in *Gazette des Beaux-Arts*, 6th ser., XXVI (1944), p. 78 and note, fig. 7.

LENT BY WELLESLEY COLLEGE LIBRARY.   PL. XXXII

69. GUILIELMUS DURANDUS. IN SENTENTIAS PETRI LOMBARDI   France (Paris), 1336

> Garrett ms. 83. In Latin. Gothic script. 2 vols., 199 and 212 vellum leaves, 15¾ x 11 inches. 2 historiated initials and illuminated borders. Binding: modern green velvet. Ex-colls.: Earl of Ashburnham (Appendix, no. 253); H. Yates Thompson (Sale, London, May 11, 1901, no. 16); Robert Garrett.

Written in Paris in 1336 by the English scribe, William of Kirkby in Lincolnshire, at the command of Simon Comitis of Naples, head of the Dominican order in Paris. A. E. Bye first noticed the connection not only of the ornament in general, but of precise drolleries with patterns used in the Belleville Breviary, Paris, Bibliothèque Nationale, ms. lat., 10483-4, which is signed by Jean Pucelle, the most distinguished illuminator to King Charles IV. The dragon-fly, often supposed to be a rebus-signature of Pucelle, is present in the Garrett manuscript as well as in the Belleville Breviary. Bye very conservatively and quite correctly attributed the manuscript to an atelier using some of the Pucelle models, rather than to the master himself. Pucelle was distinguished for a most elegant and graceful style, free and fluid of action and expressive of narrative, which was enhanced by light and delicate modelling. His incidental drolleries show a direct and tender observation of the natural characteristics of birds, beasts, insects and flowers. Although the general *mis-en-page* of the Durandus is strikingly close to the Pucelle manuscripts and the aristocratic decorative charm is there, yet the peculiar lightness, vitality and subtle modelling of veritable Pucelle works are missing.

BIBLIOGRAPHY: A. E. Bye in *Art in America*, IV (1916), pp. 98-118, figs. 1-3; De Ricci, I, p. 880, no. 83; D. Egbert in *The Princeton University Library Chronicle*, III (1942), p. 127, ill.

LENT BY PRINCETON UNIVERSITY LIBRARY, GARRETT COLLECTION.

70. ST. AUGUSTINE. DE CIVITATE DEI   France, ca. 1380

In French. Gothic script in 2 cols. 3 vols. totalling 318 vellum leaves, 18¾ x 13¼ inches. 12 miniatures; numerous illuminated initials and borders. Binding: modern red velvet. Ex-colls.: Jean, duc de Berry; H. Yates Thompson (Sale, London, March 23, 1920, II, no. 54, pl. 35); A. Chester Beatty (Sale, London, June 7, 1932, I, no. 19, pl. 25).

The French translation by Raoul de Praelles of Augustine's *City of God*, in a fine copy executed for Jean, duc de Berry, brother of King Charles V of France and the prince of medieval bibliophiles. The illustrations, by at least three different hands, are delicately drawn in *grisaille*, partly tinted in color, against grounds ornamented with diapering or rinceaux. The finest of the hands has much of the grace and freshness associated with the artist known as the Maître aux Bouquetaux. The frequent appearance of surprising freedom of pose does not necessarily indicate original invention on the part of the illustrators of this book, as the Comte de Laborde has pointed out the close relation of this manuscript to two other examples of the *City of God* from the same atelier, one in the British Museum, ms. Add. 15245, and the other, Bibliothèque Nationale, ms. fr. 22912-3. Each differs to greater or less extent, however, and the present example does not yield to the others in respect to quality or vivacity.

The first volume of this manuscript, containing chapters I to XXI, has been identified with an imperfect volume in the municipal library at Angers, ms. fr. 162.

BIBLIOGRAPHY: Comte A. de Laborde, *Les manuscrits à peintures de la Cité de Dieu*, Paris, 1902, I, pp. 241-244, no. 7, pls. VI-IX; E. Millar, *The Library of A. Chester Beatty, a Descriptive Catalogue of the Western Manuscripts*, II, Oxford, 1930, pp. 144-147, no. 73, pls. CLIX-CLXI; De Ricci, II, pp. 1695 f., no. 17, with other literature.

LENT BY PHILIP AND FRANCES HOFER.   PL. XXXIII

71. GRANDES CHRONIQUES DE FRANCE   France, end of 14th cent.

W. 139. In French. Gothic book hand in 2 cols. 497 vellum leaves, 15 x 11½ inches. 1 large and 36 small miniatures; 40 illuminated initials. Binding: early sheepskin over boards. Ex-colls.: Johannes Michel, "1592, in carcere"; Lemaire de Flicourt (1692); duc de La Rochefoucauld, Château de Roche-Guyon (Sale, Paris, July 2, 1927, no. 3).

A history of France, tracing the fortunes of the people from mythical origins down to 1380 A.D. The text is a compilation of romance, legend and fact, such as passed for history in the Middle Ages. This example, of handsome format, is illustrated with drawings in *grisaille*.

BIBLIOGRAPHY: Jacques Rosenthal, *Bibliotheca Medii Aevi Manuscripta*, (cat. 90), Munich [1928], pp. 29 f., pl.; De Ricci, I, p. 850, no. 523.

COLLECTION OF THE WALTERS ART GALLERY.

72. MISSAL FOR THE USE OF PARIS France (Paris), ca. 1380

W. 124. In Latin. Gothic script in 2 cols. with music. 295 vellum leaves, 10¼ x 7⅛ inches. 17 historiated initials; illuminated borders. Binding: modern vellum. Belonged in 17th century to the Chartreuse of Beaune.

The lightly handled modelling of the miniatures and of the grotesques that inhabit the ivy borders is a late reflection of the style inaugurated by Jean Pucelle earlier in the century. The colors are thinly laid on, but clear and light.

BIBLIOGRAPHY: De Ricci, I, p. 776, no. 119.

COLLECTION OF THE WALTERS ART GALLERY.

73. PSALTER France (Paris), ca. 1380

W. 119. In Latin. Gothic script. 187 vellum leaves, 6⅝ x 4¾ inches. 8 historiated initials; illuminated borders. Binding: old vellum.

A manuscript in the same tradition as no. 72, but more carefully executed and highly finished. Instead of grotesques, delightfully realistic birds and insects have been introduced into the ivy borders. The figures, finely modelled, appear against backgrounds minutely patterned with scroll-work or diapering.

BIBLIOGRAPHY: De Ricci, I, p. 773, no. 104.

COLLECTION OF THE WALTERS ART GALLERY.

74. BOOK OF HOURS France (Paris), ca. 1390

W. 94. In Latin. Gothic script. 186 vellum leaves, 5⅜ x 4 inches. 11 miniatures; illuminated borders. Binding: 18th century red morocco.

A once fine book illuminated by an artist in the atelier of Jacquemart de Hesdin. The delicate colors and softly modelled surface of the paintings have suffered considerably from wear.

BIBLIOGRAPHY: De Ricci, I, p. 784, no. 174.

COLLECTION OF THE WALTERS ART GALLERY.   PL. XXXIV

75. JACQUES DE LONGUYON. LES VOEUX DU PAON France, 14th cent.

In French verse. Gothic book hand. 50 vellum leaves, 12¼ x 7⅞ inches. 81 miniatures. Binding: original wooden boards recovered in modern morocco. Ex-colls.: (among others) Arundell, ca. 1500; George Manners; Robert Vaughan de Hengwrt Merion (1592-1667); John Mostine; Lord Mostyn (Sale, London, July 13, 1920, no. 126 and pl.).

This copy of the *Vows of the Peacock* is a pleasant secular manuscript of little pretentiousness, presenting in the best of its small rectangular illustrations a certain lightness and grace. The figures, simply drawn in outline upon the plain parchment, give the effect of *grisaille*, while color is achieved mainly by means of the patterned backgrounds of rose or lavender.

BIBLIOGRAPHY: De Ricci, II, p. 1337, no. 9, with previous literature.

LENT BY THE NEW YORK PUBLIC LIBRARY, SPENCER COLLECTION.

76. GUILLAUME DE LORRIS AND JEHAN DE MEUNG. ROMAN DE LA ROSE
France, early 15th cent.

In French. Batarde script in 2 cols. 191 vellum leaves, 12¾ x 9½ inches. 3 large and 106 smaller miniatures. Binding: modern morocco inlaid with earlier red velvet.

The miniatures of this most delightful example of a medieval favorite illustrate the narrative with piquancy and clarity. The figures, delicately drawn and painted with thinly laid colors, appear not against the patterned backgrounds usual at this time, but upon the uncolored vellum. Details of plants, jewelry, rich brocades and other accessories are painted in with crisp care. The whole effect is a refreshingly airy and tender presentation of this allegorical dream.

Four leaves are lacking, three of which have been supplied by modern copies.

LENT BY CARLETON RICHMOND. PL. XXXVIII

77. LE LIVRE DU ROY MODUS ET DE LA ROYNE RACIS
France, early 15th cent.

In French. Written in 2 cols. 56 vellum leaves, 12 x 8¾ inches. 34 miniatures. Binding: modern red morocco by Rivière. Ex-colls.: Lemoignon; Shirley.

The text, attributed to the Norman, Henri de Ferrières, and composed in the first half of the fourteenth century, is the earliest French prose work on sports. Originally it consisted of two parts, the *Déduits*, devoted to the chase, and the *Songe du Pestilence*, a moralization which is omitted in the present copy. The miniatures, the majority of which extend across both columns of the script, illustrate the various aspects and phases of the chase as performed in the early fifteenth century, thus providing a vivid and gay picture of contemporary life and costumes. The pictures are in *grisaille* against colored grounds, the drawing showing a mannered emphasis on rhythmically curving lines, which adds much dash to the scenes.

BIBLIOGRAPHY: The Pierpont Morgan Library, *Sports and Pastimes*, New York, 1946, pp. 9 and 11.

LENT BY THE ROSENBACH COMPANY.

78. SINGLE LEAF: ST. CHRISTOPHER
Franco-Flemish, ca. 1400

One vellum leaf, 5⅛ x 3⅜ inches. 1 miniature.

The bearded giant St. Christopher, leaning on a rustic staff, fords the stream, while on his shoulders the Christ Child makes a formal gesture of blessing. The tiny figure of the hermit holds a lamp at the left. The beautiful grey-green landscape with its distant towers and fantastically spiralling crags reflects the backgrounds in the "Très Belles Heures" of the Duc de Berry, which that bibliophile's inventory of 1401-1402 described as the work of Jacquemart de Hesdin.

LENT BY THE NATIONAL GALLERY OF ART, ROSENWALD COLLECTION.

79. BOOK OF HOURS
Southeastern France, ca. 1400

W. 237. In Latin. Gothic script. 188 vellum leaves, 6¼ x 4½ inches. 18 miniatures; numerous illuminated borders. Binding: modern stamped pigskin, covered in velvet.

The calendar of this book celebrates a number of Cluniac saints and points to a localization in the

· 30 ·

region of France between the High Alps and Provence. In conformity with such a provenance is the style of the miniatures, which are the work of an exceptionally expressive painter, who has turned from the grace and charm characteristic of most French gothic painting to an intensely dramatic presentation. His preference for swarthy complexions and his adeptness at narrative pathos reflect the strong Italian influence which is likely to be present in south French works of this period.

BIBLIOGRAPHY: De Ricci, I, p. 786, no. 186.

COLLECTION OF THE WALTERS ART GALLERY.   PL. XXXIV

80. BOOK OF HOURS   France (Paris), ca. 1400

W. 96. In Latin. Gothic script. 348 vellum leaves, 6⅛ x 4⅜ inches. 14 miniatures; illuminated borders throughout. Binding: French calf, ca. 1600, with name and arms of Jacques Aubin. Ex-coll.: P. Le Sueur, curé of Menilerreux (1742).

This book is exquisite to the touch as well as to the eye, the softest and thinnest vellum having been selected for its pages. The finely designed ivy borders are relieved occasionally by softly painted birds and insects quite naturalistic in effect, such as characterize illuminations of the last decades of the fourteenth century. The illustrations are by two hands, both very delicate in delineation and modelling, and reminiscent of the artists who worked for the Duke of Berry on such manuscripts as his "Grandes Heures" (Bibliothèque Nationale, ms. lat. 919).

BIBLIOGRAPHY: De Ricci, I, p. 785, no. 177.

COLLECTION OF THE WALTERS ART GALLERY.   PL. XXXV

81. BOOK OF HOURS OF PARIS USE   France, ca. 1410

W. 209. In Latin. Gothic script. 272 vellum leaves, 5½ x 3½ inches. 12 miniatures; illuminated borders throughout. Binding: 19th century French calf, gilt.

Despite the small scale of the illustrations and the very finely finished surface, the painter has modelled his figures with considerable vigor, using heavy drapery to give substance to his personages.

BIBLIOGRAPHY: De Ricci, I, p. 789, no. 207.

COLLECTION OF THE WALTERS ART GALLERY.   PL. XXXV

82. ST. AUGUSTINE. DE CIVITATE DEI   France (Paris), ca. 1410

In French. Gothic script. 173 vellum leaves, 17¼ x 12⅜ inches. 5 large and 59 small miniatures; numerous illuminated borders. Binding: 18th century Scottish russia, gilt. Ex-colls.: Marquess of Lothian (Sale, New York, Jan. 27, 1932, no. 10, pl.); Cortlandt Bishop (Sale, New York, April 5, 1938, no. 155); Philip S. Collins.

The text is the French translation of Raoul de Praelles that was dedicated to Charles V, King of France. This volume, an excellent example of a *de luxe* book of the period, contains only Books I to V of the work. Each Book is prefaced by a large miniature and full ivy border, while smaller column-width illustrations are dispersed through the text. The paintings are the work of several artists of the Paris school, the best of them a man of notable imagination and refinement of style.

The miniatures are marvellously brilliant in condition, presenting every brush-stroke with undiminished freshness.

BIBLIOGRAPHY: *Statistical Account of Scotland,* 1794, 1845 edit., I, p. 68; Sir Robert Kerr, *Correspondence,* 1875, II, p. 537.

LENT BY THE PHILADELPHIA MUSEUM OF ART. PL. XXXIX

83. BREVIARY OF ROME USE Northern France (Rouen), 1412

W. 300. In Latin. Gothic script. 576 vellum leaves, 8½ x 6¼ inches. 1 half-page miniature; 67 historiated initials; numerous illuminated borders with drolleries. Binding: 19th century calf.

A Breviary with Franciscan calendar and saints, executed in Rouen in Normandy. The abundant and unusual miniatures are by several hands, including one much influenced by Italian painting. This artist was responsible for the large miniature at the beginning of the book, representing the Last Judgment. A similar scene, also strongly Italianate in style, is to be found in a manuscript in the British Museum (Add. ms., 29433).

A colophon at the end states that the book was completed in 1412, but it is evident that the manuscript was in progress over a number of years. The Easter Table on the first leaf of the Breviary starts with 1398, while in the middle of the book is a calendar with Easter Sunday indicated on March 27, an Easter date which occurred in 1407.

BIBLIOGRAPHY: De Ricci, I, p. 778, no. 132.

COLLECTION OF THE WALTERS ART GALLERY. PL. XXXVI

84. BOOK OF HOURS France, 1400-1410

W. 231. In Latin. Gothic script. 167 vellum leaves, 7⅛ x 5⅛ inches, misbound. 20 miniatures; illuminated borders throughout. Binding: 19th century violet velvet. Ex-coll.: Roussin de Saint-Nicolas (1745).

The miniatures are painted in a very fine and sensitive style by a follower of Jacquemart de Hesdin. A manuscript apparently by the same artist was in the library of the Duke of Newcastle (Sale, London, Dec. 6, 1937, no. 959).

BIBLIOGRAPHY: De Ricci, I, p. 791, no. 214.

COLLECTION OF THE WALTERS ART GALLERY. PL. XXXVII

85. BOOK OF HOURS France, ca. 1415

W. 232. In Latin. Gothic script. 198 vellum leaves, 6¾ x 5¼ inches. 16 miniatures; illuminated borders throughout. Binding: 16th century French calf, gilt.

Two artists are responsible for the miniatures in this book, one a follower of Jacquemart de Hesdin, and quite possibly the same painter who illustrated no. 84. The other is close to the illuminator of the Hours of Maréchal Boucicault, in the Jacquemart-André Museum, Paris, who is sometimes identified as the painter Jacques Coene.

BIBLIOGRAPHY: De Ricci, I, p. 786, no. 181.

COLLECTION OF THE WALTERS ART GALLERY. PL. XXXVII

86. BOOK OF HOURS							France (Paris), ca. 1420

    W. 260. In Latin. Gothic script. 298 vellum leaves, 7⅝ x 5⅝ inches. 14 large and 24 small miniatures; illuminated borders and drolleries on each page. Binding: 19th century rose velvet.

A manuscript illustrated by one of the artists in the atelier of the "Boucicault Master". The book is very closely related not only in execution, but in details of the compositions, to another manuscript from this workshop: Paris, Bibliothèque Nationale, ms. lat. 10538. Possibly the same hand is at work in the two manuscripts, but in any case, the same studio patterns were employed for both, with the usual ingenious variations. In the present manuscript the artist paints with a tenderness of surface and color and with a restrained modelling that seem almost to contradict the growing interest of his contemporaries in space and plasticity.

    BIBLIOGRAPHY: De Ricci, I, p. 786, no. 185.

COLLECTION OF THE WALTERS ART GALLERY.

87. BOOK OF HOURS							France (Paris), ca. 1415-20

    W. 219. In Latin. Gothic script. 265 vellum leaves, 5½ x 10 inches. 26 miniatures; numerous illuminated borders. Binding: 15th century blind-stamped French calf; original gilded and painted edges.

A little manuscript with many unusual features. The chief artist, who shows some Flemish traits, also reveals a definite study of Italian works, as evidenced in his competent handling of the nude, willingness to undertake unusual and foreshortened poses, interest in cubic space and perspective, and in the many details revealing a fresh and close observation of nature. Because of the small scale and frequently intricate subject matter, many of the scenes have a somewhat toy-like effect. Comparable miniatures are to be found in two books exhibited at the Burlington Fine Arts Club Exhibition of Illuminated Manuscripts: nos. 204 and 205. An entirely different style characterizes the several miniatures at the end of the book, which in their soft *pointillé* technique and gothic handling of figure and drapery recall the work of Jacquemart de Hesdin, one of the chief artists of Jean, duc de Berry.

    BIBLIOGRAPHY: De Ricci, I, p. 791, no. 215. Cf. Burlington Fine Arts Club, *Exhibition of Illuminated Manuscripts*, London, 1908, pp. 99-100, pls. 131-132.

COLLECTION OF THE WALTERS ART GALLERY.					PL. XXXVIII

88. BOOK OF HOURS							France, ca. 1420-25

    W. 265. In Latin. Gothic script. 247 vellum leaves, 7⅜ x 4⅞ inches, misbound and incomplete. 14 miniatures; illuminated borders on every page. Binding: old violet velvet. Ex-coll.: Hanns Ullrich Krafft (1679).

The illuminations of this book are by two artists of great ability, who appear to have been greatly influenced by the style of the Flemish painters working in Burgundy for the duc de Berry. This is evident in the finely modelled surfaces, the particularly heavy and ample folds of the draperies, and the composition of certain scenes. That of the Flight into Egypt, in fact, closely reflects the rendering of this subject by the Fleming, Melchior Broederlam, on the altarpiece now in the museum at Dijon. Many of the scenes use finely diapered backgrounds, but others attempt landscape, and employ a *pointillé* technique to represent the qualities of air.

    BIBLIOGRAPHY: De Ricci, I, p. 790, no. 213.

COLLECTION OF THE WALTERS ART GALLERY.					PL. XXXVI

89. BOOK OF HOURS   France, ca. 1420

> W. 276. In Latin. Gothic script. 158 vellum leaves, 8 x 5¾ inches. 14 miniatures; illuminated borders on every page. Binding: 19th century purple velvet with jewelled clasps. Ex-colls.: Frédéric Spitzer (Sale, Paris, 1893, no. 3013 ?); possibly Octave Homberg collection.

Illuminated by several hands, the best of which has painted an Annunciation of charming gothic mannerism. The ivy borders are enlivened by fantastic creatures, half man and half beast, playing musical instruments. A half legible inscription on a scroll held by a grotesque on fol. 79, "Orate pro Donat" (?), appears to be the signature of one of the artists.

> BIBLIOGRAPHY: De Ricci, I, p. 789, no. 202.

COLLECTION OF THE WALTERS ART GALLERY.

90. FRAGMENT OF A BOOK OF HOURS   France, ca. 1420

> W. 221. In Latin. Gothic script. 17 vellum leaves, 6½ x 5 inches. 17 miniatures. Binding: 19th century green morocco.

A collection of miniatures from a Book of Hours, executed in an atelier that was preparing the way for the kind of painting practiced slightly later in the workshop of the Duke of Bedford. The style of these miniatures is much more refined, however, than the usual robust productions of that atelier. The artist draws with great delicacy and models so very lightly that there is little variation in plane and a very decorative distribution of color, such as is to be found in a Persian miniature of this same period.

> BIBLIOGRAPHY: De Ricci, I, p. 789, no. 203.

COLLECTION OF THE WALTERS ART GALLERY.   PL. XL

91. BOOK OF HOURS   France, ca. 1415

> W. 103. In Latin. Gothic script. 148 vellum leaves, 7¾ x 5⅝ inches. 24 large and 12 small miniatures. Binding: French gilt calf ca. 1580. Ex-colls.: Loys de Rely and Marguerite le la Fosse (late 16th cent.); Comte de Troussures.

A prayer book of fine execution and unusual representations, the miniatures being notable for originality of conception and freedom of pose. More than one hand is responsible for the illustrations. The best of them, and particularly the calendar pictures, have an energy and freshness of presentation and a command of foreshortening that suggest the kind of work that was to be characteristic of the atelier of the Rohan Master, a decade later on.

> BIBLIOGRAPHY: De Ricci, I, p. 785, no. 178.

COLLECTION OF THE WALTERS ART GALLERY.

92. BOOK OF HOURS FOR PARIS USE   France, ca. 1425

    Acc. 4560(7). In Latin. Gothic script. 221 vellum leaves, 5¼ x 4 inches. 5 large miniatures; illuminated borders. Binding: 17th century red morocco, gilt. Ex-colls.: Phillippus (15th century); Robert Gilmor II, Baltimore; J. M. Winkler, Baltimore.

A book executed in an atelier influenced by the "Boucicault Master", that was purchased in Charleston in 1807 by the early American art collector, Robert Gilmor II (see no. 42). It is perhaps the first medieval illuminated manuscript to have entered a Baltimore collection.

    BIBLIOGRAPHY: De Ricci, I, p. 235, no. 120.

LENT BY THE LIBRARY OF CONGRESS.

93. TITUS LIVIUS. DECADES   France, ca. 1425-30

    In French. Batarde script in 2 cols. 2 vols., 262 vellum leaves, 16⅞ x 11½ inches and 191 vellum leaves, 16½ x 12½ inches. 2 large and 18 smaller miniatures. Binding: 18th century russia. Ex-coll.: Marquess of Lothian (Sale, New York, Jan. 27, 1932, no. 12, pl.).

These two handsome volumes contain Books I-X and XXI-XXX respectively of Pierre Berceure's French translation of Livy's *Roman History*, which he made for Jean II le Bon, King of France.

Each volume is prefaced by a large painting, the smaller illustrations being of column width. The miniatures are by several hands very close in style to the artists who illuminated the "Salisbury Breviary" (Paris, Bibliothèque Nationale, ms. lat. 17,294), executed in Paris for John, Duke of Bedford. The miniature at the head of volume II, however, although by an excellent artist, is in a different style.

    BIBLIOGRAPHY: *Statistical Account of Scotland*, 1794, 1845 edit., I, p. 68; Sir Robert Kerr, *Correspondence*, II, 1875, p. 537.

LENT BY WILLIAM K. RICHARDSON.   PL. XLIV

94. GIOVANNI BOCCACCIO. DECAMERON   France, ca. 1460-70

    In French. Batarde script in 2 cols. 262 vellum leaves, 13¼ x 9⅜ inches. 11 miniatures; illuminated borders. Binding: 17th century green velvet with metal corner ornaments. Ex-colls.: Etienne Chevalier; Henri, Comte de Clermont-Tonnerre; the Minimes of Tonnerre (17th century); de Brienne; Bibliotheca Parisina (Sale, Paris, 1791, no. 414); Thomas Johnes of Haford; Dukes of Newcastle (Sale, London, Dec. 6, 1937, no. 934, pl.).

This copy of the *Decameron*, in the French translation by Laurent de Premierfait, appears to have been executed for Etienne Chevalier, Treasurer of France under Charles VII and Louis XI, and a very prominent man in his day (see no. 106). His monogram appears in the borders throughout the book. The charm of the illustrations has recommended the manuscript to many bibliophiles and it has had a most distinguished history, which is known to us almost without a break.

    BIBLIOGRAPHY: Dibdin, *Bibliographical Decameron*, I, cxxxiii-cxxxiv.

LENT BY WILLIAM K. RICHARDSON.   PL. XLI

95. MISSAL FOR USE OF PARIS France, 1429

 W. 302. In Latin. Gothic script in 2 cols. with music. 593 vellum leaves, 14½ x 10½ inches. 17 historiated initials; illuminated borders. Ex-coll.: Montmorency-Laval (ca. 1480).

The tiny miniatures in the initials were executed by artists of the "Bedford atelier" in Paris (see no. 99). The first initial has been removed, and elaborate arms and emblems of a member of the Montmorency-Laval family have been added on several pages.

 BIBLIOGRAPHY: De Ricci, I, p. 776, no. 121.

COLLECTION OF THE WALTERS ART GALLERY. PL. XXXVIII

96. BOOK OF HOURS France (Paris), ca. 1425

 In Latin. Gothic script. 197 vellum leaves, 9¼ x 6¾ inches. 19 large, 58 smaller miniatures. Binding: 19th century black morocco. Ex-colls.: De Buz of Villemareul de Nogent-l'Artaud; George C. Thomas, Philadelphia; William K. Richardson, Boston.

It has only recently been recognized that this manuscript is a production of the atelier that created the "Grandes Heures de Rohan" (Paris, Bibliothèque Nationale, ms. lat. 9471), one of the most remarkable and enigmatic of all French fifteenth-century Books of Hours. The works of this atelier are distinguished for highly original presentation of both narrative and symbolic scenes. Not only the iconography, but the rendering of figures in unusual poses of great expressiveness, the emphasis on intense emotion and avoidance of prettiness, set these works apart from the whole body of illumination produced by other Paris ateliers of the period. Despite the unique character of the Rohan workshop illustrations, no documents contribute to our knowledge of the individuals associated with this production. There are obviously a number of artists involved, and the sporadic reappearance of the same iconographical peculiarities in the work of different hands indicates the use of pattern-books.

The "Grandes Heures de Rohan" is, among other things, notable for the monumental scale of its illuminations, and something of this is to be seen in the present manuscript. The large scale of the figures enhances the power and emotional grandeur of the paintings. The multiplication of scenes, each main miniature being accompanied by two smaller ones with related incidents of the story, is likewise characteristic of the atelier, which delighted in casting into the narrative a wealth of casual episodes.

 BIBLIOGRAPHY: The manuscript will be discussed in detail in a forthcoming article by Erwin Panofsky in *Harvard Library Bulletin*, Spring, 1949.

LENT BY THE HARVARD COLLEGE LIBRARY. PL. XLIII

97. BOOK OF HOURS FOR USE OF TROYES France (Paris), ca. 1425

 Garrett ms. no. 48. In Latin and French. Gothic script. 105 vellum leaves, 8½ x 6¼ inches. 11 large and 33 small miniatures. Binding: modern red velvet. Ex-colls.: D. Mathieu Picquet (d.1688); John Boykett Jarman (?) (Sale, London, June 13, 1864, no. 41); Robert Garrett.

This manuscript also was executed in the Rohan atelier (see no. 96). The book, as it now stands, is incomplete, and Dr. Panofsky has recognized that the missing portion of it is a well known manuscript in the Arsènal Library in Paris (ms. 647).

The atelier's predilection for richness is reflected in the abundant use of patterned textiles for the garments, fine diapering of the backgrounds, complex ivy borders and the great number of scenes. As in the case of the previously described manuscript, each main scene is accompanied by subordinate ones. Despite the multiplicity of miniatures, a single artist seems to have executed all in the two parts of this Horae, probably the same individual who painted the marginal illustrations in a related manuscript in Cambridge, Fitzwilliam Museum, ms. 62.

BIBLIOGRAPHY: De Ricci, I, p. 873, no. 48; E. Panofsky in *Medieval Studies in Memory of A. Kingsley Porter* (ed. by W. Koehler), Cambridge, Mass., 1939, II, pp. 479-499, 6 ill., with previous literature; D. Egbert in *The Princeton University Library Chronicle*, III (1942), p. 127, ill.; Boston Museum of Fine Arts, *Arts of the Middle Ages*, Boston, 1940, no. 46. Cf. H. Martin, *Catalogue des manuscrits de la Bibliothèque de l'Arsenal*, Paris, 1885, I, p. 489, no. 647; cf. Adelheid Heimann in *Städel-Jahrbuch*, Frankfurt a.M., VII-VIII (1932), pp. 1-61.

LENT BY PRINCETON UNIVERSITY LIBRARY, GARRETT COLLECTION.   PL. XLII

98. BOOK OF HOURS FOR USE OF TROYES   France (Paris), ca. 1425

In Latin and French. Gothic script. 169 vellum leaves, 7¼ x 5¼ inches. 10 large miniatures; illuminated borders on each page. Ex-coll.: Gouault (1673).

Another product of the Rohan atelier. The miniatures in this manuscript are not painted in the large scale of the "Grandes Heures de Rohan" or of no. 96, but the connection in conception and execution is evident. The Flight into Egypt, especially, repeats the unusual representation of this scene to be found in the "Grandes Heures." In other respects, this book is closest to two other products of the atelier—British Museum, Harl. ms. 2934 and Paris, Bibliothèque St. Geneviève, ms. 1278.

LENT BY HEINRICH EISEMANN.

99. BOOK OF HOURS   France, 1430-35

W. 281. In Latin. Gothic script. 242 vellum leaves, 8 x 5½ inches. 27 miniatures; illuminated borders.

An elaborately illuminated book executed by the artists of the "Bedford atelier", so called from a magnificent Horae (British Museum, Add. ms. 18850) illuminated for John, Duke of Bedford, while he was Regent of France.

The present manuscript appears to have been made for the marriage of Jeanne de Lannoy and Thomas Malet de Berlettes, a prominent citizen and official of Lille in northern France.

BIBLIOGRAPHY: De Ricci, I, p. 797, no. 261.

COLLECTION OF THE WALTERS ART GALLERY.   PL. XL

100. BOOK OF HOURS   France (Paris), ca. 1430

W. 287. In Latin. Gothic script. 200 vellum leaves, 8⅞ x 6½ inches. 39 large miniatures and 24 in calendar; illuminated borders on every page. Binding: modern red velvet.

The abundant illustrations of this book are most interesting both from the point of view of style and iconography. The manner of painting is closely connected with that practiced in the "Bedford atelier", but the unusual conception of many of the scenes is derived directly from the tradition of the "Boucicault Master" (see no. 85). Some of the miniatures, such as the representation of St. George, practically repeat line for line compositions in the Hours of Maréchal Boucicault, executed some fifteen years earlier.

BIBLIOGRAPHY: De Ricci, I, p. 791, no. 217; E. Panofsky in *Medieval Studies in Memory of A. Kingsley Porter*, Cambridge, Mass., 1939, II, p. 486.

COLLECTION OF THE WALTERS ART GALLERY.

101. GUILLAUME DE DEGUILEVILLE. LE PELERINAGE DE LA VIE HUMAINE
France, 1437

In French. 204 vellum leaves, 14 x 10⅛ inches. 284 miniatures. Binding: 19th century French morocco by Bozerian. Ex-colls.: William Beckford; Duke of Hamilton (Sale, London, May 23, 1889); Henry H. Gibbs, first Lord Aldenham.

The text is the version in French verse of this favorite medieval allegory. The illustrations are lightly colored miniatures the width of the column, and executed by several hands, the finest of them quite delicate. The book, as it now stands, is incomplete. It has been conjectured that it originally contained well over 300 illustrations. A colophon giving the date states that this copy was executed at the order of a certain knight, Louis Martel.

LENT BY THE ROSENBACH COMPANY.

102. LE LIVRE DU PETIT ARTUS
France, ca. 1450

In French. Batarde script in 2 cols. 218 vellum leaves, 18¼ x 12 inches. 37 half-page miniatures. Binding: 18th century French mottled calf. Ex-colls.: Jacques d'Armagnac, duc de Nemours (d. 1477); Edward, Baron Thurlow; John Louis Goldsmid (Sale, London, 1815, no. 160); John North (Sale, London, 1819, III, no. 808); Robert Lang (Sale, London, 1828, no. 1949); Sir Thomas Phillipps (ms. 3633).

The hero of this romance, Arthur, son of "the good Duke Jehan de Bretagne", is named "Little Arthur" to distinguish him from "le Grand Artus", or King Arthur. The illustrations are finely handled renderings of battles, court scenes and other subjects of chivalry.

BIBLIOGRAPHY: Twenty of the miniatures were engraved as illustrations for Lord Berners' English translation of the romance edited by E. V. Utterson, *Arthur of Little Britain*, London, 1814; W. R. Leech in *Bulletin of the New York Public Library*, XXXII (1928), pp. 391-396, ill.; De Ricci, II, p. 1333, no. 114, with other literature.

LENT BY THE NEW YORK PUBLIC LIBRARY, SPENCER COLLECTION.

103. JACQUES BRUYANT. LE CHASTEL DE LABOUR
Northern France, ca. 1440

Widener ms. 1. In French verse. Batarde script. 76 vellum leaves, 8¼ x 6 inches. 46 miniatures; illuminated borders with emblems and personages. Binding: 19th century red velvet. Ex-colls.: Boutillier family of Normandy (arms); Jean Berger (ca. 1600); George C. Thomas, Philadelphia; Joseph Widener.

An allegorical poem composed in 1342, better known by the title *La Voie de Povreté et de Richesse*.

It is the earliest of a group of poems, including two English versions, all having the theme that a sufficient competence gained by hard labor is better than riches.

The illustrations are gay and amusing, and present the narrative vividly with clear delineation and bright coloring.

BIBLIOGRAPHY: [F. W. Bourdillon], *Le Livre du Chastel de Labour*, Philadelphia, 1909; A. Längfors in *Romania*, XLV (1918-19), pp. 45 ff., and LII (1926), p. 366; De Ricci, II, p. 2115, no. 1.

LENT BY THE PHILADELPHIA FREE LIBRARY, PRESENTED IN MEMORY OF JOSEPH E. WIDENER.

PL. XLI

103a. JEAN GERMAIN. LE CHEMIN DE PARADIS   France (Burgundy ?), ca. 1460

In French. French book hand. 186 paper and vellum leaves, quarto. 5 double-page colored drawings on vellum. Binding: 18th century calf. Ex-coll.: Sir Thomas Phillipps (ms. 219).

The text is an interpretation of the allegorical subject matter of two tapestries, now lost, which the author, a French prelate and counsellor of Philip the Good, Duke of Burgundy, had ordered for his church, the Cathedral of Chalon-sur-Saôn.

The illustrations, suggesting the composition of the tapestries, are large water-color drawings executed in a popular style, such as is more frequently found in German books of the period.

BIBLIOGRAPHY: Paul Durrieu, *Les manuscrits à peintures de la Bibliothèque de Cheltenham* in *Bibl. de l'Ecole de Chartes*, L (1889), p. 400.

LENT BY H. P. KRAUS.

PL. XLVIII

104. BOOK OF HOURS   France (Paris), ca. 1460-70

W. 274. In Latin and French. Gothic script. 203 vellum leaves, 8½ x 5¾ inches. 22 large miniatures and 24 smaller in calender; illuminated borders throughout. Binding: 16th century French morocco, gilt.

The miniatures in this book, the work of two artists, are unusual in composition and treatment. Each of the larger ones is divided into three or four compartments to provide for successive incidents in the narrative depicted. In some cases, however, the compartments become adjoining rooms or floors and the space is used for a continuous treatment of the story.

The painter of the first two miniatures has a delicate technique and admirable command of plastic form, perspective and lighting. The artist responsible for most of the paintings in the book has not as sure a grasp of some of these factors, but he has presented us with miniatures of the greatest interest, with subject matter that relates directly to scenes to be found in the work of Foucquet. In style he is very close indeed to the artist of W. 297 (no. 107 of this catalogue), employing the same facial types, stunted figures, exotic costumes, and detailed architectural accessories. He is, however, inferior to this artist in softness and finish of modelling, and in the rendering of form and cubic space by the modulation of light.

BIBLIOGRAPHY: De Ricci, I, p. 793, no. 232.

COLLECTION OF THE WALTERS ART GALLERY.

PL. XLVII

105. SPECULUM HUMANAE SALVATIONIS
France, ca. 1440

In French. Batarde script in 2 cols. 43 vellum leaves, 15 x 11 inches. 168 miniatures. Binding: 19th century red morocco. Ex-coll.: Sir George Holford (ms. 20).

A rarely luxurious copy of a didactic work which is generally found in unpretentious examples for popular use (see no. 139). The two rectangular miniatures at the top of each page are so planned that the one furthest to the left represents a New Testament episode, painted in full color, while the other three visible at the same time, as the book lies open, are Old Testament "prophecies" of this event, and are executed in a shadowy *grisaille*. The style is full-bodied and accomplished and the colors clear and fine. Another French manuscript of the *Speculum*, similar in style and elegance, although somewhat later in date, is ms. fr. 6275 in the Bibliothèque Nationale in Paris.

BIBLIOGRAPHY: Cf. J. Lutz and P. Perdrizet, *Speculum Humanae Salvationis*, 2 vols., Leipzig, 1907.

LENT BY THE ROSENBACH COMPANY.

106. MINIATURE FROM THE HOURS OF ETIENNE CHEVALIER, BY JEAN FOUCQUET
France, ca. 1460-70

No. 194. In Latin. Semi-batarde script (on reverse). 1 vellum leaf, 7¾ x 5¾ inches. 1 miniature; 1 half-border. Ex-coll.: Louis Fenoulhet (Sale, London, Dec. 16-18, 1946, lot 568).

A leaf from the Book of Hours of Etienne Chevalier, counsellor to King Charles VII and to King Louis XI of France, and Treasurer of France in 1452. This magnificently illustrated volume was cut apart by an unknown eighteenth-century owner and its miniatures dispersed. Forty-seven of the paintings are now known, the most recently discovered being this leaf and one other in the Paris collection of M. Georges Wildenstein, both of which came to light in 1946. The largest group of miniatures from this manuscript is the famous series of forty that is one of the chief treasures of the Chateau Condé at Chantilly. Two others are in the Louvre, one in the Bibliothèque Nationale, Paris, one in the British Museum, and one more in a London private collection. Although no specific record connects the Hours of Etienne Chevalier with Foucquet, all authorities agree in giving the work to this master, because of its close resemblance in style to the manuscript of Josephus' *Antiquités Judaïques*, now in the Bibliothèque Nationale, which is the only definitely documented work by Foucquet's hand.

This leaf contains the illustration for the Vespers of the Holy Ghost. As in the case of several other miniatures from this manuscript, Foucquet has placed the sacred scene in a French landscape, carefully portraying an actual locality. In the background flows the Seine bordering the Ile de la Cité, dominated by the Cathedral of Notre Dame, which also appears in two of the miniatures at Chantilly. In the foreground kneels a throng of clergy. Penetrating the sky is the Hand of God, which disperses a swarm of demons. Unlike the miniatures at Chantilly, which are clipped closely and pasted down on wood, in this case the entire leaf has been preserved with the foliation (fol. 89). The surface of the painting has suffered somewhat, but it is a precious example of the work of the greatest painter that France had produced up to his time. The undamaged portions are characteristic of his achievement—his faultless craftsmanship, his mastery of space composition, of plastic form, his profound observation of nature and of light, his joyous color. This leaf represents the only authentic example of Foucquet's work in America.

BIBLIOGRAPHY: Sotheby and Co., *Catalogue of Valuable Printed Books* ... (various owners), December 16th-18th, 1946, lot 568, pls. XIII-XIV (with very full description of this and the companion leaf); *Illustrated London News*, Nov. 30, 1946, p. 611. *Cf.* Trenchard Cox, *Jehan Foucquet, Native of Tours*, London, 1931; Klaus G. Perls, *Jean Fouquet*, Paris, 1940; Paul Wescher, *Jean Fouquet und Seine Zeit*, Basel, 1945, for discussion of the Foucquet problem and bibliographies of previous literature.

LENT BY ROBERT LEHMAN. PL. XLV

107. BREVIARY
France, ca. 1460-70

W. 297. In Latin. Gothic script. 273 vellum leaves, 4½ x 3½ inches. 7 large miniatures; 24 small calendar-pictures; illuminated borders. Binding: 17th century French calf. Ex-colls.: Oratorio at Nantes (ca. 1700); Peter Marié (Sale, New York, 1903, no. 563).

A charming little manuscript executed by a follower of Foucquet, apparently the same as the artist who illuminated the Hours of Olivier de Coétivy and Marie de Valois sometime between 1458 and 1473 (now Vienna, Nationalbibliothek, ms. 1929). As in the case of this latter manuscript, the miniatures of the Breviary show a good command over solid structure, perspective and lighting, but the standing figures tend to be stunted. A number of Foucquet's devices are adopted—the use of evening light for the scenes of David and Goliath, somewhat oriental turbans, occasional use of a sharp yellow in the garments.

BIBLIOGRAPHY: De Ricci, I, p. 778, no. 137. *Cf.* A. Blum and P. Lauer, *La miniature française aux XVe et XVIe siècles*, Paris, 1930, p. 75, pl. 39.

COLLECTION OF THE WALTERS ART GALLERY. PL. XLVII

108. BOOK OF HOURS
France, ca. 1450

W. 251. In Latin. Gothic script. 165 vellum leaves, 7½ x 5½ inches. 12 miniatures; illuminated borders. Binding: original wooden boards and stamped calf. Ex-colls.: Louis Charpentier (1662); Jean Boyd; Charles-Louis Frossard; Georges Hoentschel (Sale, Paris, April 14, 1910, no. 3, ill.).

The miniatures represent a moment of transition in the development of fifteenth-century French painting. The work is in a style that had grown out of the productions of the "Bedford atelier" (see no. 99) and just before the innovations of Foucquet began to have an impact upon painters of even moderate ability (see no. 106). This is basically the style that formed "Maître François" (see nos. 109, 111, 112).

BIBLIOGRAPHY: De Ricci, I, p. 792, no. 222.

COLLECTION OF THE WALTERS ART GALLERY.

109. BOOK OF HOURS
France, ca. 1470

W. 285. In Latin. Gothic script. 115 vellum leaves, 8¼ x 5½ inches. 3 large and 10 small miniatures; 24 in calendar; 2 illuminated arms of the 16th century; illuminated borders throughout. Binding: modern red velvet with old enamelled ornaments. Ex-colls.: a 16th century Medici Pope, either Leo X (1513-21) or Clement VII (1523-34); ca. 1600 in an English collection.

The miniatures are by three different artists of the school of Tours, the finest of which is the much discussed painter known as "Maître François", or the *Egregius Pictor Franciscus*, as he is called in a letter written in 1473 by the scholar Robert Gaugin to his friend, Charles de Gaucourt, the governor of Paris. This mention was in connection with a fine copy of the *City of God* that the painter had just illustrated for de Gaucourt, and which is now in the Bibliothèque Nationale in Paris (mss. fr. 18, 19). The criterion for identifying work of Maître François in other manuscripts is therefore the illustration of this St. Augustine.

The artist, active from 1463 to 1481, was prolific, and, what is more, appears to have been the center of a considerable atelier. Dr. Eleanor Spencer has undertaken the complex problem of sifting his own painting from the productions of those who worked closely after his manner.

Next to Foucquet, Maître François has been ranked as the greatest French miniature painter, and certainly he seems to have been well regarded in his time. He had nothing of the true genius of Foucquet, but he learned, doubtless from him, much about rendering of solid form, of light, of landscape and perspective. He is particularly notable for an excellent technique of crosshatching and broken strokes, wherewith he develops his effects of form and atmosphere. In the best examples from his hand, such as the manuscript shown, he has a very fine manner.

The large illustrations in this manuscript are by two other artists, one of whom has a style similar to that in British Museum Add. ms. 28785.

> BIBLIOGRAPHY: De Ricci, I, p. 794, no. 233. Cf. for Maître François: A. de Laborde, *Les manuscrits a peintures de la Cité de Dieu*, Paris, 1909, II, pp. 397-416 and plates, where the whole problem is discussed, with previous literature; E. Spencer, *The Maître François and his Atelier*, 1931 (unpublished doctoral dissertation deposited in Harvard College Library); J. Wardrop, *Egregius Pictor Franciscus* in Apollo, XV (1932), pp. 76-82, ill.

COLLECTION OF THE WALTERS ART GALLERY.   PL. XLVI

110. SINGLE MINIATURE: MEDUSA AS QUEEN   France, ca. 1460-70

No. 24.1015. Single miniature on vellum, 5 x 3½ inches.

This illustration, presumably from a manuscript of the *Memorabilia* of Valerius Maximus, represents Medusa as a lovely princess before she was transformed into a monster, in accordance with the legend. The rendering of figure and facial types, handling of space and method of modelling have many characteristics associated with the artist Maître François (see no. 109), and this work is certainly by one of his associates, if not an early production of François himself.

> BIBLIOGRAPHY: William M. Milliken in *Bulletin of the Cleveland Museum of Art*, XII (1925), p. 70, ill. p. 67; De Ricci, II, p. 1930, no. 23.1015 with further literature.

LENT BY THE CLEVELAND MUSEUM OF ART.   PL. XLVI

111. BOOK OF HOURS FOR USE OF BOURGES   France, ca. 1475

W. 214. In Latin. Gothic script. 5 large and 78 small miniatures; illuminated borders. Binding: French 16th century morocco, fanfare. Ex-coll.: De Palte (17th century).

The entire book is illustrated by Maître François (cf. no. 109), and is a characteristic example of his mature style.

> BIBLIOGRAPHY: De Ricci, I, p. 799, no. 273; and general works cited under no. 109.

COLLECTION OF THE WALTERS ART GALLERY.   PL. XLVI

112. BOOK OF HOURS   France, ca. 1470

    W. 252. In Latin. Gothic script. 192 vellum leaves, 6¾ x 4⅜ inches. 13 miniatures; illuminated borders. Binding: 16th century French olive morocco, fanfare, with arms of St. Germain de Courson impaled with de Blemur-Boette. Ex-coll.: B. H. de Fourcy (18th century).

Another and more routine example of the work of Maître François (*cf.* no. 109), executed in his "broad manner". It may be slightly earlier in date than the illustrations of the de Gaucourt *Cité de Dieu*, finished in 1473, the documented work of his hand.

    BIBLIOGRAPHY: De Ricci, I, p. 798, no. 262; and general works cited under no. 109.

COLLECTION OF THE WALTERS ART GALLERY.

113. PSALTER AND ABBREVIATED HOURS   France, 1489

    W. 286. In Latin. Batarde script. 250 vellum leaves, 8¼ x 5½ inches. 2 miniatures; illuminated borders. Binding: 19th century French brown morocco.

A Psalter with abbreviated Hours and other liturgical material for Carthusian use, written in the Chartreuse of Mont Dieu in Champagne by Friar Guillaume Joret at the order of the Prior, Louis de Busco.

The miniatures, which include a representation of the Prior kneeling before the Virgin, are by Jacques de Besançon. Jacques was a pupil of Maître François (*cf.* no. 109), and the closest in style of those associated with him. He appears to have collaborated on some of the important commissions assigned to his master, and it is hardly surprising that Durrieu, one of the foremost scholars of the nineteenth century, confused him completely with Maître François himself. Subsequent scholarship, and particularly the analytical studies of Eleanor Spencer, have now dissolved much of this confusion. The documented point of departure for studying his style is a service book made and presented by him in 1485 to his guild of St. John the Evangelist of the church of Saint-André-des-Arts in Paris.

Jacques de Besançon was one of the competent miniaturists of the late fifteenth century who turned to illuminating the woodcuts of printed books, as the new craft began to offer serious competition to manuscript production. His hand has been recognized in some of the *de luxe* copies of books printed by Antoine Verard, especially those prepared for presentation to Charles VIII.

    BIBLIOGRAPHY: De Ricci, I, p. 803, no. 296. *Cf.* for Jacques de Besançon, P. Durrieu, *Un grand enlumineur parisien: Jacques de Besançon*, Paris, 1892; E. Spencer, *The Maître François and his Atelier*, 1931 (unpublished doctoral dissertation deposited in Harvard College Library), pp. 103-119.

COLLECTION OF THE WALTERS ART GALLERY.

114. BOOK OF HOURS   France, ca. 1470-80

    W. 207. In Latin. Batarde script. 97 vellum leaves, 4¼ x 3 inches. 6 large and 34 small miniatures. Binding: modern blue velvet.

A tiny book reflecting the influence of the school of Tours. All the figures are represented in white garments, although the rest of the miniature in each case is rendered in full color. It is a semi-*grisaille* treatment that was favored by the Tours artists for a period of time.

    BIBLIOGRAPHY: De Ricci, I, p. 794, no. 238.

COLLECTION OF THE WALTERS ART GALLERY.

115. BOOK OF HOURS FOR USE OF TOURS France, ca. 1470

Ms. 096.3. In Latin. Gothic script. 140 vellum leaves, 5½ x 3¾ inches. 9 miniatures. Binding: red morocco, gilt by Matthews. Ex-coll.: Joseph J. Cooke (Sale, New York, 1883, II, no. 1566).

Executed by several artists of the school of Tours with a predilection for the use of black in garments, which is exceptional in French manuscripts of this period.

BIBLIOGRAPHY: De Ricci, I, p. 158, no. 7.

LENT BY TRINITY COLLEGE, HARTFORD. PL. LI

116. BOOK OF HOURS France, ca. 1480

Garrett ms. 55. In Latin. Gothic script. 124 vellum leaves, 6⅞ x 4¾ inches. 15 miniatures; illuminated borders. Binding: French olive morocco, ca. 1600. Ex-colls.: Marguerite de Rohan; Charles Sauvageot (Sale, Paris, Dec. 3, 1860, no. 44); A. Firmin-Didot (Sale, Paris, 1882, no. 16, 2 pls.); Marcel Thévenin (Sale, Paris, March 4, 1903, pp. 3-23, no. 1); Robert Garrett.

An exceptionally fine manuscript of the period, executed for Marguerite de Rohan, wife of Jean d'Orléans, comte d'Angoulême, the best miniatures being by a competent painter of the Tours school. His style is strong and monumental, but characterized by a gentle softness. He builds up the plasticity of his forms both by a fine *pointillé* technique and by close hatching in the shadows and the golden highlights. His formulae of atmospheric lighting and twilight dusk in certain compositions reveal the inheritance of Foucquet inventions. Several of the miniatures display a dramatic invention of representation worthy of the master himself. The two finest miniatures are simply panel paintings that chance to be on the pages of a book: the widowed Marguerite in a sensitive and telling portrait, and on the opposing page the half-length figure of Christ blessing.

This manuscript has been attributed in a general way to Foucquet, but as early as 1903, Bouchot suggested a close relation to Bourdichon, if not an attribution to his early period. He pointed out resemblances with a triptych of the Crucifixion in Loches, which has been connected tentatively with Bourdichon. There is no question but that the same models and patterns did play some part in certain passages of both works. Very recently, Wescher has attributed the manuscript to Bourdichon without qualification.

BIBLIOGRAPHY: Cf. P. Burty in *Gazette des Beaux Arts*, IX (1861), pp. 55-56; H. Bouchot, *Exposition des primitifs français*, Paris, 1904, pl. LXXI; De Ricci, I, p. 874, no. 55; D. Egbert in *The Princeton University Library Chronicle*, III (1942), p. 128, ill.; P. Wescher, *Jean Fouquet und seine Zeit*, Basel, 1945, pp. 85-86, figs. 65-66; H. Bouchot, *Le livre d'heures de Marguerite de Rohan, comtesse d'Angoulême*, Paris, 1903, ill.

LENT BY PRINCETON UNIVERSITY LIBRARY, GARRETT COLLECTION. PL. XLVII

116a. BOOK OF HOURS OF TOURS USE France, ca. 1470-80

Ms. acc. 4560,8. In Latin. Gothic script. 145 vellum leaves, 7½ x 5½ inches. 4 large miniatures; illuminated borders. Binding: 17th century black morocco. Ex-coll.: Susan Minns (Sale, New York, May 2, 1922, no. 410, ill.)

The illustrations are by a follower of Foucquet, who has made use of the master's methods of representing exterior and interior space and lighting, and has introduced his accustomed renaissance features, such as colored marble columns, shell niches and inscribed entablatures.

BIBLIOGRAPHY: De Ricci, I, p. 235, no. 121.

LENT BY THE LIBRARY OF CONGRESS.

117. BOOK OF HOURS France, ca. 1470

W. 210. In Latin. Gothic script. 128 vellum leaves, 5 x 3¼ inches, incomplete and misbound. Historiated borders on each page. Binding: 19th century French morocco, gilt. Ex-coll.: de Cornuau.

An unusual little book each page of which is surrounded by a border of foliage enlivened with courtly figures, peasants, grotesques and animals, all executed in *grisaille* and dull gold. The work is by several hands, of the Tours school, the best of them being artists of considerable skill. Despite the complexity of the borders there is no repetition, except that the two sides of each leaf show duplicate designs, doubtless enforced by the transparency of the vellum. Some of the borders are unfinished and show the under-drawing. Two other leaves of this book belong to Sir Sydney Cockerell.

BIBLIOGRAPHY: De Ricci, I, p. 803, no. 292.

COLLECTION OF THE WALTERS ART GALLERY.

118. GUILLAUME DE NANGIS. CHRONIQUE DES ROIS DE FRANCE France, ca. 1470

W. 306. In French. Gothic book hand in 2 cols. 325 vellum and paper leaves, 15½ x 11 inches. 8 miniatures. Binding: 19th century red morocco. Ex-colls.: Joseph Barrois (ms. 465); Earl of Ashburnham (Sale, London, 1901, no. 418).

The outside leaf of the first gathering of this history is of vellum and carries a miniature and illuminated border in a competent, but routine style. The real interest of the manuscript lies in the fine pen drawings, tinted with color lightly enough so that the vivacity of the draughtsmanship is not obscured. Illustrations of this kind, very abundant in German books of the fifteenth century, are relatively seldom met with in French works.

BIBLIOGRAPHY: De Ricci, I, p. 851, no. 526.

COLLECTION OF THE WALTERS ART GALLERY.

119. DIRC VAN DELFT. DE TAFEL VAN DEN KERSTEN GHELOVE

Netherlands (Utrecht ?), early 15th cent.

W. 171. In Dutch. Gothic script. 167 vellum leaves, 7⅜ x 5⅜ inches. 34 historiated initials. Binding: modern red velvet.

This treatise on Christian faith was composed in 1404 for Duke Albrecht of Bavaria, Count of Holland, by his chaplain, Dirc van Delft. This manuscript contains only the first thirty-four chapters (out of a possible fifty-seven) of the *Winterstuc*. On the first pages are the arms of the Bavarian Counts of Holland. The miniatures are by two artists, the more accomplished of them extraordinarily skillful in constructing form and expression entirely by means of soft modelling in light and shade, a completely "painterly" technique. The second hand, competent, but harder and more dependent upon outline, is close to the illustrator of the early copy of the *Somerstuc* of Dirc's treatise in the Pierpont Morgan Library (M. 691). The two books are very similar indeed in style and format, but are not parts of the same manuscript. Also related to this second artist is the illustrator of the Dirc van Delft manuscript in the British Museum (Add. ms. 22288), much larger in format than the Walters book. The same textual peculiarities, with a few exceptions, are to be found in both the Walters and London manuscripts.

BIBLIOGRAPHY: De Ricci, I, p. 823, no. 397; G. J. Hoogewerff, *De Noord-Nederlandsche Schilderkunst*, The Hague, 1936, I, p. 583, note; A. Byvanck, *La miniature dans les Pays-Bas septentrionaux*, Paris, 1937, p. 21; L. M. Daniëls, *Meester Dirc van Delf, O.P. Tafel van den Kersten Ghelove*, Antwerp and Utrecht, 1939, I, pl. 8, pp. 72-76, p. 272, note to p. 79 (a complete textual description).

COLLECTION OF THE WALTERS ART GALLERY.   PL. L

120. BOOK OF HOURS   Netherlands (Utrecht), ca. 1410

W. 185. In Latin and Dutch. Gothic script. 283 vellum leaves, 5 x 3¾ inches. 12 large miniatures and 1 historiated initial; illuminated initials and border. Binding: 18th century vellum. Ex-coll.: Definnes, of Orlencourt, near St. Omer.

The miniatures are painted in a fluent, rapid style, lightly modelled. In some cases the figures ignore the frame and emerge into the margin. The border sprigs of trefoils and daisies are sparse and simple.

In somewhat similar style is ms. 18,392 in the Bodleian Library, Oxford.

BIBLIOGRAPHY: De Ricci, I, p. 787, no. 191.

COLLECTION OF THE WALTERS ART GALLERY.

121. BOOK OF HOURS   Netherlands (Utrecht), ca. 1430

W. 168. In Latin. Gothic script. 223 vellum leaves, 6¼ x 4½ inches. 11 full-page miniatures and 20 historiated initials; illuminated borders. Binding: original stamped calf over boards.

Illuminated by several artists, including one very close in style to the Master of Zweder van Culemborg (cf. no. 128). The decoration, with little half-figures of angels and clusters of violets in the borders framing the pictures resembles a fine Missal at the University of Munster (ms. 41) also illuminated by the Zweder Master.

BIBLIOGRAPHY: De Ricci, I, p. 794, no. 235. Cf. for Munster manuscript: A. Byvanck, *La miniature dans les Pays-Bas septentrionaux*, Paris, 1937, pp. 148 f., pls. XXXIX-XLI.

COLLECTION OF THE WALTERS ART GALLERY.   PL. L

122. BOOK OF HOURS   Netherlands (Utrecht), ca. 1435

W. 188. In Dutch. Gothic script. 18 historiated initials; illuminated borders. Binding: modern rose velvet.

A well executed manuscript, closely related in painting style and decoration to no. 121, but less elaborate in its scheme of illumination.

BIBLIOGRAPHY: De Ricci, I, p. 791, no. 216.

COLLECTION OF THE WALTERS ART GALLERY.

123. BOOK OF HOURS   Flanders, ca. 1460-70

    W. 208. In Latin. Batarde script. 152 vellum leaves, 4⅜ x 3¼ inches. 11 miniatures. Binding: original stamped calf over boards.

A little book that represents the influence of the panel paintings of the chief Flemish artists upon the shop-productions of the illuminators, some of the pictures being based upon the compositions of Petrus Christus and others.

    BIBLIOGRAPHY: De Ricci, I, p. 799, no. 269.

COLLECTION OF THE WALTERS ART GALLERY.

124. BOOK OF HOURS FOR USE OF UTRECHT   Netherlands, ca. 1440

    W. 165. In Latin. Gothic script. 152 vellum leaves, 5¾ x 3⅝ inches. 18 full-page miniatures. Binding: original stamped calf over boards. Ex-coll.: Rev. W. J. Loftie.

One of a group of similar books, executed apparently at Delft, in striking and expressive grisaille technique, lightly relieved by color. The angularity of the poses and drapery folds and the sharp contrasts of the modelling recall Netherlands wood-carvings of this same period.

    BIBLIOGRAPHY: Burlington Fine Arts Club, *Exhibition of Illuminated Manuscripts*, London, 1908, no. 243, pl. 149; A. W. Byvanck and G. J. Hoogewerff, *La miniature hollandaise*, The Hague, 1922-25, p. 24, no. 45, pl. XIII, fig. 54 (ownership wrongly ascribed); De Ricci, I, p. 787, no. 192.

COLLECTION OF THE WALTERS ART GALLERY.

125. BOOK OF HOURS FOR USE OF ARRAS   Flanders, ca. 1425

    W. 166. In Latin and Flemish. Gothic script. 186 vellum leaves, 6¼ x 4⅝ inches. 13 full-page miniatures; historiated initials; numerous drolleries; illuminated borders. Binding: original stamped pink leather mounted in modern binding.

One of a group of books produced, generally for export, in an atelier in Malines or Ghent. This Horae was made for Elizabeth, daughter of Godfrey van Munte and wife of Daniel Rym (d. 1431), both members of prominent Ghent families.

Other manuscripts from the same atelier include a Book of Hours made for Jean sans Peur, Duke of Burgundy (Paris, Bibliothèque Nationale, ms. lat. nouv. acq. 3055); Pierpont Morgan manuscripts 46 and 439; Providence, John Carter Brown Library, ms. 3, and many others. They all are characterized by abundant and vigorous foliate ornament, amusing drolleries, and a competent, decorative painting style, still essentially gothic.

    BIBLIOGRAPHY: De Ricci, I, p. 787, no. 190; V. Leroquais, *Un Livre d'Heures de Jean sans Peur*, Paris, 1939, p. 53 (erroneously alluded to as ms. 170).

COLLECTION OF THE WALTERS ART GALLERY.

126. BOOK OF HOURS   Flanders, ca. 1425

    W. 170. In Latin. Gothic script. 183 vellum leaves, 6½ x 4¾ inches. 27 large miniatures and 8 historiated initials. Binding: 16th century stamped calf over boards by Joris de Gavere in Ghent.

Executed in the same Ghent or Malines atelier as no. 125.

    BIBLIOGRAPHY: De Ricci, I, p. 787, no. 189.

COLLECTION OF THE WALTERS ART GALLERY.

127. MISSAL   French Flanders, ca. 1435

>In Latin. Gothic script. 30 vellum leaves, 13 x 9 inches. 25 miniatures; 5 historiated initials; illuminated borders. Binding: modern vellum.

A fragment of a Missal executed in one of the ateliers near the Franco-Flemish border that maintained a flourishing production, especially for export. The style is decorative, although somewhat routine. The iconography, however, is the most interesting feature of the atelier, being very eclectic, and revealing the process by which elements of representation were transferred from one region to another through the pattern-books of the most productive guilds. (Cf. no. 129.)

The present manuscript retains elements of the "Bedford atelier" as well as of the so-called "gold-scroll" group. The introduction of the main illustration into the margins is an interesting feature.

LENT BY MR. AND MRS. NELSON GUTMAN.

128. MISSAL FOR CARTHUSIAN USE   Netherlands (Utrecht), ca. 1430

>W. 174. In Latin. Gothic script in 2 cols. 250 vellum leaves, 10⅝ x 7½ inches. 56 miniatures and 59 historiated initials. Binding: contemporary stamped calf over wooden boards.

A very richly illuminated book, with illustrations by two of the foremost Dutch miniature painters of the first half of the fifteenth century. The great full-page Crucifixion is by the artist known as the "Master of Zweder van Culemborg", from a manuscript that he illuminated for Zweder, who became Bishop of Utrecht in 1425. He also is responsible for many of the smaller miniatures in this Missal, while others were carried out by an artist who shows careful study of the works of the Van Eycks, an artist generally termed the "Arenberg Master" or the "Master of Catherine van Cleef". The manuscript is very close in the style of illumination and in its general interest to a Latin Bible in the Fitzwilliam Museum, Cambridge, and to the Egmondt Breviary in the Pierpont Morgan Library (M. 87), a Missal illuminated at the Carthusian monastery of Nieulicht near Utrecht.

>BIBLIOGRAPHY: De Ricci, I, p. 776, no. 122; A. W. Byvanck, *La miniature dans les Pays-Bas septentrionaux*, Paris, 1937, p. 66, note 3.

COLLECTION OF THE WALTERS ART GALLERY.   PL. XLIX

129. BOOK OF HOURS   French Flanders, ca. 1425

>W. 211. In Latin. Gothic script. 234 vellum leaves, 4⅝ x 3¼ inches. 21 miniatures; illuminated borders. Binding: modern red velvet.

This little book is a member of the general group of manuscripts described under no. 127. Although, as in the case of all of them, the technique is somewhat routine in character, the iconography is of the greatest interest and contains unusual features drawn from French, Italian, Flemish and Lower Rhenish art.

>BIBLIOGRAPHY: De Ricci, I, p. 789, no. 201.

COLLECTION OF THE WALTERS ART GALLERY.

130. BOOK OF HOURS   Flanders, ca. 1485

    W. 439. In Latin. Batarde script. 300 vellum leaves, 7¾ x 4½ inches. 14 large miniatures and 32 historiated initials; numerous historiated borders. Binding: original stamped calf laid in modern binding.

Made for a member of the family of Cleves and La Marcke, who is depicted in the frontispiece, possibly Engelbert of Cleves who married Charlotte de Bourbon in 1489. The style of the miniatures is not of the greatest fineness but it is strong and the subject matter is frequently of unusual interest.

    BIBLIOGRAPHY: De Ricci, I, p. 805, no. 307.

COLLECTION OF THE WALTERS ART GALLERY.

131. BOOK OF HOURS   Flanders, ca. 1500

    W. 430. In Latin. Gothic script. 155 vellum leaves, 4⅜ x 2⅝ inches. 12 miniatures. Binding: modern French inlaid morocco.

The miniatures are executed in a dark *grisaille* relieved with slight color. The motto of the original owner, "Je Lay de Veu", is worked into the border of each miniature.

    BIBLIOGRAPHY: De Ricci, I, p. 807, no. 312.

COLLECTION OF THE WALTERS ART GALLERY.

132. BOOK OF HOURS   Flanders, ca. 1465

    W. 190. In Latin. Batarde script. 139 vellum leaves, 7 x 4¾ inches. 9 large miniatures and 8 historiated initials. Binding: modern green velvet. Ex-coll.: Joannes Rietmakers (1663).

The small scenes in initials are executed in *grisaille* and gold on black grounds in the manner of the infinitely more elaborate prayer book on black vellum made for Galeazzo Maria Sforza (Vienna, Nationalbibliothek, ms. 1856). These initials are in fact closely related to the marginal medallions in that manuscript both in subject and technique, so that at least a common atelier is indicated, and this book may be considered a more routine production of the same shop.

The larger illustrations in the present book are done in *grisaille* on dark colors, the general color scheme being not very different from that prevailing in the main miniatures of the Sforza manuscript. The style, however, is much more highly modelled and less individual than in the Sforza book, and the figure types are closer to those of the so-called "Girart Master".

    BIBLIOGRAPHY: De Ricci, I, p. 794, no. 234.

COLLECTION OF THE WALTERS ART GALLERY.

133. BOOK OF HOURS   Netherlands (Utrecht), ca. 1480

    In Dutch. Gothic script. 192 vellum leaves, 5⅜ x 4 inches. 4 full-page miniatures and 6 historiated initials; illuminated borders. Binding: 17th century vellum. Ex-coll.: C. W. Reynell.

A later example of the school of Utrecht which demonstrates how generally conservative were the developments in Holland in miniature painting, as well as in the general decoration of books. Similar in style and date is British Museum Add. ms. 29,887.

LENT BY DIMITRI TSELOS.   PL. LI

134. IMAGE DU MONDE   Flanders, 1489

      W. 199. In French. Batarde script. 132 vellum leaves, 10½ x 7¾ inches. 37 miniatures. Binding: modern French morocco.

A "scientific" synopsis of the elements of astronomy, natural history, the seven arts, the forces of nature, etc., illustrated by astronomical diagrams as well as by *grisaille* illustrations. At the end of the volume the scribe, who dates his work February 20, 1489, states that the text was originally compiled for John, duke of Berry in 1245 [sic] and that in 1444 it was enlarged and put in order at the request of "Jehan le Clerc, librarier et bourgois de Bruges".

      BIBLIOGRAPHY: De Ricci, I, p. 845, no. 504; W. Nelson Francis, *The Book of Vices and Virtues* (Early English Text Society), London, 1942, p. XX, (the author includes the Walters manuscript in his list of manuscripts of *Le Miroir du Monde*, due to the fact that the scribe gives this title to his work, but our codex has nothing to do with the old French allegories that are the subject of his discussion).

COLLECTION OF THE WALTERS ART GALLERY.

135. JEHAN DE WAVRIN. CHRONIQUES D'ANGLETERRE   Flanders, ca. 1490

      W. 201. In French. Batarde script. 331 vellum leaves, 17¼ x 13⅜ inches. 6 large miniatures; illuminated borders. Binding: 18th century French calf. Ex-coll.: Robert Blathwayt, Dyrham Park, Chippenham (Sale, London, Nov. 20, 1912, no. 125, ill.).

This is volume IV of a luxurious copy of Wavrin's *Chronicle of England*, of which volumes II, III and V belonged in the seventeenth century to William III of Orange and are now in the Royal Library at The Hague.

The miniatures are the work of a fine Flemish painter, and are of unusually high calibre for historical illustration.

      BIBLIOGRAPHY: De Ricci, I, p. 851, no. 527, with previous literature.

COLLECTION OF THE WALTERS ART GALLERY.   PL. XLIV

136. BOOK OF HOURS FOR USE OF ROME   Flanders, ca. 1490

      W. 176. In Latin. Gothic script. 164 vellum leaves, 3⅛ x 2 inches. 9 large and 37 small miniatures; illuminated borders throughout. Binding: 18th century Russian morocco, gilt. Ex-colls.: Souchtelen, St. Petersburg; A. Polovtsoff (Sale, Paris, Nov. 14, 1910, I, no. 479); Cornuau.

A tiny book of silky vellum, whose chief charm is in the naturalistic and carefully studied flowers, birds and insects that are strewn through the borders.

      BIBLIOGRAPHY: De Ricci, I, p. 807, no. 317.

COLLECTION OF THE WALTERS ART GALLERY.

137. LECTIONARY OF THE BIBLE AND CHURCH FATHERS

                                                                            Germany (Rhineland), 2nd half of 14th cent.

      W. 148. In Latin. Gothic script. 283 vellum leaves, 11¾ x 8¼ inches. 6 large and 23 smaller miniatures; 4 drawings on flyleaves. Binding: 16th century German stamped pigskin over boards.

The miniatures are in a vigorous gothic style on heavy burnished gold grounds. Some of the marginal ornamental strips appear to have been added later, or by less skilled hands. Of particular interest are some nearly contemporary pen and ink drawings on flyleaves, several of which repeat some of the figures and scenes in the main miniatures, with slight adaptations suggesting that they might be projects for triptychs, statues, etc.

The representation of Brigittine nuns in one of these sketches indicates that the book was early in a Brigittine convent, and doubtless was executed there.

BIBLIOGRAPHY: De Ricci, I, p. 823, no. 395.

COLLECTION OF THE WALTERS ART GALLERY.   PL. LIII

138. LECTIONARY OF THE GOSPELS   Germany (Rhineland), ca. 1300

Ms. acc. 558564. In Latin. Transitional minuscule script. 172 vellum leaves, 12½ x 9 inches. One large historiated initial. Binding: original thick wooden boards with deep compartments for ornamental plaques, now missing. Ex-colls.: Rev. Edwin A. Dalrymple, Baltimore; Nathaniel D. Sollers, Baltimore.

A book written in a large archaic script showing only incipient gothic characteristics. The large historiated initial, representing Christ enthroned among the four symbols and the four Evangelists writing, appears to be the work of an artist from the region of the lower Rhine or even Flanders.

BIBLIOGRAPHY: De Ricci, I, p. 901, no. 2.

LENT BY THE LIBRARY OF CONGRESS.   PL. LIII

139. SPECULUM HUMANAE SALVATIONIS   Germany, 14th cent.

Ms. Z.109.073. In Latin verse. Gothic script. 103 vellum leaves, 11 x 19 inches. About 200 drawings, of which 30 are missing. Binding: original pigskin over wooden boards. Ex-coll.: Elihu Yale.

An unpretentious, didactic manuscript for popular use, abundantly illustrated with rough drawings—a type of book that was produced prolifically in Germany during the fourteenth and fifteenth centuries. Despite its humble character, this book holds particular interest for the history of American collecting, since it was probably the first medieval illuminated manuscript to enter an American library. It was presented in 1714 by Governor Elihu Yale to the newly founded college that later was named after him.

BIBLIOGRAPHY: *Yale Library Gazette*, VII, no. 1, (July, 1932); De Ricci, I, p. 167, no. 27.

LENT BY YALE UNIVERSITY LIBRARY.

140. PRAYER BOOK   Austria, ca. 1440

W. 163. In Latin. Gothic script. 181 vellum leaves, 5 x 3¾ inches. 30 miniatures; 3 historiated initials; numerous illuminated borders. Binding: 17th century stamped calf over boards. Ex-colls.: Possibly Leonhard von Laymingen; Baldassare Boncompagni, Rome.

A book illustrated for an Austrian bishop, with arms believed to be those of Leonhard von Laymingen, Bishop of Passau on the Danube from 1423 to 1451. The figure of a kneeling bishop is prominent throughout the miniatures. These are thinly colored so that the drawing shows through the paint, and include many unusual subjects. A number of the scenes show the high mountains of the Tyrol in the background. Large, vigorous acanthus leaves sprout from initials and curl around the margins.

BIBLIOGRAPHY: De Ricci, I, p. 815, no. 359.

COLLECTION OF THE WALTERS ART GALLERY.

141. SINGLE MINIATURE: THE HOLY TRINITY   Bohemia, ca. 1430

Historiated initial U. Vellum, 6¼ x 7⅛ inches. Ex-coll.: Edward Schultze.

God the Father, represented as a gentle, white-haired giant, his downcast eyes glancing thoughtfully to one side, places his hands lightly on the shoulders of the diminutive figure of Christ standing before him and holding the Cross, on which alights the grey dove of the Holy Spirit. The gentleness of the mood is carried out by the extreme delicacy of the style and the coloring. All strongly plastic effects of light and shade are avoided, and only a very delicate modulation of the planes exists, subtly accented in some places with gold highlights.

BIBLIOGRAPHY: *Cf.* Edith Hoffmann, *Cseh Miniaturok*, Budapest, 1918.

LENT BY THE NATIONAL GALLERY OF ART, ROSENWALD COLLECTION.   PL. LII

142. THOMAS AQUINAS. HISTORIA DE CORPORE CHRISTI Austria (Vienna), early 15th cent.

In Latin. Gothic script. 43 vellum leaves, 11¼ x 15⅜ inches. 2 miniatures; 1 illuminated border. Binding: 18th century Austrian stamped pigskin. Ex-coll.: Emperor Charles VI (1718).

This manuscript of the office of the feast of Corpus Christi was written and illuminated for William the Affable, Duke of Austria (1370-1406). It is dated between 1403 and 1406 by the presence of the arms of his consort, Joan of Anjou, whom he married in 1403. The finely executed miniature shows the duke kneeling in prayer in his armor, while a standard bearer holds his crested helm. An intricate gold rinceau enriches the blue background. Below are the shields of Anjou-Sicily-Jerusalem and Austria. The miniature has been attributed to the court illuminator, Nicolas of Brünn, who was one of the illuminators of a Durandus *Rationale* executed for Duke William (Vienna, Nationalbibliothek, cod. 2765).

BIBLIOGRAPHY: *Cf.* Karl Oettinger in *Jahrbuch der Preussischen Kunstsammlungen*, LIV (1933), pp. 221 ff.

LENT BY H. P. KRAUS.

143. RUDOLF VON EMS. WELTCHRONIK   Germany, 1402

In German. Cursive German book hand in 2 cols. 353 paper leaves, 11½ x 8¼ inches. About 287 colored drawings. Binding: 18th century half calf and paper boards. Ex-coll.: Reichsgraf Toerring-Gutenzell.

This "Chronicle of the World" by Rudolf von Ems, a scholarly Swiss poet of the thirteenth century, is a rhymed version of the Bible, supplemented by additions from other religious and secular works. Planned on a most extensive scale, it was interrupted by the author's death, and various subsequent writers attempted to complete it. The work remained popular into the fifteenth century and over forty manuscripts of it have survived.

The present example is supplied with an abundance of colored drawings, notable for their narrative charm and vigor of execution. Placed unframed upon the rough white paper, some occupy a column's width, others sweep informally across the page and into the margins. Always, however, the arrangement of script and picture results in a fine and unified page design. A rubricated note in the scribe's hand, occurring at the end, may be translated: "The book was completed in the Year of our Lord MCCCCII on the eve of the Conception of the Virgin".

> BIBLIOGRAPHY: C. G. Boerner Co., *Catalogue CX*, Leipzig, 1912. Cf. K. Goedecke, *Grundriss zur Geschichte der deutschen Dichtung*, 2nd ed., Dresden, 1884, I, pp. 120, 126-128; W. Golter, *Die deutsche Dichtung im Mittelalter*, Stuttgart, 1912, pp. 250-253.

LENT BY THE NEW YORK PUBLIC LIBRARY, SPENCER COLLECTION.   PL. LV

144. EBERHARD WINDECKE. DES KAISERS SIGISMUNDS BUCH   Germany, ca. 1440-50

> In German. Cursive book script. 306 paper leaves, 15¾ x 10½ inches. 173 miniatures. Binding: early 19th century English brown morocco, gilt. Ex-colls.: Von Ebner-Eschenbach, Nuremberg; Dr. Johann Kloss, Frankfurt a. M. (*ca.* 1820); Sir Thomas Phillipps (ms. 10381).

The text is a collection of documents, biographical records, news reports, popular satirical and political poems compiled by Eberhard Windecke of Mainz, renowned chronicler of the reign of Emperor Sigismund. This manuscript is illustrated with very large colored drawings executed with strength and vigor, characteristic of German secular graphic art at its best.

> BIBLIOGRAPHY: Potthast, *Bibl. Medii-Aevi*, 2nd ed. II, 1116 (ms. Cheltenham); Eberhard Windecke, *Denkwürdigkeiten zur Geschichte des Zeitalters Kaiser Sigmunds*, Berlin, 1893, ed. by W. Altmann: cod. C-E (critical edition of the text); J. Aschbach, *Geschichte Kaiser Sigismunds*, Hamburg, 1838-45, IV, pp. 448-465; Droysen, *Eberhard Windeck* in *Abhandlungen der sächsischen Gesellschaft der Wissenschaften, Phil.-hist. Kl.*, III (1857), pp. 149-229; Reifferschneid, *Des Kaiser Sigismund Buch von E. Windeck u. seine Ueberlieferung* in *Nachrichten der Göttinger Gesellschaft der Wissenschaften*, (1887), pp. 522-545; Wyss, *Eberhard Windeck und sein Sigmundbuch* in *Centralblatt für Bibliothekswesen*, XI (1895), pp. 433-483.

LENT BY H. P. KRAUS.

145. APOCALYPSE   Germany, early 15th cent.

> Ms. 15. In Latin. Gothic script. 18 vellum leaves, 13 x 9⅛ inches. 36 miniatures. Binding: 17th century French vellum. Ex-colls.: Abbey of Citeaux; James Lenox (acquired 1874).

This codex presents an interesting example of the kind of popular manuscript that furnished the prototypes for the block books of the fifteenth century. Without any pretense to elegance, the artist has drawn the figures clearly and vigorously and enlivened them with delicate tints of yellow, green, red, etc. Excerpts from the text are scattered over the backgrounds, and red inscriptions in banderolles clarify the significance of the figures.

> BIBLIOGRAPHY: Quaritch, *General Catalogue*, 1874, no. 141; De Ricci, II, p. 1318, no. 15. On the general subject of the relation of certain types of Apocalypse manuscripts to the block books, see Gertrud Bing, in *Journal of the Warburg and Courtauld Institutes*, V (1942), pp. 143-158.

LENT BY THE NEW YORK PUBLIC LIBRARY, MANUSCRIPT DIVISION.

146. BIBLIA PAUPERUM South Germany, ca. 1420

In German. Gothic book hand. 19 vellum leaves, 11½ x 8¼ inches. 39 half-page drawings.

The half-page illustrations are drawn in outline with a pen in a light and fluent style, enlivened by thin washes of coloring. A scene from the New Testament occupies a central roundel on each page, while subsidiary roundels contain busts of the prophets. On either side appear scenes from the Old Testament which are considered prophetic symbols of the central episode.

LENT BY THE NEW YORK PUBLIC LIBRARY, SPENCER COLLECTION.

147. ULRICH VON RICHENTHAL. CHRONIK DES KONSTANZER KONZILS
Germany (Constance), ca. 1450-60

In south German dialect. Gothic book hand in 2 cols. 521 paper leaves, 16 x 12¼ inches. 115 colored drawings; 837 coats of arms. Binding: original wooden boards and sheepskin. Ex-coll.: Graf Gustav von Königsegg und Aulendorf (near Constance).

This is an eye-witness account of the Church Council held at Constance from 1414 to 1418, the author having kept a diary of all interesting events, as well as of his impressions of contemporary life in the city of Constance.

The drawings are characteristic examples of Upper Rhenish illustration of the period, the freely executed outlines being tinted with thin washes of color. They are unframed, and are placed very informally with relation to the text, sometimes spreading across two pages. Since the scenes include remarkably faithful portrayals of actual Constance buildings, it is probable that the drawings were derived from sketches made on the spot, as Karl Kup has pointed out.

BIBLIOGRAPHY: Karl Kup in *Bulletin of the New York Public Library*, XI (1936), pp. 303-320, 4 pls.; De Ricci, II, p. 1342, no. 32, with previous literature.

LENT BY THE NEW YORK PUBLIC LIBRARY, SPENCER COLLECTION. PL. LIV

148. PSALTER AND ABBREVIATED HOURS Germany (Rhineland), 2nd half of 15th cent.

Ms. 4560(3),16. In Latin. Gothic script. 261 vellum leaves, 7½ x 5½ inches. 23 ornamented initials and many figures in borders. Binding: original 15th century stamped calf over boards. Ex-colls.: Sister Jutken Schomans; Rev. E. A. Dalrymple, Baltimore.

An unpretentious little Psalter with abbreviated Hours and Canticles that was executed in a Brigittine convent, probably near Cologne. The first initial is in a good Rhenish style, with softly modelled acanthus and use of gold and silver. The rest of the ornament is in a highly decorative provincial manner that is similar to the work of "Pennsylvania Dutch" craftsmen in this country. There is much use of elaborately flourished pen decoration, large initials with red and blue ornament, and an abundance of amusing figures and animals drawn in outline and colored with flat hues.

BIBLIOGRAPHY: De Ricci, I, p. 232, no. 113.

LENT BY THE LIBRARY OF CONGRESS.

149. PSALTER   England, ca. 1300

    Garrett ms. 35. In Latin. Large insular gothic script. 188 vellum leaves, 10¼ x 7¼ inches. 13 full-page miniatures; 10 historiated initials. Binding: 18th century English calf. Ex-colls.: Barne Roberts (ca. 1500); Robert Garrett.

The figures in the full-page miniatures that precede the text are of large scale and characterized by vigorous and effective drawing, rather than delicacy. The manuscript is enriched by backgrounds and ornament of heavy burnished gold, sometimes simply tooled, and also of silver, which has not tarnished.

    BIBLIOGRAPHY: De Ricci, I, p. 870, no. 35; Boston Museum of Fine Arts, *Arts of the Middle Ages*, Boston, 1940, no. 41; D. Egbert in *The Princeton University Library Chronicle*, III (1942), p. 126, ill.

LENT BY PRINCETON UNIVERSITY LIBRARY, GARRETT COLLECTION.   PL. LVIII

150. AEGIDIUS COLUMNA. DU GOUVERNMENT DES PRINCES   England, ca. 1300

    W. 144. In French. Gothic script. 121 vellum leaves, 11¾ x 8¼ inches. 10 miniatures and historiated initials; illuminated initials and partial borders. Binding: English russia, ca. 1815 by Faulkner (with Goldsmid arms). Bought in London in 1463 for a monastery of St. Gualterus. Ex-colls.: Ebenezer Mussel (Sale, London, May 30, 1766, no. 90); William Bayntun (Sale, London, June 4, 1787); John Louis Goldsmid (Sale, London, Dec. 11, 1815, no. 293); Joseph Barrois; Earl of Ashburnham (Sale, London, 1901, no. 241); C. Fairfax Murray.

The text was originally composed in Latin about 1280 at the command of Philip the Bold, King of France, for the instruction of his son, Philip the Fair, by Egidio Colonna. The author, also called Gilles de Rome (1247-1316), was a pupil of Thomas Aquinas and himself a famous scholastic and philosopher. This French translation by Henri de Gauchy was made almost immediately afterwards, probably before 1285, the year when Philip the Fair ascended the throne. Though only a few early copies have survived, the treatise was greatly renowned in its time, as indicated by the present manuscript, which was written and illuminated in England shortly after the completion of the French version.

The text sets forth the ideals for conduct of a prince, his responsibilities and proper relations with his family, courtiers and subjects. The illustrations are executed with skill and grace, in a style that is characteristic of English productions around 1295 to 1300.

    BIBLIOGRAPHY: De Ricci, I, p. 846, no. 507. Cf. J. P. Molenaer, *Li Livres du Gouvernment des Rois*, a 13th century French version of Egidio Colonna's Treatise, New York-London, 1899; *Histoire Littéraire de la France*, XX, pp. 168-174.

COLLECTION OF THE WALTERS ART GALLERY.

151. BOOK OF HOURS   England (East Anglia), ca. 1300

    W. 105. In Latin. Gothic script. 56 vellum leaves, 8¼ x 5½ inches. 12 full-page miniatures and 15 historiated initials. Binding: modern red morocco.

The miniatures of this fragmentary Hours, once extremely fine works in the style of one of the most distinguished English manuscripts, the Psalter of Robert De Lisle (British Museum, Arundel ms. 83), have been ruined by water. Enough of the original surface remains to show the mannered sway of the figures, the very softly modelled folds of the drapery, sprinkled with delicate patterns, the intricate diapered or gold tooled backgrounds. Most notable is the relatively monumental scale of the figures and the unusual subjects of several of the pictures.

BIBLIOGRAPHY: De Ricci, I, p. 785, no. 175.

COLLECTION OF THE WALTERS ART GALLERY.   PL. LIX

152. THE WINDMILL PSALTER   England (Canterbury ?), late 13th cent.

M. 102. In Latin. Gothic script. 168 vellum leaves, 12¾ x 8¾ inches. 11 large historiated initials and numerous grotesques. Binding: modern pigskin over boards. Ex-colls.: Lord Aldenham; William Morris.

This book ranks among the best known English manuscripts of the period and certainly is one of the most delightful that has come down to us. The illustration consists entirely of historiated or elaborately ornamented initials and a wealth of fantastic line-endings. The complex B introducing the first Psalm embraces the Tree of Jesse, and occupies an entire leaf. An unusual feature is that on the opposite page the succeeding E of the word "Beatus" is also given great prominence, being peopled with figures enacting the Massacre of the Innocents, and a downswooping angel bearing a scroll inscribed with the rest of the first words of the Psalm. The background and edges of the letter are enriched with fluent pen-tracery in colored inks, of a most complex and lacy pattern. At the top is the windmill that has given the Psalter its name.

All the paintings in the book, as well as the extraordinary line-endings, appear to be the work of a single artist who is a most expressive and unique personality. His figures are characterized by great freedom of pose and movement, the hands graceful and prehensile, the round-cheeked faces moulded in a kind of pale *grisaille*, the draperies modelled with a most delicate and luscious surface. Particularly unusual are the colors, in which a beautiful rose red, a luminous blue, and a strange, golden tan shot with green are notable.

BIBLIOGRAPHY: Belle da Costa Greene and Meta P. Harrsen, *Exhibition of Illuminated Manuscripts. . .*, New York, 1934, no. 45, fig. 7, pl. 42; De Ricci, II, p. 1385, no. 102, with previous literature.

LENT BY THE PIERPONT MORGAN LIBRARY.   PL. LVI

153. PSALTER AND HOURS   England, ca. 1300

W. 102. In Latin and Norman French. Gothic script. 105 vellum leaves, 10½ x 7¼ inches. 37 historiated initials; numerous line-endings and drolleries, of which 34 rank as miniatures. Binding: modern red velvet.

A manuscript made for a foundation of Augustinian monks, probably that of St. Julian near St. Albans Abbey, from which it was founded. Two artists are responsible for the illuminations, which include many of unusual interest. The line-endings are particularly diverse and imaginative, and some of these, as well as some of the drolleries, are executed on surprisingly large scale, often characteristic of English manuscripts of this period. The more accomplished of the two artists is very expressive and graceful of outline and patterns his surfaces with great delicacy. He is equally expressive in minute paintings and in large ones. His style at its best approaches the artist of no. 152.

BIBLIOGRAPHY: De Ricci, I, p. 784, no. 169.

COLLECTION OF THE WALTERS ART GALLERY.   PL. LVIII

154. THE TICKHILL PSALTER England (Nottinghamshire), ca. 1310

In Latin. Gothic script in 2 cols. 155 vellum leaves, 13 x 8¾ inches. 482 miniatures, including 7 full-page historiated initials. Binding: green morocco, ca. 1780 by Scott of Edinburgh. Ex-colls.: Augustinian Priory of Worksop (now Radnor); Marquess of Lothian, Newbattle Abbey (Sale, New York, Jan. 27, 1932, no. 7, facs.)

One of the richest and most interesting examples of English gothic illumination, this Psalter was written for the Priory of Worksop near Nottingham. A fifteenth-century inscription on the flyleaf attributes its writing and "gilding" to the hand of John Tickhill, Prior of Worksop from 1308 to 1314. The Prior did not do the abundant illustrations of the manuscript, however. These are the work of a travelling group of lay artists, as Dr. Egbert has demonstrated in his exhaustive monograph. Seven other English manuscripts executed during the first quarter of the fourteenth century, the chief of which is the Psalter of Queen Isabella in Munich, were done by the same travelling atelier, using the same pattern-books, for prominent interrelated families, nearly all of which were connected with Nottinghamshire. One of the most interesting features of the Tickhill Psalter is that its ambitious program remained unfinished, so that it preserves for us every stage of the illuminator's procedure, from the first rough sketch to the finished miniature. The plan was to embellish the lower margin of each page with a continuous series of Biblical illustrations. The completed portion stresses episodes in the lives of David and Solomon, an unparalleled series, which shows direct dependence upon the version of the Biblical narrative recounted in Petrus Comestor's *Historica Scholastica*.

BIBLIOGRAPHY: De Ricci, II, p. 1340, no. 26; Donald Drew Egbert, *The Tickhill Psalter*, New York, 1940, with complete bibliography on p. 127.

LENT BY THE NEW YORK PUBLIC LIBRARY, SPENCER COLLECTION. PL. LVII

155. TABLE OF CONSANGUINITY AND GENEALOGY OF CHRIST England, 14th cent.

W. 80. In Latin. Gothic script. Vellum roll, 14 ft. 2½ inches x 16½ inches. Colored drawings.

This roll is illustrated with drawings, lightly colored, in a sure and graceful style, many of them in circular medallions.

BIBLIOGRAPHY: De Ricci, I, p. 824, no. 404.

COLLECTION OF THE WALTERS ART GALLERY.

156. GUILLAUME DE DEGUILEVILLE. GRACE DIEU (THE PILGRIMAGE OF THE SOUL)
England, ca. 1430

In English. Gothic book hand. 136 vellum leaves, 10⅝ x 7½ inches. 26 miniatures. Binding: 15th century doeskin over boards. Ex-colls.: Sir Thomas Cumberworth of Somerby, Lincolnshire (ca. 1430-50); Agnes Radcliffe; Marrick Nunnery, Yorkshire; John Cowper; Henry Percy, Earl of Northumberland (1564-1632); Lord Leconfield of Petworth, Sussex (Sale, London, 1928, no. 76, 3 pls.).

Only six manuscripts are known of this English translation of the popular *Pélerinage de la Vie Humaine* in which the poet, in a vision, sees his soul visiting in turn Purgatory, Hell and Paradise. As is often the case with popular manuscripts, and particularly those executed in England during the fifteenth century, there is no great elegance of material or style. However, the miniatures have a certain insouciant charm and a gayety of color.

The manuscript was probably made about 1430 for Sir Thomas Cumberworth of Somerby in Lincolnshire, who willed it in 1450 to his chantry priest. Its subsequent history down to the present time is recorded by numerous ownership entries in the book.

BIBLIOGRAPHY: V. H. Paltsits in *Bulletin of the New York Public Library*, XXXII (Nov. 1928), pp. 715-720; De Ricci, II, p. 1339, no. 19, with additional literature.

LENT BY THE NEW YORK PUBLIC LIBRARY, SPENCER COLLECTION.   PL. LX

157. GEOFFREY CHAUCER. THE CANTERBURY TALES   England, ca. 1440-50

In English. 11 vellum leaves, 11⅞ x 8 inches. 2 miniatures; borders; ornamented initials. Ex-colls.: Grandson of Alfred Harley, 6th Earl of Oxford (Sale, July 23, 1896); W. A. White.

These leaves together with two others (in the John Rylands Library, Manchester, England) form the so-called Oxford manuscript, a fragment of what must have been one of the finest illuminated copies of the Canterbury Tales. While the borders are executed in the conventional mid-century English style, the outline drawings depicting the pilgrims on horseback are sensitively and expressively drawn.

BIBLIOGRAPHY: John M. Manly and Edith Rickert, *The Text of the Canterbury Tales*, Chicago, 1940, I, pp. 396-398; Rosenbach Company, *An Exhibition of Fifteenth Century Manuscripts and Books in Honor of the Six Hundredth Anniversary of the Birth of Geoffrey Chaucer*, New York, 1940, p. 8.

LENT BY THE ROSENBACH COMPANY.   PL. LIX

158. JOHN LYDGATE. FALLS OF PRINCES.   England, ca. 1460

In English. 212 vellum leaves, folio. 7 miniatures; about 260 illuminated initials. Binding: late 17th or early 18th century calf. Ex-coll.: Sir Thomas Phillipps (ms. 4254).

The text composed in the third decade of the fifteenth century by the monk, John Lydgate, a follower of Chaucer, is an adaptation in verse of Boccaccio's *De casibus virorum et feminarum illustrium*. The manuscript is among the most elaborately decorated early copies of the work. The miniatures are executed by an artist strongly influenced by Flemish painting.

BIBLIOGRAPHY: Henry Bergen, *Lydgate's Fall of Princes*, Washington, 1927, IV, pp. 88-92; Rosenbach Company, *An Exhibition of Fifteenth Century Manuscripts and Books in Honor of the Six Hundredth Anniversary of the Birth of Geoffrey Chaucer*, New York, 1940, pp. 14-15.

LENT BY THE ROSENBACH COMPANY.

159. MAGNA CHARTA WITH STATUTES   England, ca. 1470

In Law-French and Latin. English book hand. 476 vellum leaves, 12¼ x 8¼ inches. 3 historiated initials; numerous illuminated initials and borders. Binding: modern red velvet, in 3 vols. Ex-colls.: Sir James Dyer (1562); Owen D. Young.

A handsome copy of the Magna Charta with a compilation of subsequent laws up to the eighth year of the reign of King Edward IV. It is generously adorned with ornamented initials and with the vigorous, colorful acanthus and vine borders characteristic of English illumination of the time. The historiated initials show kings holding court.

BIBLIOGRAPHY: De Ricci, II, p. 1854, no. 1.

LENT BY WILLIAM K. RICHARDSON. PL. LX

160. BIBLE Hungary, ca. 1335-1340

Ms. Pre-acc. 1. In Latin. Gothic script in 2 cols. 2 vols., 352 and 394 vellum leaves, 17½ x 12½ inches. 122 historiated initials; 2 elaborately historiated borders; numerous marginal ornaments. Binding: 19th century English blue morocco. Ex-colls.: Demeter Nekcsei-Lipócz, Count of Bács, Hungary; Henry Perkins (Sale, Hanworth Park, 1873, no. 174, ill.).

A monumental two-volume Bible, executed for Demeter Nekcsei-Lipócz, Count of Bács, a prominent official in the court of Charles Robert of Anjou, King of Hungary (1310-1342). Meta Harrsen, in a detailed study of this distinguished manuscript, has identified the original owner and attributed it to a Hungarian court atelier headed by a miniature painter from Bologna. She has pointed out the constant mutual relations between Italy and Hungary under the regime of the Neapolitan-born Charles Robert.

Three hands may be distinguished in the sumptuous illumination of the two volumes. Although the Italian influence is strong throughout, the work is characterized by a fantasy, a strong, crisp modelling and a dramatic intensity that differentiates it from the usual Bolognese productions of the period.

To this same atelier is attributed a richly illustrated Passional, now divided among three collections: the Pierpont Morgan Library, ms. 360, Vatican lat. ms. 8541 and Léonce Rosenberg collection, Paris, nos. 72, 73.

BIBLIOGRAPHY: De Ricci, I, p. 180, no. 1; Meta Harrsen, *The Bible of Demeter Nekcsei-Lipócz, Count of Bács in Hungary*, printed by the Government Printing Office for the Library of Congress (in press).

LENT BY THE LIBRARY OF CONGRESS. PL. LXII

161. PONTIFICAL North Italy, ca. 1380

In Latin. Gothic script. 147 vellum leaves, 14¾ x 10½ inches. 21 miniatures; 58 historiated initials; illuminated borders. Binding: English straight-grain purple morocco, ca. 1830. Ex-colls.: Andrea Calderini, Bishop of Ceneda in Vittoria Veneto (1378-1385); Meschatin La Faye family of Forez (ca. 16th century); Bossange; H. Yates Thompson (Sale, London, June 3, 1919, no. 15); Frank B. Bemis.

A magnificent volume of handsome format and large script, with abundant rubrication, flourished pen-ornaments in colored inks and a series of acanthus borders, miniatures and historiated initials painted in a strong and accomplished style. The miniatures present numerous interesting and unusual scenes of liturgical objects being blessed, rendered with great attention to the vestments and other details. Many of the miniatures in the latter part of the book are by later and less interesting hands, quite possibly working on unfinished sketches placed in the book by the original artist.

BIBLIOGRAPHY: De Ricci, I, p. 949, no. 1, with previous literature.

LENT BY HARVARD COLLEGE LIBRARY, DEPARTMENT OF GRAPHIC ARTS. PL. LXIV

162. ANTIPHONARY Italy (Florence), ca. 1375

> W. 153. In Latin. Gothic script with many recent alterations; music. 56 vellum leaves, 24 x 16½ inches. 8 miniatures in initials; numerous ornamented initials. Binding: 19th century half morocco. Ex-colls.: A. Firmin-Didot (Sale, Paris, 1884, no. 8); Marshall C. Lefferts (check-list, 1901, p. 55).

A choir book executed in Florence for a church dedicated to Saints Peter and Paul. The miniatures, some of monumental scale, are by three able artists who were followers of Orcagna. The colors, their pristine brilliance and crispness undimmed, are laid over a very heavy layer of burnished gold leaf grounded on gesso to give salience. The surface of the gold has been richly tooled.

In addition to the historiated initials are numerous large letters executed in elaborate designs of red and blue.

BIBLIOGRAPHY: De Ricci, I, p. 780, no. 148.

COLLECTION OF THE WALTERS ART GALLERY. PL. LXIII

163. ANTIPHONARY Italy (Siena), 1345

> No. 1928.117. In Latin. Gothic script. 346 vellum leaves, 20⅞ x 13⅜ inches. 40 historiated initials; illuminated borders. Binding: modern black morocco. Ex-coll.: Walter V. R. Berry (d. 1928).

The forty historiated initials have been attributed by Berenson to Lippo Vanni, on the basis of comparison with a choir book in Siena known by documents to have been illuminated by Lippo in 1345. They are painted in a fluid, sketchy style that Berenson considers characteristic of Tuscan miniature painting of the fourteenth century—a style which he finds reflected in certain of the panel paintings of Lippo Vanni that are to be dated in the same years in which he was active as a miniaturist. One of these, very close indeed to Lippo's miniature-painting manner, is a little triptych in the Walters Art Gallery. The Antiphonary provides thus an exceptionally valuable example of the relation between book illustration and panel painting in the Middle Ages.

BIBLIOGRAPHY: B. Berenson in *Gazette des Beaux-Arts*, IX (1924), pp. 257-285, ill.; *idem* in *Studies in Medieval Painting*, New Haven, 1930, pp. 39-61, 14 figs.; *Exposition du Livre Italien*, Paris, 1925, p. 45, no. 167; De Ricci, I, p. 1050, no. 1928.117.

LENT BY FOGG ART MUSEUM, HARVARD UNIVERSITY. PL. LXIV

164. LEAF: STATUTES OF THE GOLDSMITHS' GUILD North Italy (Bologna), 1383 ?

> In Latin. 1 vellum leaf, 14 x 18⅛ inches. 1 miniature; 1 historiated initial; armorials.

A leaf containing the prologue and beginning of the Statutes and Ordinances of the Goldsmiths' Guild of the city of Bologna, possibly the set promulgated in 1383. At the top is a majestic painting of the Virgin and Child enthroned between the standing figures of St. Petronius and St. Alle, both in episcopal vestments. The style is very close to that of Niccolò da Bologna (cf. no. 165).

BIBLIOGRAPHY: For history of statutes of the Goldsmiths' Guild of Bologna, see S. J. A. Churchill and C. G. E. Bunt, *The Goldsmiths of Italy*, London, 1926, pp. 81-85, 166.

LENT BY THE NATIONAL GALLERY OF ART, ROSENWALD COLLECTION. PL. LXV

165. SINGLE MINIATURE: THE CRUCIFIXION BY NICCOLO DA BOLOGNA

Italy (Bologna), late 14th cent.

No. 24.1013. Single leaf from manuscript, vellum, 10¼ x 8 inches. 1 miniature. Ex-colls.: Probably Dukes of Anjou (Anjou arms); Count Louis Paar (Sale, Rome, 1889, no. 266); Arthur Sambon, Paris; Léonce Rosenberg, Paris.

The painting is by the hand of the most important Bolognese miniaturist of the Trecento, Niccolò da Bologna (active ca. 1369-ca. 1402). It is inscribed: "Nicolaus F.", a signature used by this artist in his later years. The rather monumental figures with broad expressive faces, the draperies terminating in small zig-zag folds, as well as the background ornamented with heavy golden arabesques, are all characteristic of Niccolo's style, as are the whitish flesh tones and the color contrasts employed in the garments.

BIBLIOGRAPHY: A. Venturi in *Archivio stor. dell'arte*, II (1889), pp. 91-92; S. de Ricci, *Catalogue d'une collection de miniatures . . . de M. L. Rosenberg*, Paris, 1913, p. 20, no. 49, pl. VI; William M. Milliken in *Bulletin of the Cleveland Museum of Art*, XII (1925), p. 69, ill.; idem in *Art in America*, XIV (1926), pp. 219-233; De Ricci, II, p. 1930, no. 24.1013; Cleveland Museum of Art, *Twentieth Anniversary Exhibition*, Cleveland, 1936, p. 59, no. 136.

LENT BY THE CLEVELAND MUSEUM OF ART. PL. LXV

166. JOHANNES CLIMACUS. SCALA DEL PARADISO

Italy, late 14th cent.

W. 157. In Italian. Gothic script. 196 vellum leaves, 9½ x 6½ inches. 1 historiated initial and border. Binding: 19th century English green morocco. Ex-colls.: Nicolo da Martino; Howell Wills (Sale, London, July 11, 1894, no. 482).

An Italian version of a well-known guide for monastic life originally written in Greek. This copy is distinguished by a historiated border and an initial containing a representation of the author, which is by a painter of unusual ability.

BIBLIOGRAPHY: De Ricci, I, p. 843, no. 495.

COLLECTION OF THE WALTERS ART GALLERY.

167. SCENES FROM THE BIBLE

Northern Italy, 2nd half of 14th cent.

Later captions in Italian. 48 vellum leaves, octavo. 48 full-page miniatures. Binding: 15th century Italian stamped morocco.

A series of illustrations in several hands, all with northern characteristics. Some of the most effective scenes are painted with black or dark backgrounds, and the modelling is built up upon dark under-painting for skin and draperies.

The borders and inscriptions are a later addition.

BIBLIOGRAPHY: Z. Haraszti in *More Books, the Bulletin of the Boston Public Library*, XXIII (1948), p. 252.

LENT BY THE BOSTON PUBLIC LIBRARY.

168. SINGLE MINIATURE; THE VIRGIN WITH SAINTS PETER AND PAUL

Italy (Siena), 14th cent.

No. 65. Vellum, 6 x 6¼ inches. Miniature within initial V.

The figures are represented at three-quarter length, the Apostles glancing upward at Christ, who appears in the clouds above.

BIBLIOGRAPHY: Maggs, *Catalogue 404* (1921), no. 92, pl. XLIX; De Ricci, II, p. 1706, no. B.22.

LENT BY ROBERT LEHMAN.

169. SUETONIUS. LIVES OF THE TWELVE CAESARS   Italy (Milan), 1433

Kane ms. 44. In Latin. Modified roman script. 169 vellum leaves, 9¾ x 7½ inches. 12 miniatures; 1 historiated border; 12 ornamented initials. Binding: 16th century Italian calf, with the emblems of the printer Gabriele Giolito' de Ferrari. Ex-colls.: Robert Hoe (Sale, New York, 1912, II, p. 401, no. 2511); Mrs. Phoebe A. D. Boyle (Sale, New York, 1923, no. 323); Grenville Kane.

This collection of the biographies of the Roman emperors from Julius Caesar to Domitian was composed by Suetonius at the beginning of the second century A. D. It remained one of the most popular classical works throughout the Middle Ages and the Renaissance.

This manuscript, which has retained its pristine freshness to an almost miraculous degree, was probably executed for a member of the Visconti family of Milan or one of its branches. One of the Visconti emblems, the knotted veil, appears twice in the ornament, and the book is signed and dated 1433 by the scribe, Milanus Burrus, who is known to have worked for the Visconti. He wrote another copy of the same text for a Visconti owner, which is now in the Fitzwilliam Museum, Cambridge, McClean ms. 162. *Cf.* also Paris, Bibliothèque Nationale, ms. ital. 131, as well as no. 170 of this catalogue. An early owner was Guiniforte della Croce, whose arms were painted over earlier bearings on the first page and whose name appears on the flyleaf.

The style of the miniatures resembles in a general way that of the Fitzwilliam manuscript, except that the delineation and modelling of the planes seem harder in the present example, possibly due to some extent to the unworn condition of the surface. A manuscript that may be in part, at least, executed by the same miniaturist is the Breviary made between 1428 and 1447 for Marie de Savoy, wife of Philippe-Marie Visconti (now Chambéry, Bibl. Munic., ms. 4).

BIBLIOGRAPHY: De Ricci, II, p. 1897, no. 44, with previous literature. *Cf.* V. Leroquais, *Les Breviaires Manuscrits des bibliothèques publiques de France*, Paris, 1934, I, pp. 255-260, pls. LXXV-LXXXI.

LENT BY PRINCETON UNIVERSITY LIBRARY, KANE COLLECTION.   PL. LXVI

170. LEONARDO BRUNI (ARETINO). DE PRIMO BELLO PUNICO   Italy (Milan), 1444

Lewis ms. 54. In Latin. Modified roman script. 78 vellum leaves, 8½ x 6 inches. Illuminated border; 3 ornamented initials. Binding: 15th century Italian stamped calf. Ex-colls.: Trivulzio-Belgioso-Trotti (Sale, 1885); Thomas F. Richardson; John F. Lewis.

This book is signed by the same scribe as no. 169, but was written in 1444. The arms, motto and emblems, which are exactly the same as in the Fitzwilliam Museum manuscript, McClean 162, indicate that this volume likewise was done for a member of the Visconti family of Milan. There are no miniatures in this book, but the style of the border ornament with its playful *putti* is so close to that of the Fitzwilliam manuscript as to suggest that the same artist is responsible for both.

BIBLIOGRAPHY: Edwin Wolf, 2nd, *European Manuscripts in the John Frederick Lewis Collection*, Philadelphia, 1937, pp. 60 f., no. 54, ill.; De Ricci, II, p. 2059, no. 184, with previous literature.

LENT BY THE PHILADELPHIA FREE LIBRARY, JOHN FREDERICK LEWIS COLLECTION.

171. OFFICES OF THE VIRGIN — Northern Italy (Milan), ca. 1440

W. 323. In Latin. Gothic script. 180 vellum leaves, 4⅞ x 3¼ inches. 18 miniatures and historiated initials; illuminated borders with figures. Binding: Italian straight-grain red morocco, ca. 1800.

A little manuscript evidently made for a marriage, with abundant armorials scattered throughout the book. Unfortunately, attempts to identify them have been unsuccessful. The miniatures are executed in the manner of the so-called Zattavari school, and show the somewhat gaudy coloring but delicious drawing of this atelier, and its charming habit of representing a world in which everyone is forever young. The artist of this manuscript is particularly skillful and inventive, handling his figures with complete command of foreshortening and free movement. His technique is very delicate and his conceits refreshing. Unusual features are the two miniatures representing St. Ambrose, mounted on a horse and in episcopal robes, galloping over fighting armies.

BIBLIOGRAPHY: De Ricci, I, p. 813, no. 349.

COLLECTION OF THE WALTERS ART GALLERY. PL. LXVI

172. ESPOSIZIONE SOPRA LA CANTICA — Italy (Milan), ca. 1440-50

In Italian. Gothic script in 2 cols. 71 vellum and paper leaves, 11 x 8 inches. 45 miniatures; 1 border with figures. Binding: modern English green morocco, gilt, by Lloyd. Ex-colls.: Sta. Chiara, Murano (15th century); Sister Anastasia Lanardi (17th century).

An exceptionally interesting manuscript also connected with the Zattavari school, and displaying its youthful figures, interest in perspective and fluent handling of unusual poses. The color, however, is less gay than in the typical Zattavari productions, while the technique of both drawing and coloring is likewise more expressionistic and less polished than in characteristic examples of the school. The coloring is at its best on the paper pages, where it achieves a sober and harmonious luminosity. The subjects, highly symbolic, are all of great iconographical interest. The handling of space and plastic form varies from a dream-like serenity to a passionate exaggeration.

LENT BY PHILIP AND FRANCES HOFER. PL. LXVI

173. OFFICES OF THE VIRGIN, ETC. — Italy (Naples), ca. 1480

W. 328. In Latin. Gothic script. 215 vellum leaves, 6¾ x 5⅛ inches. 7 miniatures; 6 historiated initials; illuminated borders. Binding: French black morocco, ca. 1815.

An elaborately illuminated manuscript characterized by complex gold vine borders with birds and animals. Another manuscript of the same type and incorporating the same heraldic motto, "Spera in Dio", is in the Walters Art Gallery, ms. 329.

BIBLIOGRAPHY: De Ricci, I, p. 813, no. 350.

COLLECTION OF THE WALTERS ART GALLERY.

174. PSALTER WITH CISTERCIAN LITANY   Southern Italy (Naples), ca. 1460

W. 330. In Latin. Semi-roman script. 203 vellum leaves, 8⅝ x 6⅛ inches. 2 large and 5 small miniatures; illuminated borders; numerous "white-vine" initials. Binding: original wooden boards and stamped black leather; remains of 13th century silver-gilt clasps with grotesques in relief.

A richly embellished book on fine vellum, illustrated in a hard but very competent and decorative style.

BIBLIOGRAPHY: De Ricci, I, p. 774, no. 109.

COLLECTION OF THE WALTERS ART GALLERY.

175. SINGLE MINIATURE: ASSUMPTION OF THE VIRGIN   Italy (Florence), late 14th cent.

No. 30.105. Historiated initial G on vellum, 13¾ x 13⅛ inches. Ex-colls.: W. Y. Ottley (Sale, London, 1938, no. 182); Edouard Kann, Paris.

The initial in orange-red, lined with yellow and decorated with leaf scrolls in blue, grey and various shades of green frame the monumental figures of Christ and the Virgin, flanked by saints and worshipped by music-making angels. In the background are winged cherubs surmounted by angels carrying crowns of flowers. Figure types, brilliant coloring, composition and style suggest an artist of the Florentine school anticipating the manner of Lorenzo Monaco.

BIBLIOGRAPHY: A Boinet, *La collection de miniatures de M. Edouard Kann*, Paris, 1926, p. 25, no. XXVI, pl. XXIV and colored frontispiece; William M. Milliken in *Bulletin of the Cleveland Museum of Art*, XVII (1930), pp. 131-133, ill.; De Ricci, II, p. 1932, no. 30.105.

LENT BY THE CLEVELAND MUSEUM OF ART.   PL. LXVII

176. SINGLE MINIATURE: VIRGIN SURROUNDED BY ANGELS

Italy (Florence), 15th cent.

No. 28.652. Fragment of a leaf from an Antiphonary, vellum, 16½ x 11¾ inches. Historiated initial G and floral border. Ex-coll.: Marczell von Nemes.

The conservative composition, the fresh but delicate coloring with almost imperceptible modelling and the gentle charm of the figures reveal the influence of Fra Angelico upon contemporary Florentine miniaturists.

BIBLIOGRAPHY: De Ricci, II, p. 1931, no. 28.652; William M. Milliken in *Bulletin of the Cleveland Museum of Art*, XXXII (1945), pp. 5-7.

LENT BY THE CLEVELAND MUSEUM OF ART.

177. LECTIONARY OF THE GOSPELS   Northern Italy (?), mid 15th cent.

   In Latin. Gothic script. 114 vellum leaves, 14⅛ x 10½ inches. 4 historiated initials; 1 full and three partial borders. Binding: contemporary Italian stamped morocco. Ex-colls.: Aeneas Silvius Piccolomini; Earl of Ashburnham (Appendix, no. 17); H. Yates Thompson (Sale, London, March 23, 1920, no. 61, pl. 46); A. Chester Beatty (Sale, London, May 9, 1933, no. 63, pl. 39).

This delicately executed work is difficult to localize. The four historiated initials showing the Evangelists writing are completely gothic in style, but the script is Italianate in character. The Piccolomini arms show indications of having been inserted after the manuscript was designed. The cardinal's hat indicates that they refer to Aeneas Silvius Piccolomini, who was cardinal from 1456 to 1458, just before being elevated to the papacy as Pope Pius II.

   BIBLIOGRAPHY: De Ricci, II, p. 1341, no. 29, with previous literature.

LENT BY THE NEW YORK PUBLIC LIBRARY, SPENCER COLLECTION.   PL. LXI

178. TWO MINIATURES: PENTECOST AND CHRIST AS KING   North Italy, early 15th cent.

   Nos. 99-100. Historiated initials A and B from an Antiphonary. Vellum, 4½ x 4½ and 3¼ x 3⅝ inches, respectively.

These two initials appear to be by the same hand as a miniature owned by the Cleveland Museum of Art, attributed to the school of Stefano da Verona. The delicacy of style, the gothic character of the figures and the almost iridescent color are characteristic of the Veronese school.

LENT BY ROBERT LEHMAN.   PL. LXVIII

179. LEAF FROM AN ANTIPHONARY   Northern Italy, first half of 15th cent.

   In Latin. One vellum leaf, folio size. Historiated initial M and border.

The Annunciation to the Virgin, who is seated on a cushion in a garden and clad in an azure mantle over a rich red dress. The angel, with a light blue robe and rose wings, is somewhat Byzantine in type and silhouette. In lightness, delicacy and prettiness, however, the figure belongs to the Italian Renaissance. Behind is a darkening green landscape lit delicately with a gold light, while in the sky God and his cherubim appear etched in gold. The illustration is attributed to the master known as Belbello da Pavia, one of the foremost Italian miniaturists of the first half of the fifteenth century.

   BIBLIOGRAPHY: Cf. P. Toesca, La pitture e la miniature in Lombardia, Milan, 1912, pp. 536-549, 582, and esp. figs. 443-449, tav. XXXII, frontispiece; P. D'Ancona, La miniature italienne, Paris, 1925, pp. 51-53, pl. XLVII.

LENT BY THE NATIONAL GALLERY OF ART, ROSENWALD COLLECTION.   PL. LXVII

180. STIGMATIZATION OF ST. FRANCIS   Italy (Ferrara), 2nd half of 15th cent.

   Historiated initial from Antiphonary. Vellum, 7¼ x 6¾ inches. Ex-coll.: Eduard Simon (Sale, Berlin, 1929, no. 2).

The initial G frames St. Francis kneeling in a landscape coldly modelled in northern light, his robe delicately, but sharply picked out with gold highlights. The painting style is reminiscent of that of Cosimo Tura.

Three other miniatures from the same Antiphonary are known, one in the Berlin Kupferstichkabinett and two formerly in the Edouard Kann collection.

BIBLIOGRAPHY: P. Wescher in *Berliner Museen, Beiblatt zum Jahrbuch der Preussischen Kunstsammlungen,* LI (1930), no. 4, pp. 78-81, ill. p. 80, fig. 3; A. Boinet, *La Collection des Manuscrits de M. E. Kann,* Paris, 1926, no. 39, pl. XXXVII.

LENT BY THE NATIONAL GALLERY OF ART, ROSENWALD COLLECTION. PL. LXVIII

181. SINGLE MINIATURE: ST. JEROME IN THE WILDERNESS

North Italy, 2nd half of 15th cent.

No. 47.64. Miniature from a manuscript, vellum, 7 x 9½ inches. Ex-coll.: Von Beckinrath, Berlin.

This painting resists a definite attribution as to artist or place of execution. Various of its stylistic elements are characteristic of the school of Ferrara showing the influence of Cosimo Tura, others suggest a Lombard artist. However, the northern origin of the miniature is obvious in the structure of the landscape with its strange rock formation, in the cool light and above all in the sharply outlined figure of the saint depicted in a passionate pose.

BIBLIOGRAPHY: H. J. Hermann in *Wiener Jahrbuch der Kunsthistorischen Sammlungen,* XXI (1900), p. 94, fig. 70; William M. Milliken in *Bulletin of the Cleveland Museum of Art,* XXXV (1948), pp. 19-21, ill.

LENT BY THE CLEVELAND MUSEUM OF ART.

182. VERGIL. OPERA Italy (Ferrara ?), ca. 1450-60

Garrett ms. 110. In Latin. Roman script. 252 vellum leaves, 10⅝ x 6¾ inches. 2 partial borders; 16 large and numerous smaller initials. Binding: 18th century Italian vellum. Ex-colls.: Valerius Miccus (16th century); Robert Garrett.

The borders consist of well articulated "white-vine" ornament on blue, red and green dotted grounds, the tendrils delicately shaded to give roundness. The arms of the first owner, probably a member of the Bianchini family of Ferrara, are finely executed.

BIBLIOGRAPHY: *A Vergilian Exhibition* in *Bulletin of the New York Public Library,* XXXIV (1930), pp. 511 f., ill. p. 490; De Ricci, I, p. 886, no. 110.

LENT BY PRINCETON UNIVERSITY LIBRARY, GARRETT COLLECTION.

183. PTOLEMY. GEOGRAPHY North Italy, ca. 1460

Ms. 97. In Latin. Roman script in 2 cols. 102 vellum leaves, 16¼ x 11 inches. 27 maps; numerous ornamented initials. Binding: modern tooled calf. Ex-colls.: Hieronymus Guilielmus Ebner of Eschenbach (Sale, Nuremberg, 1813); Anton Apponyi of Vienna; Count Louis Apponyi (Sale, London, 1892, no. 1016).

The maps, prepared by Donnus Nicolaus Germanus, go back to Ptolemy (ca. 90-168 A.D.), except for the world map, which is attributed to Agathodaemon, an ancient Alexandrian geographer. The book is written evenly on smooth, soft, polished vellum in two columns, with elegantly executed white-vine initials and a half border in the text part. The text is further enlivened by captions in gold and silver and some precise geometrical diagrams. The maps, on heavier vellum, are thickly painted and gilded. According to the Reverend Dr. Joseph Fischer, "This codex furnishes the original copy for the maps in the important Roman editions of Ptolemy of the years 1478, 1490, 1507 and 1508, in which the Ptolemaic maps are reproduced more accurately than in most other editions."

BIBLIOGRAPHY: Martin Raidelius, *Commentatio critico-literaria de Claudii Ptolemaei Geographia ejusque codicibus*, Nuremberg, 1737, pp. 26-33; J. Fischer, *An Important Ptolemy Manuscript with Maps in the New York Public Library* in C. G. Herbermann, *Historical Records and Studies*, VI, 2 (1913), pp. 216-234; E. L. Stephenson and J. Fischer, *The Geography of Claudius Ptolemy, translated into English . . . including reproductions of the maps from the Ebner Manuscript. . .*, New York, 1932; De Ricci, II, p. 1330, no. 97; *Bulletin of the New York Public Library*, XLI (June, 1937), p. 456, no. 6.

LENT BY THE NEW YORK PUBLIC LIBRARY, MANUSCRIPT DIVISION.

184. ROBERTUS VALTURIUS. DE RE MILITARI   North Italy, 3rd quarter of 15th cent.

In Latin. Semi-gothic script with corrections in roman. 208 leaves, paper and vellum, 11 x 8¼ inches. 78 drawings. Binding: 19th century calf. Ex-coll.: Wilfrid M. Voynich.

An illustrated manuscript of the renowned work on military art and machines of war that was composed by Valturius in Rimini, probably between 1446 and 1456, and dedicated to Sigismond Malatesta. Compared to the other twenty known manuscripts of the text, this copy presents a number of points of distinction. Its text has been abundantly corrected throughout in one or possibly two hands contemporary with the scribe, and most of these corrections are embodied in other manuscript copies and in the first printed edition of the text issued in Verona in 1472. Moreover, the sepia drawings, close though they are to the famous woodcuts of the 1472 edition, show some interesting divergences and are accompanied by written directions for their location in the text and for corrections of details—all of which are properly reflected in other and later copies. The conclusion reached by Dr. Erla Rodakiewicz in an unpublished study of the manuscript is that this copy shows the features of a prototype and represents an early phase of the text, and so, presumably, is a manuscript worked over by the author himself. In this case, it represents an interesting instance of a renaissance scientific or technical illustrated book in the course of production.

BIBLIOGRAPHY: De Ricci, II, p. 1848, no. 14. Cf. E. Rodakiewicz, *The Editio Princeps of Roberto Valturio's "De Re Militari" in Relation to the Dresden and Munich Manuscripts* in *Maso Finiguerra*, XVIII-XIX (1940), pp. 15-82, and literature cited.

LENT BY THE LIBRARY OF CONGRESS, ROSENWALD COLLECTION.   PL. LXXII

185. GIOVANNI MARCANOVA. ANTIQUITATES   North Italy, 1465

Garrett ms. 158. In Latin. Roman script in 2 cols. 209 vellum leaves, 14¼ x 10¼ inches. 15 full-page and numerous text drawings. Binding: 18th century Italian vellum. Ex-colls.: The humanist Muretus; Collegio Romano, Rome, until 1870; Robert Garrett.

This work is a kind of encyclopedia of material illustrating Roman history and supplementing and explaining archaeological data. The author (1410-1467) was an Italian philosopher, physician, poet and amateur antiquarian, who was active in several north Italian cities. This work, the second version of his *Antiquities*, consists of a collection of inscriptions, selections from Latin authors, and an album of wash drawings of sculpture, architectural elements, etc. Facsimiles of lapidary inscriptions are given in capitals in imitation of incised letters and spaced as on the monuments, sometimes contained within delicate outlines suggesting slabs, urns, or sarcophagi. In many cases the ornamental arrangement of the text and the decorative use of diagrams and outlines resembles the pages of Colonna's *Hypnerotomachia Poliphili*, printed by Aldus in 1499.

BIBLIOGRAPHY: Holmes Van Meter Dennis in *Memoirs of the American Academy in Rome*, VI (1927), pp. 113-126; Elizabeth B. Lawrence, *ibid.*, pp. 127-131, pls. 23-48; De Ricci, I, p. 897, no. 158, with previous literature. Cf. C. Hülsen, *La Roma Antica di Ciriaco d'Ancona*, Rome, 1907, pp. 2-3.

LENT BY PRINCETON UNIVERSITY LIBRARY, GARRETT COLLECTION.   PL. LXXII

186. AELIANUS. DE INSTRUENDIS ACIEBUS   Italy, ca. 1480

In Latin. Roman script. 83 vellum leaves, 11⅜ x 8⅝ inches. Illuminated borders, initials and diagrams. Binding: original Italian red morocco, blind-tooled. Ex-colls.: Matthias Corvinus ?; Count Anton Apponyi; Count Louis Apponyi (Sale, London, Nov. 10, 1892, no. 9); Robert Hoe (Sale, New York, 1912, II, no. 2417).

According to Aelianus, his comprehensive work on military tactics was inspired by a conversation of the author with Frontinus, famous Roman military strategist (see no. 187 of this catalogue). The present manuscript comprises an excerpt from this work as well as Onosander's *De optimo imperatore*. The book is adorned with borders peopled by children and birds, illuminated initials and numerous handsome diagrams of military formations executed in gold, silver and colors.

The attribution to the library of Corvinus is uncertain, since the emblem at the foot of the first page is hitherto unrecorded among the Corvinus symbols. It has been pointed out that Francesco Massaro saw an Aelianus in that library in 1520. In any case, this book is sufficiently sumptuous to have suited the taste of King Matthias.

BIBLIOGRAPHY: De Ricci, I, pp. 959 f., no. 16, with previous literature.

LENT BY WILLIAM K. RICHARDSON.

187. ONOSANDER. DE OPTIMO IMPERATORE   Italy (Naples), 2nd half of 15th cent.

In Latin. Italic script. 176 vellum leaves, 8⅛ x 5⅝ inches. 4 illuminated pages; illuminated initials. Binding: early 19th century blue morocco. Ex-colls.: probably Alphonse of Aragon, King of Naples; G. Libri (Sale, London, March, 1859, no. 740); Sir Thomas Phillipps (ms. 23619).

This brief but comprehensive treatise on the duties of a general was composed by Onosander, a Greek philosopher of the first century A.D. It was translated into Latin for Pasiello Maliepiero, Doge of Venice (1457-62), by his secretary, Nicolo Sagundino. This translation was also used for the first printed edition of the work published in 1494. An inscription at the beginning of the present manuscript indicates that this copy was dedicated by the translator to Alphonse of Aragon, King of Naples.

In addition to Onosander's text, the codex contains Frontinus' *Rei Militari Libri*, a work on strategy by a Roman general who was once governor of Britain. At the beginning of each tract is a finely drawn and colored "white-vine" border and on the opposite page an inscription handsomely framed and lettered in alternating lines of blue and gold capitals. The manuscript is signed at the end by a scribe active in Naples: "P. Hippolyti Lunensis manu."

LENT BY PHILIP AND FRANCES HOFER.

188. HEBREW RITUAL   North Italy, ca. 1480

  Garrett ms. 26. In Hebrew. 150 vellum leaves (partly misbound), 4½ x 3⅛ inches. 2 full-page and 26 smaller miniatures; ornamented borders. Binding: 18th century Italian intarsia with mother-of-pearl and ivory, displaying the initials and arms of alleged 14th century owners, Cardinal Gotio Battaglia and Galeotto Malatesta. Ex-colls.: Marco Battaglini, Bishop of Cesena (ca. 1716); Monastery of Conventuals at Montescudo near Rimini; Earl of Ashburnham (Appendix no. 231, Sale, London, May 1, 1899, no. 26); Robert Garrett.

The illustrations of Jewish religious life are executed in a characteristic renaissance style, clear and bright of color, and with a developed handling of plasticity and volume.

The errors in De Ricci's listing of the manuscript arise from the fantastic eighteenth-century forgery exposed by Dr. Panofsky: a letter on an originally blank leaf of the book, purporting to indicate that the text is by Maimonides (Rhamban) and the illustrations by Giotto; and also that the book was presented by Cardinal Gotio Battaglia to Galeotto Malatesta and "approved" by Pope Benedict in 1338.

  BIBLIOGRAPHY: De Ricci, I, p. 869, no. 26; E. Panofsky in *Journal of the Walters Art Gallery*, IV (1941), pp. 27-44 (with complete illustration) and V (1942), pp. 124-125.

LENT BY PRINCETON UNIVERSITY LIBRARY, GARRETT COLLECTION.

189. HYGINUS. DE SIDERIBUS TRACTATUS   North Italy, ca. 1450

  In Latin. Humanistic hand. 80 vellum leaves, 9¼ x 5⅞ inches. 38 miniatures. Binding: 18th century Italian vellum. Ex-colls.: Duke di Cassano Serra, Naples (Sale, London, Feb. 5, 1828, no. 128); Sir Thomas Phillipps (ms. 6972); A. Chester Beatty (Sale, London, May 9, 1933, no. 60, pls. 35-36).

A humanist manuscript of exceptional charm and refinement. The thirty-eight vignettes depicting the legendary characters of the constellations are executed with delicate beauty of line and color, the stars being indicated in gold in their appropriate places. Each of the unframed figures is set off upon the white vellum by a shadow of shredded blue.

The text is the work of a mythographer who flourished about 25 B.C. and who based his astronomy largely on the Hellenistic poet, Aratos. The latter wrote poetically of the myths associated with the namesakes of the constellations, but used the serious scientific catalogue of the stars drawn up by the Greek astronomer, Eudoxios of Knidos in the fourth century B.C.

  BIBLIOGRAPHY: De Ricci, II, p. 1341, no. 28, with previous literature.

LENT BY THE NEW YORK PUBLIC LIBRARY, SPENCER COLLECTION.   PL. LXXIII

190. VALERIUS MAXIMUS. FACTORUM ET DICTORUM MEMORABILIUM, LIBRI IX
                                                              Italy (Naples), ca. 1470-85

  In Latin. Semi-roman script. 197 vellum leaves, 13½ x 9⅛ inches. 1 full and 10 single borders; 133 illuminated initials. Binding: 18th century Italian calf. Ex-colls.: Robert S. Holford; Sir George Holford.

This luxurious manuscript was executed for one of the foremost bibliophiles of the Renaissance, Ferdinand I of Aragon, King of Naples. It is written in a fine script, surrounded by margins of monumental width, on vellum selected for its whiteness, evenness of texture and remarkable softness to the touch. The full border of the first page and the partial borders that mark the opening of each book are ornamented in the humanist taste with representations of candelabra, coins, engraved gems, garlands, *putti*, and other classical motives, often executed in *camaieu d'or* and relieved against grounds of shredded blue, lavender, rose, etc. The work is notable for the integration of all these favorite humanistic motives into the page design, and for the luminosity of color and exquisite finish of the painting. The texture of some of the colors suggests the admixture of oil or gum as a medium. The resulting gloss, combined with the rich use of gilding, enhances the metallic effect of the ornament.

BIBLIOGRAPHY: V. H. Paltsits in *Bulletin of the New York Public Library*, XXXIII (1929), pp. 847-853, 5 figs.; De Ricci, II, p. 1339, no. 20, with further literature.

LENT BY THE NEW YORK PUBLIC LIBRARY, SPENCER COLLECTION. PL. LXXI

191. AESOP'S FABLES   Italy (Florence), ca. 1480

In Greek. 75 vellum leaves, 7⅞ x 4⅞ inches. 135 miniatures; 1 historiated three-quarter border. Binding: 19th century Grolieresque morocco by C. Smith. Ex-colls.: Rev. Theodore Williams (Sale, London, April 1827); Sir Thomas Phillipps, ms. 23609 (Sale, London, July 1, 1946, no. 26 A).

The fables are written in a single column within wide margins, the beginning of each story being marked by ornamental initials on squares of burnished gold leaf and delicate foliate border sprays in typical Florentine style. The illustrations, unusually numerous for a classical text, are shaped to fit advantageously into empty spaces in the lines of writing, often extending into the margins. They are competently executed by two artists, characteristically Florentine in the types and poses of the figures, the skillful modelling, foreshortening and architectural perspective, as well as in the use of clear, bright colors. There is a predilection for landscape extending into a blue distance. The incidents of the fables are set forth in considerable detail and with dramatic skill.

LENT BY THE NEW YORK PUBLIC LIBRARY, SPENCER COLLECTION. PL. LXXV

192. LIVY. DE SECUNDO BELLO PUNICO   Italy (Florence), ca. 1475

In Latin. Roman script. 223 vellum leaves, 14⅛ x 9⅜ inches. 1 border; 1 historiated and 9 "white-vine" initials. Binding: blue morocco by Bradel l'Aîné. Ex-colls.: Matthias Corvinus, King of Hungary; Chrétien-François de la Moignon (1735-89) (Sale, Paris, 1791, no. 205); Sir Thomas Phillipps, ms. no. 3010; A. Chester Beatty (Sale, London, May 9, 1933, no. 59, pl. 34).

This manuscript, which preserves the well-balanced proportions and wide margins of its original format, was made for Matthias Corvinus, King of Hungary (1442-1490), one of the great bibliophiles of the Renaissance. It is signed by the scribe, Johannes Franciscus Martius of San Gimigniano, who also wrote for Corvinus two other manuscripts containing other parts of Livy's *History*.

The first page introduces the King's arms at the foot of a three-quarter white-vine border. The large initial shows a medallion portrait of Livy in *camaieu d'or*, suggesting a bronze relief.

BIBLIOGRAPHY: A. De Hevesy, *La Bibliothèque du Roi Matthias Corvin*, Société Française de Reproductions de Manuscrits à Peintures, Paris, 1923, p. 66, no. 45; De Ricci, II, pp. 1340-1341, no. 27, with other literature.

LENT BY THE NEW YORK PUBLIC LIBRARY, SPENCER COLLECTION. PL. LXIX

193. ST. AUGUSTINE. DE CIVITATE DEI   Italy (Florence), ca. 1470

> In Latin. Roman book hand. 322 vellum leaves, 14¼ x 10⅛ inches. 2 full borders; 2 historiated initials. Binding: 15th century Italian blind stamped morocco. Ex-coll.: Edward A. Parson, New Orleans (Sale, London, May 9, 1933, no. 2, pls. III-IV).

A splendid renaissance manuscript, fine of vellum and of writing. Its two full borders show animals and *putti* inhabiting the intricate "white-vine" pattern on particolored grounds. The second border includes an interesting allegorical miniature, while the initial frames a representation of St. Augustine gazing at the vision of the City of God, here depicted as Florence itself.

> BIBLIOGRAPHY: De Ricci, II, pp. 1341-1342, no. 30, with previous literature.

LENT BY THE NEW YORK PUBLIC LIBRARY, SPENCER COLLECTION.   PL. LXX

194. VITE DE' SANTI   Northern Italy, 15th cent.

> In Italian. Modified roman script. 200 vellum leaves, 13½ x 9⅜ inches. 181 miniatures and "white-vine" border. Binding: 18th century Italian vellum. Ex-coll.: Sir Thomas Phillipps (ms. 2636).

This codex represents an interesting example of a renaissance book in the process of illustration. The finished miniatures are of fine quality, gay in color, with the modelling heightened by gold. The stages of preparation seen range from the first light silver-point sketch, through the determination of the outline in ink, the washes of under-color, successive laying on of tones and the progressive working up of the modelling to the finished product.

LENT BY PHILIP AND FRANCES HOFER.

195. VERGIL. OPERA   Italy (Naples), ca. 1500

> W. 400. In Latin. Italic script. 220 vellum leaves, 5½ x 2¾ inches. 2 full-page miniatures; 1 historiated and 2 architectural borders. Binding: modern Italian brown morocco.

A fine little pocket-size Vergil, containing the *Bucolics*, *Georgics* and *Aeneid*. The two full-page illustrations are painted in *camaieu d'or* on lavender-stained leaves, with some use of green, blue and red for the landscape. Silver, now oxidized, was employed as highlights on flesh. The effect is very shadowy, as of a dream-picture. Similar lavender leaves painted in precisely the same style, and quite possibly by the same hand, occur in a larger Vergil in the University Library at Leiden (ms. B.P.L. 63). Other features of this manuscript are also to be found in the Walters Vergil: the architectural frames with *putti* that surround the initial text pages of the separate works, and the craggy landscape used as a historiated frame. In the Walters manuscript such a frame, with men plowing, woodcutters, olive trees and bee-hives, introduces the *Georgics*. A similar landscape frame occurs in a luxurious Livy written at Naples for the bibliophile and scholar, Andrea Matteo III Acquaviva, Duke of Atri.

> BIBLIOGRAPHY: De Ricci, I, p. 832, no. 440. Cf. A. W. Byvanck, *Les principaux manuscrits à peintures . . . dans les . . . Pays-Bas*, Soc. Franç. de reprod. de mss. à peintures, Paris, 15e année (1931), pp. 81 f., pls. XXII-XXIII; *Beschreibendes Verzeichnis der illuminierten Handschriften in Osterreich*, Leipzig, 1933, VI, 4, pp. 68 f., pls. XXIX-XXX.

COLLECTION OF THE WALTERS ART GALLERY.   PL. LXXIV

196. VERGIL. OPERA　　　　　　　　　　　　　　　　　　　　　　　　Italy, ca. 1500

 Ms. 2945.1400. In Latin. Italic script. 225 vellum leaves, 5¾ x 3 inches. 6 miniatures; illuminated initials, etc. Binding: 19th century French brown morocco. Ex-colls.: Spanish coll.; A. Firmin-Didot (Sale, Paris, 1878, no. 10); Junius S. Morgan.

The format, page design and script of this little manuscript are the same that the printer Aldus adopted for his pocket classics. Each work commences with a fine renaissance letter modelled in monochrome with the effect of relief, while the introductory lines are in alternating rows of gold and blue capitals. The opening page of each book shows at the bottom a delicate vignette executed with well-modelled figures and landscapes of vast distances, despite the small scale.

 BIBLIOGRAPHY: *A Vergilian Exhibition* in *Bulletin of the New York Public Library*, XXXIV (1930), p. 512; De Ricci, II, p. 1182, no. 41.

LENT BY PRINCETON UNIVERSITY LIBRARY.　　　　　　　　　　　　　　　　PL. LXXIV

197. GREEK POETS　　　　　　　　　　　　　　　　　　　　　　　Italy, late 15th cent.

 In Greek. 250 vellum leaves, 8½ x 5⅜ inches. 1 historiated initial; illuminated half-border, with a small miniature. Binding: 19th century brown morocco, gilt by C. Lewis. Ex-colls.: The Rev. Theodore Williams; Sir Thomas Phillipps (ms. 3503).

This anthology of Greek poetry consists of Orpheus, *Argonautica* and *Hymns*, Proclus, *Hymns*, Homer, *Hymns*, Moschus, *Eros Drapetes* and Aratus, *Phainomena*. Rubricated headings and initials of Greek workmanship ornament the text pages. The fine Greek script has been recognized as that of the famous scribe, Johannes Rhosos (fl. 1457-1515), who worked for such great bibliophiles of the day as Cardinal Alessandro Farnese, Lorenzo de' Medici and Cardinal Bembo. The Bodleian Library in Oxford possesses other manuscripts by this scribe, and these are signed.

The first page is enriched in a good renaissance style with an initial framing a picture of Orpheus playing a fiddle to the animals. In the lower margin is a circular miniature of the ship of the Argonauts.

 BIBLIOGRAPHY: *Cf.* H. Omont, *Facsimiles de Manuscrits Grecs des XVe et XVIe siècles*, Paris, 1887, p. 13, pl. 30.

LENT BY HARVARD COLLEGE LIBRARY, DEPARTMENT OF GRAPHIC ARTS.

198. RUY DE PINA. CHRONICLES OF KING DUARTE . . . CHRONICLE OF KING JOHN II
　　　　　　　　　　　　　　　　　　　　　　　　　　　　　Portugal, early 16th cent.

 In Portuguese. Gothic script. 124 vellum leaves, 15½ x 11⅜ inches. Numerous partial borders and drolleries; 130 calligraphic initials. Binding: 19th century purple morocco by Townsend. Ex-colls.: William Bragge (Sale, London, 1876, no. 151); Sir Francis Cook; Wyndham F. Cook.

The book contains two of the most famous chronicles of fifteenth-century Portugal, exceptional in their frankness and distinguished as important literary and historical records. The author, Ruy de Pina (1440-1521), having served for many years as envoy to Castile and the Vatican, was an eyewitness to most of the important political events of his era. While his sole authorship of the Chronicle of King Duarte's reign (1433-1438) is disputed, the history of John II, finished in 1504 and including records of negotiations with Columbus, is entirely Pina's work.

The manuscript, of handsome format, is written on heavy cream parchment in a large script in brown ink and ruled in red. It is decorated with complex calligraphic initials which develop into partial borders and background ornaments. These decorations are not illuminated, but are free and accomplished pen drawings, depicting drolleries, fruit, birds, flowers, insects, reptiles, etc.

BIBLIOGRAPHY: De Ricci, II, p. 1698, no. 28.

LENT BY PHILIP AND FRANCES HOFER.

199. MINIATURE: ENTRY INTO JERUSALEM   Northern Italy, 15th cent.

No. 63. Initial D on vellum, 16⅛ x 13¾ inches. Ex-coll.: Edouard Kann, Paris.

The initial, from an Antiphonary, is of monumental size. The turbulent rendering of Christ's white robes has caused the work to be attributed to Liberale da Verona or Girolamo da Cremona. A closely similar initial exists in one of the chorali in the Piccolomini Library in the Cathedral of Siena.

BIBLIOGRAPHY: A. Boinet, *La collection de miniatures de M. Edouard Kann*, Paris, 1906, p. 30, no. XXXIV, pl. XXXIII; De Ricci, II, p. 1712, no. B.20.

LENT BY ROBERT LEHMAN.

200. DIO CASSIUS. LIFE AND REIGN OF OCTAVIUS CAESAR   Italy (Rome), ca. 1535-50

In Greek. Minuscule script. 68 vellum leaves, 4¾ x 2¾ inches. 2 illuminated pages. Binding: early 19th century French straight grain morocco in red. Ex-colls.: Cardinal Alessandro Farnese; Stefano Evodio Assemani, Librarian of the Vatican (1707-1782).

The text is an excerpt from the *History of Rome* by Dio Cassius, Roman senator and celebrated historian, who was active in the latter part of the second and the early third century A.D. Born a Roman citizen in Asia Minor, Dio spent most of his life in Rome, composing his works in Greek, the scholarly language of the time.

The present manuscript was commissioned by Cardinal Alessandro Farnese (1520-1589), a man of great learning and artistic taste. The tiny volume shows delicate penmanship and wide, finely balanced margins. The two headpieces feature classical cameos or sculpture and naturalistically rendered iris. The lower part of each of the two illuminated pages is decorated with Alessandro's coat of arms surmounted by the cardinal's hat and inscribed with his name and title as Vice-Chancellor of the Church, an office he received in 1535. Comparison with signed manuscripts indicates that this example is the work of the well-known Greek scribe, Giovanni Onorio de Maglie, of Lecce, who was employed in the Vatican from 1535 to 1550, and was noted for his elegant calligraphy.

BIBLIOGRAPHY: Cf. E. Müntz, *La Bibliothèque du Vatican au XVe siècle*, 1886, p. 101; P. Franchi de' Cavalieri and J. Lietzmann, *Specimina Codicum Graecorum Vaticanorum*, Bonn, 1910, p. XVI, pl. 48; H. Omont, *Facsimiles des manuscrits grecs du XVe au XVIe siècles*, Paris, 1887, p. 12, pl. 28.

LENT BY PHILIP AND FRANCES HOFER.   PL. LXXIV

201. BOOK OF HOURS OF ROME USE   Northern Italy, ca. 1500

   In Latin. Roman script. 184 vellum leaves, 6¾ x 4⅞ inches, incomplete. 7 large initials, several historiated. Binding: 17th century Italian morocco, gilt. Ex-coll.: A. Chester Beatty (Sale, London, May 9, 1933, no. 64, pl. 40).

A renaissance Horae of soft vellum and fine script. The first few lines of text in each section are written in capitals alternately red, blue and gold, introduced by large initials featuring miniatures or elaborate ornament.

   BIBLIOGRAPHY: De Ricci, II, p. 1694, no. 11.

   LENT BY PHILIP AND FRANCES HOFER.

202. VINCENTIUS DEMETRIUS VOLTIUS. PORTOLANO   Italy (Leghorn), 1598

   In Italian. 6 double vellum leaves, 14¼ x 9¼ inches. 5 double page charts; illuminated title page and full-page arms. Binding: contemporary red morocco, gilt. Ex-coll.: J. J. Fletcher, Boston.

A characteristic example of the illuminated navigation charts in use from the fourteenth to the end of the sixteenth century. This volume is signed on the third page by the well-known cartographer, Voltius (or Volcius) of Ragusa, who states that he executed the work on July 18, 1598 in the region of Leghorn. Five other portolanos by Voltius are known.

   BIBLIOGRAPHY: Cf. A. E. Nordenskiöld, *Periplus, an essay on the early history of charts. . .*, Stockholm, 1897, p. 68.

   LENT BY PHILIP AND FRANCES HOFER.

203. BOOK OF HOURS   Flanders, ca. 1500

   In Latin. Gothic script. 209 vellum leaves, 4 x 3⅛ inches. 16 large and 16 small miniatures. Binding: black shagreen with silver ornaments. Ex-colls.: J. de Bure l'aîné (Sale, Paris, 1853, no. 67); A. Firmin-Didot (Sale, Paris, 1879, no. 26); Baron S. de La Roche-Lacarelle (Sale, Paris, 1888, no. 19); Eugène Paillet (Sale, Paris, 1902, no. 1); Robert Hoe (Sale, New York, 1911, I, no. 2138); Felix M. Warburg, in whose memory it was presented to the Library of Congress.

A little Horae with miniatures of the greatest charm and delicacy by more than one hand. Several fairly unusual representations are included.

   BIBLIOGRAPHY: De Ricci, II, pp. 1850 f., no. 13.

   LENT BY THE LIBRARY OF CONGRESS.   PL. LXXVIII

204. BOOK OF HOURS   Flanders (Bruges ?), ca. 1490

   In Latin (and Spanish). Gothic script. 117 vellum leaves, 5¾ x 4 inches. 7 large and 24 small miniatures; 19 historiated initials; 7 historiated borders; numerous illuminated borders. Binding: 19th century black morocco, gilt, by Zaehnsdorf. Ex-colls.: D. Bonaventura de Rubeis; William A. White.

Illuminated at the end of the fifteenth century, before the influence of the ambitious illustrative projects of the Grimani Breviary had overwhelmed the more serene and subtle trends in Flemish painting, this book contains miniatures of a refinement and beauty that are unsurpassed by any Flemish manuscripts now in this country. It is said to have been made for Joanna the Mad of Castile, mother of Emperor Charles V. There is a prayer in Spanish in the section of this same book that now belongs to Mrs. Adrian Van Sinderen of Brooklyn.

The illustrations are in a style of great clarity and refinement of finish, the landscapes fresh and rolling, the drapery handled without any touch of banality. A notable feature is the color, which is clear, but restrained in brilliance, with a liberal use of pearly grey and pale lavender. Most of the borders employ the tenderly painted flowers, birds, jewels and damasks that are to be found in other fine books of the time. Particularly delightful, however, are the historiated borders, each containing a series of little scenes, amplifying the legend of the saint whose full-page picture adjoins. These are painted softly around the text, and do not undertake the perspective tricks which characterize some of the later developments of the school (cf. no 207).

The miniatures resemble the style of the anonymous artist known as the Master of Maria of Burgundy, after a prayer book for that princess which is now ms. 78 B 12 in the Kupferstichkabinett, Berlin. Figure and facial types, coloring, refinement of finish, all correspond to the works assigned to this master. A further very close relationship is with a fine manuscript formerly in the Huth collection and now in the British Museum (ms. Add. 38,126), which contains several miniatures almost identical with certain ones in this book and some of which, at least, appear to be by the same hand.

BIBLIOGRAPHY: B. Quaritch, *Examples of the Art of Book Illumination*, V-X, London, 1892, pls. 39-43; British Museum, *Catalogue of the Fifty Manuscripts and Printed Books Bequeathed to the British Museum by Alfred H. Huth*, London, 1912, no. XIII, pp. 16-19; *Trésor de l'art flamand . . . Mémorial de l'exposition d'art flamand ancien à Anvers, 1930*, Paris, 1932, II, p. 47, pl. LXV; De Ricci, I, p. 1056, no. 3, II, p. 1205, no. 6, p. 2306, last item. Cf. F. Winkler, *Die flämische Buchmalerei*, Leipzig, 1925, pp. 39 f., 103-113, pls. 10, 57-65.

LENT BY MRS. WILLIAM EMERSON. PL. LXXVII

205. SCENES FROM THE LIFE OF CHRIST — Flanders, ca. 1500

In Spanish. Gothic script. 12 vellum leaves, 3¾ x 2¼ inches, mounted in a modern frame. Ex-coll.: Mrs. George Cupples.

A very fine series of miniatures by a Flemish artist whose style is close to that of no. 203. The text on the reverse of the leaves is written in Spanish.

BIBLIOGRAPHY: Z. Haraszti in *More Books, the Bulletin of the Boston Public Library*, III (1928), pp. 73-74; De Ricci, I, p. 924, no. 35.

LENT BY THE BOSTON PUBLIC LIBRARY.

206. SINGLE MINIATURE: THE ANNUNCIATION — Flanders, early 16th cent.

No. 72. Vellum, 6⅞ x 5½ inches.

The increasing tendency to introduce into the pages of books what are essentially independent paintings, treated without relation to the general book design, is exemplified in this fine Annunciation, executed in the tradition of Memling and Gherard David. It is not without significance that such works as this so often have been cut out and preserved as the individual paintings that they really are. Inversely it can be assumed that some miniatures on vellum in this style were from the first intended as separate works and never were inserted in books (cf. nos. 212, 213).

LENT BY ROBERT LEHMAN.   PL. LXXVIII

207. TWO MINIATURES: PIETA; ST. BRIGITT   Flanders (Ghent), ca. 1515

Nos. 102-3. 2 vellum leaves, 7½ x 5⅛ inches. Ex-coll.: Frederick, Marquess of Londonderry (1856).

The Pietà with the Virgin, unattended, holding the body of Christ at the foot of the Cross, is surrounded by a border showing the Three Marys at the Tomb and the "Noli Me Tangere".

St. Brigitt is shown writing her *Revelations* in her study, attended by an angel, while through the window she sees a vision of Christ. The border shows rustic figures on a country road.

Both pictures are painted by an artist working in the tradition initiated by the Grimani Breviary, now in the Library of San Marco, Venice. The style and handling of the scenes approximates that of the Hortulus Animae (Vienna, Nationalbibliothek, ms. 2706) or the Breviary of Eleanor of Portugal in the Pierpont Morgan Library (ms. 52). As in the case of these other manuscripts, the historiated borders to be found in the Grimani Breviary or in no. 204 of this catalogue have been treated as whole paintings upon which the main illustration has been imposed in the form of an additional and independent painting, a development of Flemish fascination with the representation of spacious landscape vistas.

Nine other illustrations from this same manuscript are scattered in various collections.

BIBLIOGRAPHY: De Ricci, II, p. 1716, no. C.30.

LENT BY ROBERT LEHMAN.

208. BOOK OF HOURS   Flanders, ca. 1500

W. 423. In Latin. Gothic script. 213 vellum leaves, 2¾ x 2 inches. 9 full-page miniatures; illuminated borders. Binding: 18th century Italian engraved silver.

A tiny book on the extremely thin, silky vellum favored in the sixteenth century Flemish ateliers. The dull gold borders are strewn with large flowers, carefully studied after nature.

BIBLIOGRAPHY: De Ricci, I, p. 806, no. 308.

COLLECTION OF THE WALTERS ART GALLERY.

209. BOOK OF HOURS   Flanders, ca. 1510

W. 427. In Latin. Gothic script. 219 vellum leaves, 3¾ x 2½ inches. 15 large and 5 small miniatures; illuminated borders. Binding: modern red velvet.

The carefully observed renderings of flowers in the chief borders of this manuscript are more finely executed than in the average examples, but the chief charm of the book lies in the refreshing treatment of all the intervening pages. The uncolored margins are strewn in each case with a few tenderly observed flowers, birds, jewels or other objects, a treatment found also in the well-known Croy prayerbook in Vienna (ms. 1858).

BIBLIOGRAPHY: De Ricci, I, p. 807, no. 316.

COLLECTION OF THE WALTERS ART GALLERY.

210. BOOK OF HOURS   Flanders, ca. 1530

W. 425. In Latin. Gothic script. 58 vellum leaves, 3½ x 2½ inches. 45 miniatures; illuminated borders. Binding: modern French inlaid morocco with old enamel plaques. Ex-coll.: Peter Marié (Sale, New York, 1903, no. 567).

An attractive renaissance prayer book, the borders feature not only the usual carefully studied flowers, insects and birds, but jewels and renaissance architectural motives. The handling of lighting and of distant landscape in the miniatures is good, despite the tiny scale of the paintings.

BIBLIOGRAPHY: De Ricci, I, p. 807, no. 313.

COLLECTION OF THE WALTERS ART GALLERY.

211. BOOK OF HOURS   Flanders, ca. 1500

W. 428. In Latin and Flemish. Gothic script. 222 vellum leaves, 3¾ x 2¾ inches. 17 large and 29 small miniatures; illuminated borders. Binding: original wooden boards and stamped calf by Ludovicus Bloc.

The miniatures are well executed, and the borders are composed with the characteristic designs of naturalistic flowers, birds, jewelry and similar motives.

BIBLIOGRAPHY: De Ricci, I, p. 807, no. 315.

COLLECTION OF THE WALTERS ART GALLERY.

212. SIXTY-FOUR MINIATURES BY SIMON BENING   Flanders (Bruges), ca. 1520

W. 442. 64 miniatures on vellum, each 3⅛ x 2⅜ inches, mounted in the form of a quadriptych. Ex-coll.: Charles Stein (Sale, Paris, May 10, 1886, no. 241, with 4 pls.).

A remarkable series of scenes painted in the best style of the Sanders-Bening school, and usually attributed to the hand of Simon Bening (see no. 213). The subjects commence with the meeting of Joachim and Anna at the Golden Gate and continue through the story of Christ and of the Virgin to a final scene showing the Day of Judgment. Many scenes seldom represented in painting are included and many unusual conceptions of familiar subjects, the whole forming a kind of repertory of all the inventions of the school, as Dr. Paul Wescher has pointed out.

Although the size of the miniatures corresponds with the format of the small prayer books being turned out in Ghent and Bruges during the early sixteenth century (cf. nos. 203, 204, 214), the great number of scenes make it unlikely that this series ever formed part of such a book. Destrée considers that these miniatures were from the beginning intended to be mounted on a quadriptych and that the present frame may be contemporary. In any case, this series emphasizes the easy interchange between the separate paintings and the book-paintings at the beginning of the sixteenth century in Flanders, when not only the style, but the material and format could be the same for both purposes, and the same artists were active in both fields.

BIBLIOGRAPHY: A. Darcel in *Gazette des Beaux-arts*, XXXIII (1886), p. 132; L. Kaemmer and H. G. Ströhl, *Ahnenreihen aus dem Stammbaum des portugiesischen Königshauses*, Stuttgart, 1903, p. 26, pls. I-IV; J. Destrée, *Les Heures de Notre Dame dites de Hennessy*, Brussels, 1923, pp. 19-23, pls. doc. 1-4; F. Winkler, *Die Flämische Buchmalerei des XV und XVI Jahrhunderts*, Leipzig, 1925, pp. 139 f., pl. 83 (by error these are attributed to the Royal Library in Madrid, although the existence of the former Stein miniatures is noted in the list on p. 140); De Ricci, I, p. 809, no. 324, II, p. 2291, last note on page; Worcester Art Museum—Philadelphia Museum of Art, *Exhibition of Flemish Painting*, Worcester and Philadelphia, 1939, no. 50, ill.; Wadsworth Atheneum, *Life of Christ*, Hartford, 1948, no. 184, figs. 15-16; *Art News*, March, 1948, p. 27, reproducing 12 scenes (Passion), erroneously captioned.

COLLECTION OF THE WALTERS ART GALLERY. PL. LXXIX

213. SELF PORTRAIT BY SIMON BENING Flanders (Bruges), 1558

No. 191. Vellum, 3⅛ x 2 inches. Ex-colls.: Bonnier, Lille; Count Straszewicz (Sale, Lille, Mar. 8, 1837); Paul Delaroff, Leningrad; Eugene Pelletier, Paris.

Simon Bening, born in 1483 in Ghent and active in Bruges, where he died in 1561, is considered the last great miniaturist of the Flemish school.

This self portrait, painted in Bening's old age, was not conceived as a book illustration, but—in spite of its small size—as an independent painting. It is in the same format as the individual pictures of the group of sixty-four painted by him, shown as no. 212 in this exhibition. Beneath the portrait is inscribed: "SIMON BENNIK. ALEXANDRI. F. SE IPSV. PIGEBAT. ANO. AETATIS. 75. 1558". The artist is shown at half length, holding his spectacles and looking toward the spectator. Behind him is a leaded window, and nearby is an easel with colors and a painting. Another example, very similar, once in the Salting collection, is now in the Victoria and Albert Museum.

BIBLIOGRAPHY: De Ricci, II, p. 1718, no. C.29. *Cf.* W. H. J. Weale in *Burlington Magazine*, VIII (1906), pp. 356 f.; Burlington Fine Arts Club, *Exhibition of Illuminated Manuscripts*, London, 1908, p. 118, no. 241, pl. 144; P. Durrieu, *La miniature flamande*, Brussels, 1921, pl. 87; P. Wescher in *The Art Quarterly*, IX (1946), p. 208.

LENT BY ROBERT LEHMAN.

214. BOOK OF HOURS Flanders (Bruges), early 16th cent.

W. 426. In Latin and Flemish. Batarde script. 214 vellum leaves (including 15 blanks), 3 x 2¼ inches. 7 full-page miniatures; illuminated borders. Binding: violet velvet with 16th cent. silver-gilt ornaments.

One of the delicately wrought little prayer books that were produced by Bruges artists working in the general style of the Grimani Breviary atelier. Despite the exquisite finish of the painting, and the skill at rendering atmospheric distances on so small a scale, these books follow the production methods of the workshop and repeat scenes or select elements from patterns that have been used over and over again. This book duplicates some of the details to be found in Morgan ms. 451, an Horae of the same format that was made in Bruges in 1531.

BIBLIOGRAPHY: De Ricci, I, p. 810, no. 332.

COLLECTION OF THE WALTERS ART GALLERY. PL. LXXVIII

215. BOOK OF HOURS France, ca. 1515

W. 452. In Latin. Roman script. 155 vellum leaves, 6⅞ x 4¼ inches. 24 large and 3 small miniatures; illuminated borders. Binding: 16th century French brown morocco. Ex-coll.: Robertet.

This renaissance manuscript is illuminated by an artist who has derived his style from Bourdichon (cf. no. 116), but has not retained the large scale with which Bourdichon sought to give solidity to his figures.

BIBLIOGRAPHY: De Ricci, I, p. 811, no. 338.

COLLECTION OF THE WALTERS ART GALLERY.

216. OVID. HEROIDES Italy (Naples), ca. 1500

In Latin. Modified roman script. 110 vellum leaves, 6⅜ x 5⅝ inches. 19 full-page miniatures; 1 full border. Binding: 18th century Italian red morocco, gilt. Ex-colls.: Richard Heber; Sir Thomas Phillipps (ms. 8416).

Dull gold frames with hanging trophies enclose scenes elaborate in their architectural and landscape effects, painted in bright colors in the somewhat rapid technique that characterizes certain of the manuscripts illuminated by Neapolitan artists for the Duke of Atri, Andrea Matteo III Acquaviva (1458-1529). Cf. no. 195 of this catalogue. An unidentified cardinal's arms have been painted over the bearings of the original owner of the manuscript, enough traces of which are visible to suggest that it is a coat quartering Aragon.

BIBLIOGRAPHY: Cf. H. J. Hermann, Miniaturhandschriften aus der Bibliothek des Herzogs Andrea Matteo III Acquaviva, Vienna, 1898; Beschreibendes Verzeichnis der Illuminierten Handschriften in Osterreich, Leipzig, 1933, VI, 4, pp. 68-71, no. 36, pls. XXIX-XXX.

LENT BY HARVARD COLLEGE LIBRARY, DEPARTMENT OF GRAPHIC ARTS.

217. NOMS, ARMES ET BLASONS DE LA TABLE RONDE France, early 16th cent.

W. 463. In French. Batarde script. 155 vellum leaves, 10¾ x 7½ inches. 148 illuminated coats of arms. Binding: 19th century purple morocco. Ex-colls.: De Quevalin; Bibliothèque de Dinan (1840); Baron Achille Seillière (Sale, London, 1887, no. 602).

The book includes two texts: the *Noms, armes et blasons des chevaliers et compagnons de la Table Ronde,* and *La Forme quon tenoit des Tournoys.* The first part lists and extolls severally the knights of the Round Table, and describes the arms of each, which also are illustrated. The *Forme quon tenoit des Tournoys* is a treatise based upon the *Livre des Tournois* by Roi Renée, and recently has been attributed to the authorship of the ill-fated Jacques d'Armagnac, duc de Nemours. The work describes the rules and procedures for a tournament.

BIBLIOGRAPHY: De Ricci, I, p. 848, no. 515; E. Sandoz in *Speculum*, XIX (1944), pp. 389-420.

COLLECTION OF THE WALTERS ART GALLERY.

218. DESCRIPTION DES DOUZE CESARS France, ca. 1520

W. 467. In French. Batarde script. 40 vellum leaves, 8¼ x 5½ inches. 16 large miniatures. Binding: modern French inlaid morocco. Ex-coll.: Comte de Lignerolles (Sale, Paris, 1894, I, no. 31).

Description des douze Césars abbregés avecques leurs figures faites et pourtraictes selon le naturel is the title given by the scribe to this work, which is really an abridged version of Suetonius' work on the *Twelve Caesars*, but extended to the time of Antoninus Pius. Each emperor is depicted "according to life" in profile against a blue background within a round frame. The general style of the painting is that of the school of Bourdichon, but the portraits seem based at least ultimately on ancient models—probably coins or gem-carvings. The book is a characteristic example of French humanistic taste, and several similar manuscripts are known, although the others go no further than the canonical Twelve Caesars.

BIBLIOGRAPHY: De Ricci, I, p. 827, no. 417.

COLLECTION OF THE WALTERS ART GALLERY.

219. HOURS FOR USE OF BOURGES France (Bourges), 1506

In Latin. Roman script. 148 vellum leaves, 5¼ x 2¾ inches. 1 large and 40 small miniatures. Binding: white vellum by Charles Lewis, ca. 1825. Ex-colls.: Jean Lallemant the Younger (d. 1548); Henri de Tillard Bissy, Bishop of Toul (ca. 1720); Pierre Fournier; Robert S. Holford; Sir George Holford (Sale, London, 1927, II, no. 393).

This little book was executed for Jehan Lallemant the Younger, Seigneur de Marmagnac, who was Mayor of Bourges in 1510, and held a series of other important public offices. The family mansion built by his father, and today still one of the show places of Bourges, is notable for the use of numerous emblematic and symbolic motives in its ornament. This predilection for a mysterious personal symbolism is evident in the books owned by the Lallemants, of which three are included in this exhibition.

This manuscript was executed in 1506 and its very beautiful roman script of undeviating evenness has caused it to be ascribed to the renowned calligrapher and type-designer, Geoffroy Tory. The miniatures, all painted with great finish of detail, are both heraldic and enigmatic in subject. The single full-page miniature represents a red lion holding on his head the apocalyptic Book of Seven Seals, inscribed with the motto "Delear Prius". In his mouth he holds a plumed helmet from which hangs an escutcheon with the Lallemant arms quartering those of the younger Lallemant's grandparents. The other forty miniatures are small framed rectangles featuring alternately a hair shirt and the Book of Seven Seals with the motto. All miniatures appear against backgrounds of a black curtain strewn with a semée of gold letters and torn to reveal a lining of diagonal red and white stripes. A closely similar manuscript is described under no. 220.

BIBLIOGRAPHY: E. P. Goldschmidt, *Les Heures de Jean Lallemant written by Geoffroy Tory in 1506*, London, 1928; De Ricci, I, p. 665, no. 1.

LENT BY THE LIBRARY OF CONGRESS, ROSENWALD COLLECTION.

220. HOURS FOR USE OF BOURGES   France (Bourges), early 16th cent.

 W. 446. In Latin. Italic script. 93 vellum leaves, 6 x 3½ inches. 14 large and 4 small miniatures. Binding: early 19th century yellow straight grain morocco by Simier. Ex-colls.: Jean Lallemant the Younger (d. 1548); Cochran (1837), no. 46.

Also executed for Jean Lallemant the Younger, this manuscript is in every respect similar to no. 219. The vellum and format are equally elegant, the script in this case is a beautiful italic. The tiny rectangular miniatures featuring a hair shirt or a motto-bearing book against striped or letter-strewn backgrounds appear in the early pages. The main illumination, however, consists of enlargements of these to full or three-quarter page size. On this scale we see again the black curtain strewn mysteriously with all the letters of the alphabet in disorder, torn to show a red and white striped lining and, through the hole, the hair shirt. Alternating with these are miniatures displaying a blue seraph holding a red volume inscribed with the motto "Delear Prius", while the background, half black and half striped in red and white, is strewn with gold knots. Added to each of these large miniatures is a new feature—a tiny golden glory enclosing a microscopic religious scene—the subject being the appropriate illustration for each respective division of the Horae.

 BIBLIOGRAPHY: De Ricci, I, p. 812, no. 341.

COLLECTION OF THE WALTERS ART GALLERY.

221. OFFICES OF THE VIRGIN FOR USE OF BOURGES   France (Bourges), 1524

 In Latin. Roman script. 113 vellum leaves, 8⅞ x 5⅝ inches. 16 large and 24 small miniatures; 16 illuminated borders. Binding: 18th century French red morocco by Dérome. Ex-colls.: (among others) P. Girardot de Préfond (Sale, Paris, 1757, no. 42); Duc de La Vallière (Sale, Paris, January 12, 1784, I, no. 303); Prince Michel Petrovitch Galitzin (Sale, Paris, March 3, 1825, no. 14); Duke of Hamilton (Sale, London, May 23, 1889, no. 58, pl. IX); Robert Hoe (Sale, New York, April 24, 1911, I, no. 2142); Cortlandt F. Bishop (ms. 9).

A very fine manuscript in the French renaissance style, painted in the same atelier as no. 222, but larger in format and the scenes more complex in composition. Both are characterized by the courtly mannerism of the figures, a wealth of charming incident in the scenes, and delicately executed landscapes and interior backgrounds. The manuscript has been ascribed to Geoffroy Tory, doubtless because of the fine roman script. The date, 1524, appears in the frame of one of the miniatures.

 BIBLIOGRAPHY: De Ricci, II, p. 1656, no. 9, with previous literature.

LENT BY THE LIBRARY OF CONGRESS, ROSENWALD COLLECTION.   PL. LXXVI

222. BOOK OF HOURS FOR TOULOUSE USE   France, 1524

 W. 449. In Latin. Roman script. 170 vellum leaves, 8¾ x 4 inches. 28 large and 5 small miniatures. Binding: French red morocco ca. 1800.

Executed for an Abbot Bertrand in the same atelier as no. 221 and in the same year. The two books are very similar indeed in style, presenting the same luminous coloring, soft surface modelling, and successful rendering of atmospheric distances in the landscapes. The calendar pictures, omitted in no. 221, are in this manuscript particularly delightful scenes of domestic and rural life in renaissance France.

 BIBLIOGRAPHY: De Ricci, I, p. 811, no. 339.

COLLECTION OF THE WALTERS ART GALLERY.   PL. LXXVI

223. BOOK OF HOURS FOR ROME USE   French Flanders (St. Amand), 1537

>Lewis ms. 109. In Latin and French. Batarde script. 146 vellum leaves, 5½ x 4⅛ inches. 11 large miniatures. Binding: modern red morocco. Ex-colls: François Duquesne; duke of Orléans (?); J. B. Jarman (Sale, London, 1864, no. 76); William Bragge (Sale, London, 1876, no. 350); Robert Hoe (Sale, New York, 1912, II, no. 2468).

A renaissance book that represents a later and more provincial phase of the style seen in nos. 221 and 222, having accomplished designs but carried out with less softness of surface and harmony of color than in those two examples. An interesting development is the use of architectural borders of complex silhouette, rendered with scrollwork and occasional figures, resembling the frames in the well-known Book of Hours of Henry II in the Bibliothèque Nationale, Paris (ms. lat. 1429).

A colophon gives exceptionally full information about the book. It was executed in 1537 at the Abbey of St. Amand for François Duquesne.

>BIBLIOGRAPHY: E. Wolf, 2nd, *European Manuscripts in the John Frederick Lewis Collection*, Philadelphia, 1937, no. 109, pls. XXI-XXII; De Ricci, II, p. 2040, no. 92.

LENT BY THE PHILADELPHIA FREE LIBRARY, JOHN FREDERICK LEWIS COLLECTION.

224. BOOK OF HOURS   France, ca. 1540

>W. 451. In Latin. Batarde script. 168 vellum leaves, 7⅛ x 4¼ inches. 7 large miniatures; illuminated initials; historiated calendar borders. Binding: 17th century French morocco, gilt. Ex-colls.: Jean Lallemant the Younger; Girardot de Préfond; Duke of Hamilton (ms. 317).

The miniatures of this book, like the others executed for Jean Lallemant the Younger, are again somewhat enigmatic. They consist of a series of nearly identical round towers, with door and windows locked and barred, standing upon a chest and surmounted by an anvil supporting a helmet with the crest of the Lallemant colors. A man looking through the barred windows waves an inscribed scroll, and various elements of the picture bear symbolic inscriptions. The whole is set in a delightfully wild landscape, lightly drawn and delicately colored. Each picture is differentiated chiefly by a tiny golden glory in the sky, holding a microscopic scene, similar to the series to be found in no. 220. It is possible that the towers refer to a period of imprisonment suffered by Lallemant between 1535 and 1537, when his enemies charged him with misusing public funds as Receiver General of Languedoc. He was later exonerated.

The script and the illuminated letters in this manuscript are still gothic and do not partake at all of the advanced renaissance character of nos. 219 and 220.

Lallemant ownership is attested by a heraldic page very similar to that in no. 219, and by numerous family obituary notes at the end of the book.

>BIBLIOGRAPHY: De Ricci, I, pp. 810 f., no. 335.

COLLECTION OF THE WALTERS ART GALLERY.

225. BOOK OF HOURS FOR USE OF BOURGES   France, 1544

>Lewis ms. 87. In Latin. Batarde script. 63 vellum leaves, 6⅝ x 4¼ inches. Marginal figures. Binding: modern silk brocade. Ex-colls.: Jean Lallemant the Younger; Alphonse Labitte; W. C. Crane (Sale, New York, Dec. 9, 1912, I, no. 384).

The sole decoration of this manuscript consists of seraphim painted one in each of the three outer margins of each page, alternately red and blue. These are similar to the seraphim that hold the apocalyptic book with the motto "Delear Prius" in some of the miniatures of no. 220. Jean Lallemant has written at the end a note to the effect that the book was received by him June 12, 1544. He died four years later, as we know from an obituary note inserted by one of his children in no. 224 of this catalogue.

BIBLIOGRAPHY: E. Wolf, 2nd, *European Manuscripts in the John Frederick Lewis Collection*, Philadelphia 1937, no. 86.

LENT BY THE PHILADELPHIA FREE LIBRARY, JOHN FREDERICK LEWIS COLLECTION.

226. HISTORY OF THE HOUSE OF SAVOY — Italy, 1580

W. 464. In Latin. 21 vellum leaves, 9⅛ x 13¼ inches. 21-full-page illustrations. Binding: modern dark red morocco by Gruel.

A luxuriously illuminated album illustrating in contemporary fashion the great personnages of the House of Savoy and the chief events in the history of the family. The paintings, very skillful but somewhat gaudy in style and color, apparently are the work of a Flemish mannerist, who had absorbed much of Italian style. The most interesting pictures are those that represent military events, which are depicted in a panoramic manner that is reminiscent of tapestry designs. The Italian cities, such as Turin, shown in these scenes are represented accurately enough to suggest that the artist was familiar with the localities.

BIBLIOGRAPHY: De Ricci, I, p. 827, no. 419.

COLLECTION OF THE WALTERS ART GALLERY.

227. ARCHITECT'S PATTERN-BOOK — France, 2nd half of 16th cent.

In French. Civilité script. 88 vellum leaves, 9 x 12 inches. 81 drawings. Binding: contemporary French calf with painted strapwork. Ex-colls.: Count Robert Lichnowsky; Baron Alphonse de Rothschild.

An unpublished book containing monochrome wash drawings in pen and ink of the architectural orders, projects for ecclesiastical and secular buildings, arches, mantelpieces, etc. The edifices depicted are of an eclectic style, largely derived from Italian architectural books of the time. French captions in *lettres de civilité* indicate the type and purpose of the various projects.

LENT BY PHILIP AND FRANCES HOFER.

228. CYPRIEN VON LEOWITZ. ECLIPSES LUMINARI — South Germany, ca. 1553

In Latin and German. Humanistic and gothic book hands. 68 paper leaves, 17¼ x 14 inches. 61 large illuminated astronomical drawings; 7 miniatures. Binding: 18th century half calf.

This handsome volume, with its precisely executed astronomical drawings, finely colored, contains prognostications of eclipses of the sun and moon from 1555 to 1559. Below several of these diagrams are watercolor paintings showing the activities of men that will be interrupted at the place and time of the prophesied eclipse. The shadows to be cast by the unusual light, the planets to be seen at the time of the occurrence are very carefully indicated. The book was composed for Prince Otto Henry, Count Palatine, Duke of Bavaria.

LENT BY PHILIP AND FRANCES HOFER. PL. LXXX

229. MODUS SCRIBENDI   Austria (Melk ?), ca. 1440

 In Latin. Gothic script. 16 paper leaves, 8¾ x 5¾ inches. Binding: modern red morocco. Ex-coll.: Stanley Morison.

One of only six known medieval manuals of calligraphy, it is especially important for its text, probably written in the Abbey of Melk.

 BIBLIOGRAPHY: Stanley Morison, *A Fifteenth Century Modus Scribendi from the Abbey of Melk*, Cambridge, (England), 1940; Steinberg in *Library*, March, 1943.

LENT BY PHILIP AND FRANCES HOFER.

230. CORNELIUS GRAPHEUS (OR SCHRYVER). LETTER TO ALBRECHT DÜRER

 Flanders (Antwerp), February 23, 1524

 In Latin. Cursive script. 1 paper leaf, 17½ x 13½ inches. Ex-colls.: Willibald Pirckheimer; Royal Society, London.

An example of letter-calligraphy by a scribe active as Town Secretary of Antwerp in the first half of the sixteenth century. The fact that it was written to Albrecht Dürer, himself interested in letter forms, and that it was later in Pirckheimer's possession gives added interest.

 BIBLIOGRAPHY: Sir Martin Conway, *Literary Remains of Albrecht Dürer*, Cambridge, (England), 1889.

LENT BY PHILIP AND FRANCES HOFER.

231. CALLIGRAPHIC SPECIMEN BY BERNARDINO CATTANEO   Italy (Siena), 1545

 In Italian. Cursive script. 20 vellum leaves, 5¾ x 8 inches. Binding: contemporary Italian morocco, gilt. Ex-colls.: Edward Raleigh; T. Posthumous Hoby (17th cent.); Stephen Penny; Charles J. Harford.

Italian verses written for Edward Raleigh, an Englishman. Flowing Italian cursive of this type had an influence on calligraphy in England which is still felt to this day.

LENT BY PHILIP AND FRANCES HOFER.

232. CALLIGRAPHIC SPECIMEN BY ESTHER INGLIS   England (London), 1606-7

 In Latin and French. 101 paper leaves, 4 x 5¾ inches. 1 miniature; numerous colored drawings. Binding: contemporary English calf, gilt. Ex-colls.: Thomas Egerton, Lord Ellesmere; W. L. Boynes (ca. 1850); W. A. White.

This *Argumenta in Librum Psalmorum*, dedicated to Thomas Egerton, Grand Chancellor of England in 1606, is a somewhat elaborate example of the work of the gifted calligrapher, Esther Inglis. Each page shows a different variety or size of script, including mirror-writing and microscopic lettering. Each Psalm is ornamented with a flower carefully drawn and colored.

 BIBLIOGRAPHY: Dorothy J. Jackson, *Esther Inglis, Calligrapher, 1571-1624*, New York, 1937, no. 18.

LENT BY PHILIP AND FRANCES HOFER

233. CALLIGRAPHIC SPECIMEN BY FRIAR DIDACE   France (Paris), 1647

> In Latin and French. Elaborate flourished script. 90 paper leaves, 6¼ x 4¼ inches. Binding: contemporary olive morocco, gilt.

Litaniae a l'Honore Beatissimae Virginis Mariae—a prayer distributed over the pages of the book in a large and elaborately flourished display script, in colors and gold. The composition of the phrases, a few words to a page, is highly decorative and varied. The appeal of the book is enhanced by the signature: "Par son Tres obeisant & Tres Obligé Serviteur Frere Didace de Paris pauvre petit Capucin tres Indigne. En nostre Convent de s Maretz ce Vingt-huictiesme Decemb' 1647."

LENT BY PHILIP AND FRANCES HOFER

PLATES

d̄ne ds uirtutum conuerte nunc respice
decaelo et uide et uisitar uineam istam et dirige
ec eam quam plantauit dextera tua
et super filium hominis quem confirmasti tibi
                an cles   opcyrie iadolescines
Incensa igni et effosa manu: ab increpat
ione uultus tui peribunt
                                            open pen
Fiat manus tua super uirum dexterae tuae
et super filium hominis quem confirmasti
tibi. et non discedimus abs te
Uiuificabis nos et nomen tuum inuocabimus
D̄ne ds uirtutum conuerte nos et ostende
faciem tuam et salui erimus

              Exp̄ ps lxxix in pro tr colariorum
              blissiaþ
EXULTATE
              gefylstan   fingaþ
        adiutori nostro iubilate dō iacob
                      gefean
Sumite psalmum et date tympanum
psalterium iucundum cum cithara
    fingaþ of fyþe   menþes of byman
Canite inintio mensis tubae: in die
      michum
insigni sol̄mnitatis uestrae
Quia praeceptum in isrl est et iudicium dō iacob
Testimonium in ioseph posuit eum dum exiret de terra
                                                    aegypti

II

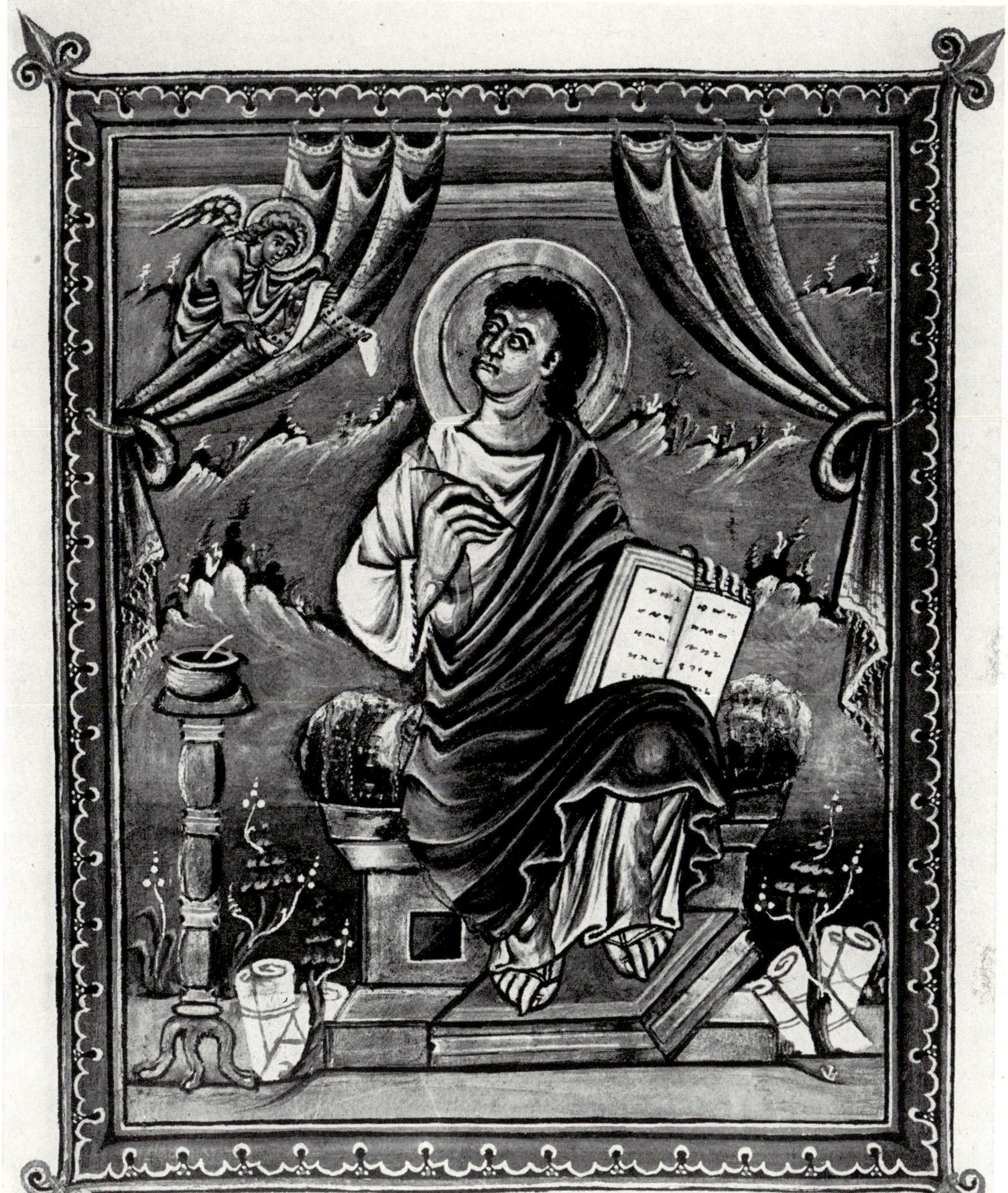

4

IV

V

6

6

VI

10

11

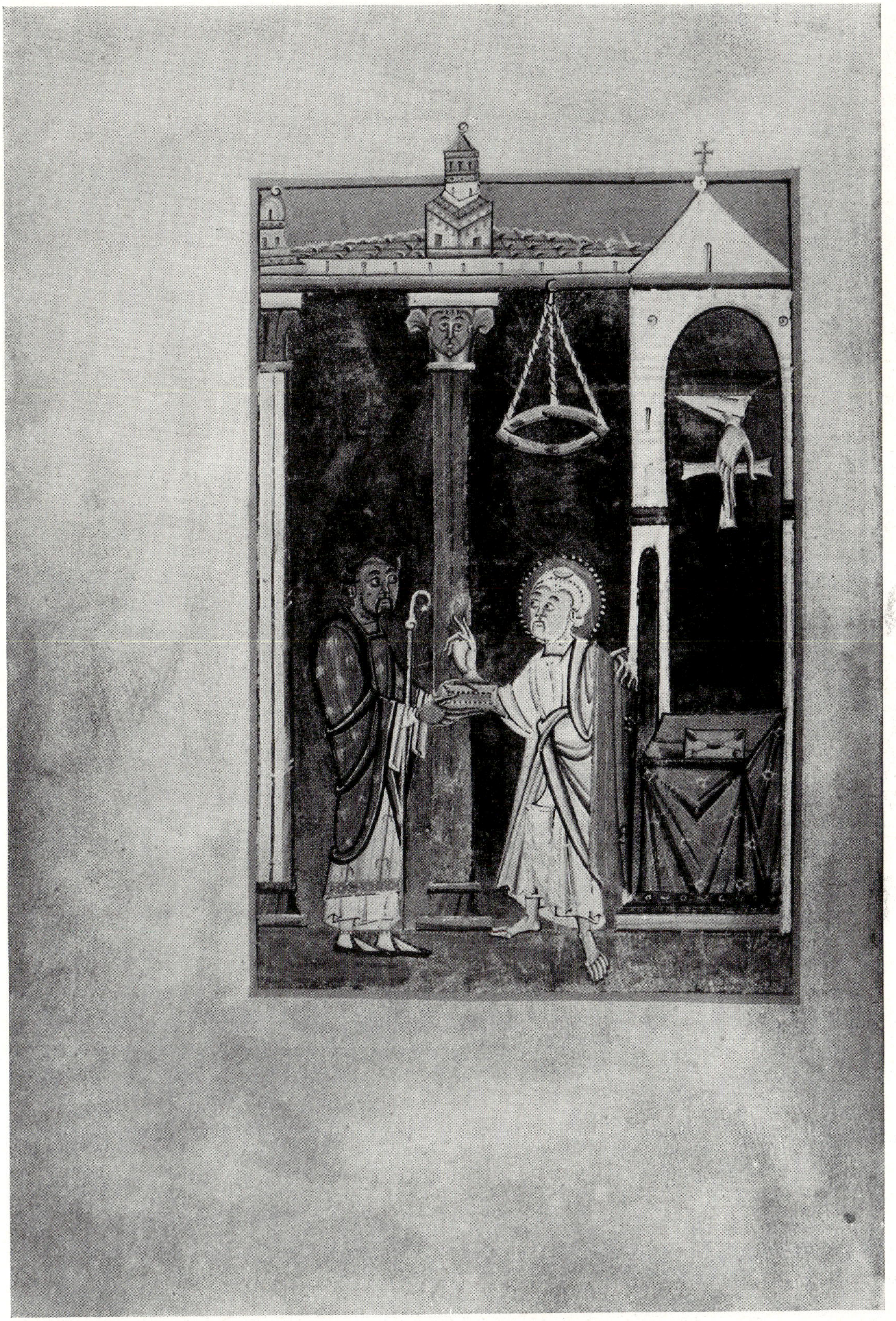

12

VIII

IX

16

14

XI

18

XII

17

13

XIII

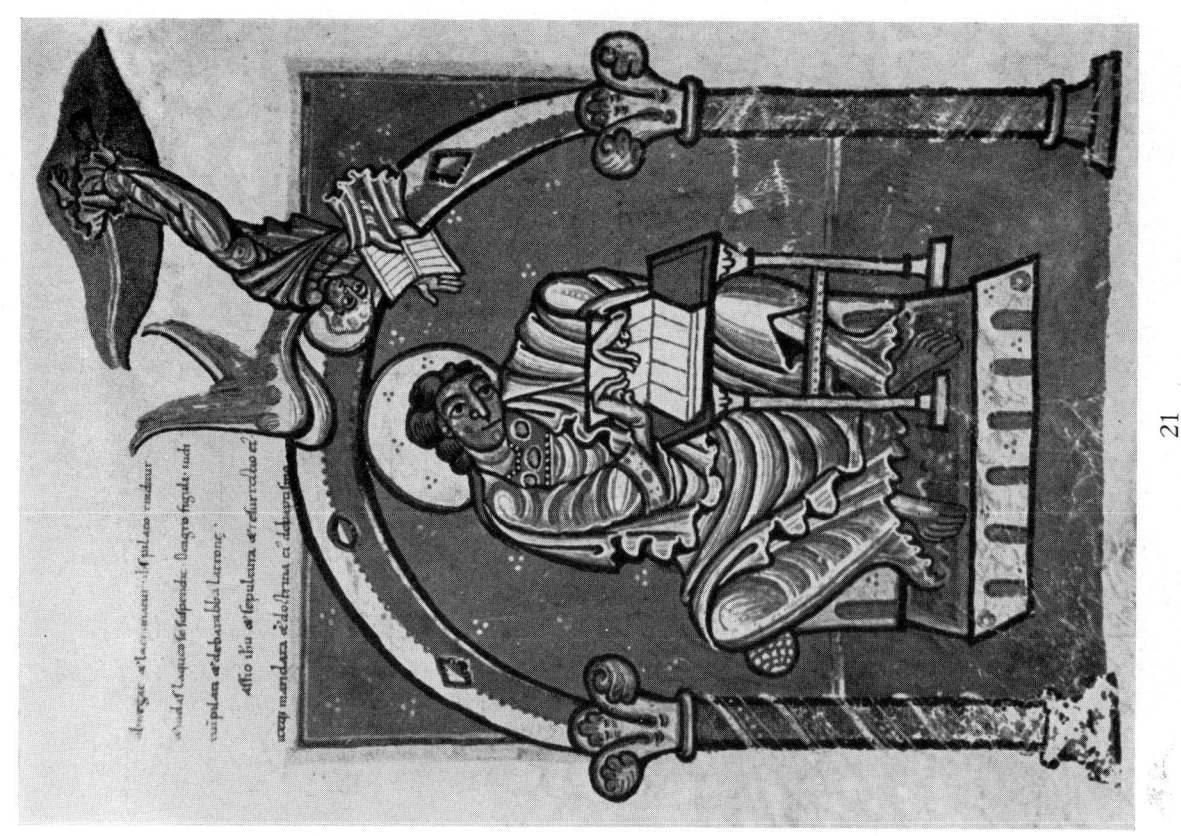

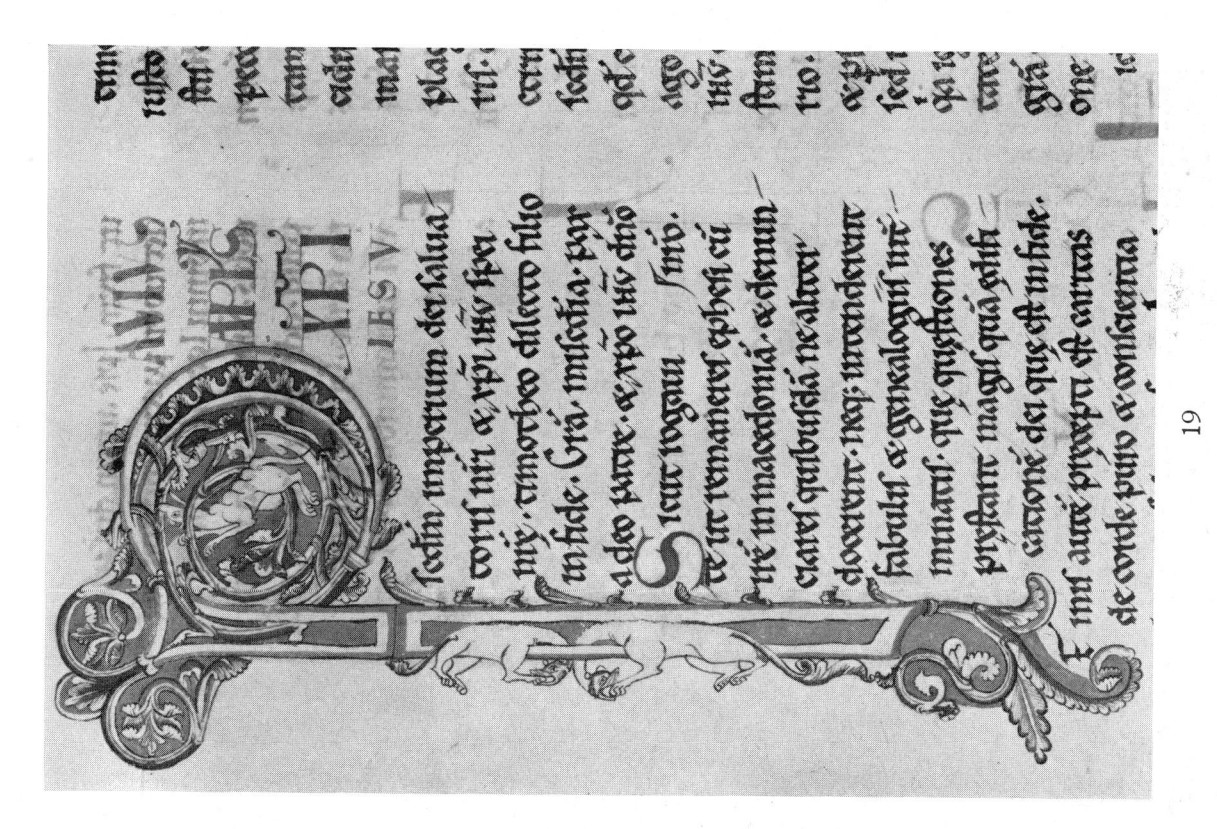

XIV

22

23

XV

31

32

XVI

XVII

33

XVIII

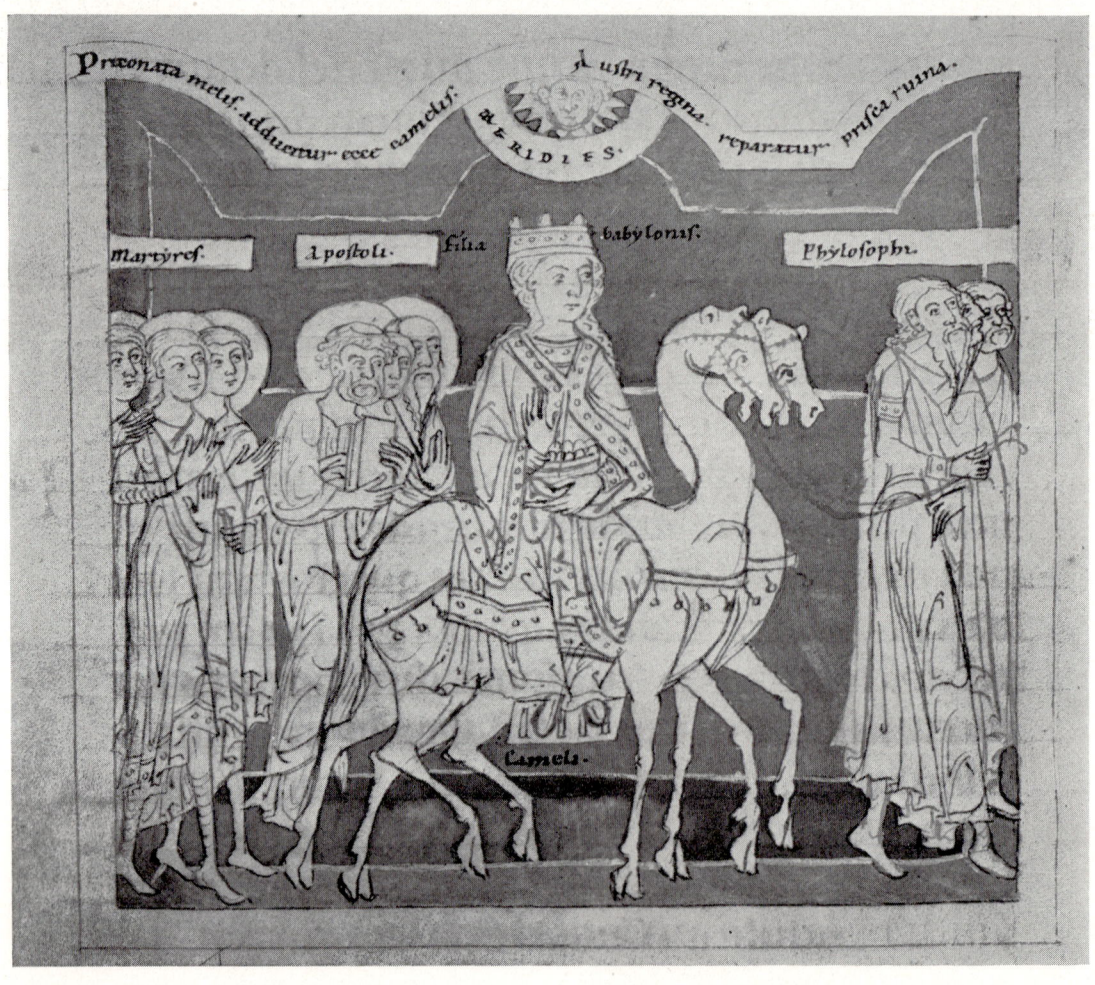

Above: 30   *Below:* 27

XIX

XX

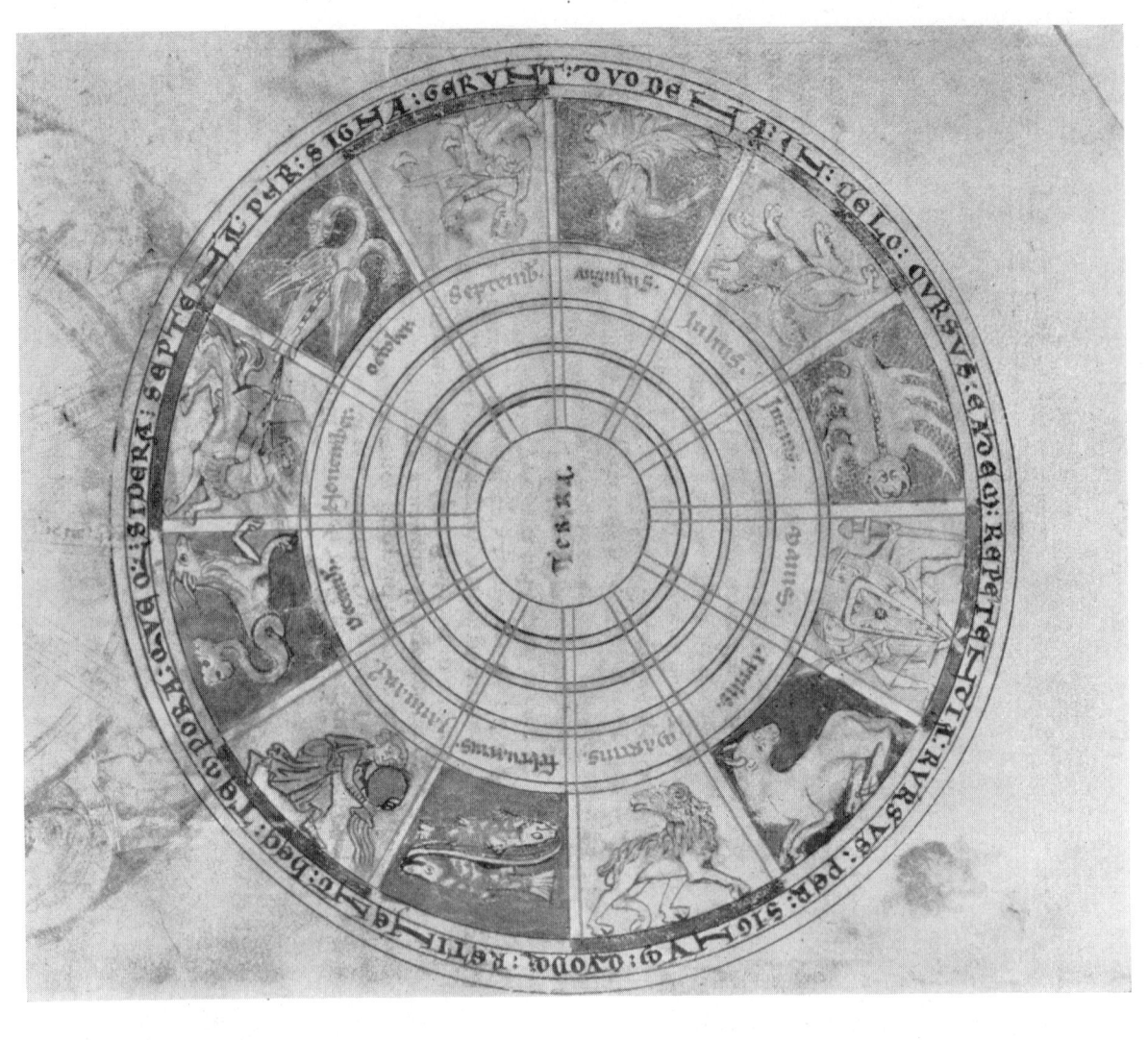

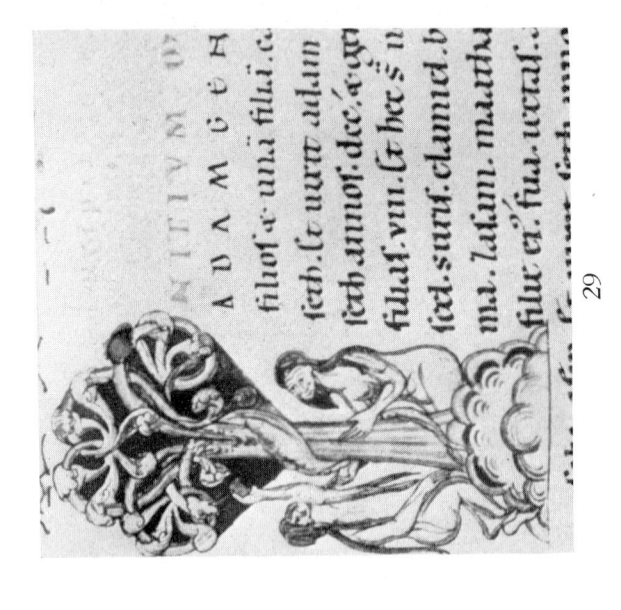

XXI

41

24
24

XXII

XXIII

XXIV

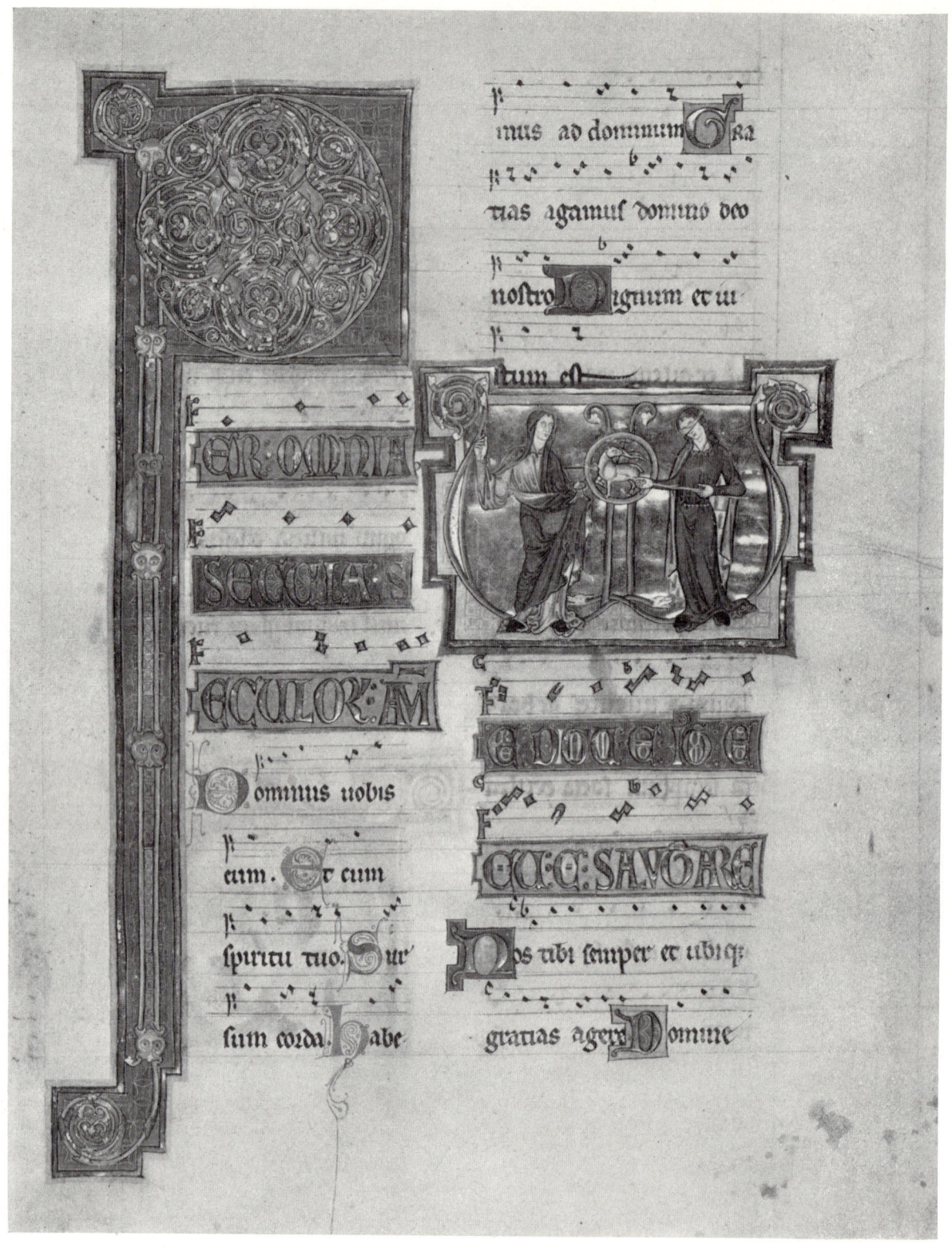

XXV

pplo tritus effugiss, et latitant cum sex milibus. Saul aut non
nisi cum sexcentis uiris eet in campo. et sedet sub malo grana
to. Jonathas filius suus cum unico armigo eo antignorante patre
p prerupta montiu ac saxorum ascedit ad hostium statoes. atqe ex
eis quos primo egressu repit miraclosam uictoriam reportauit.

raliter cum post uictoriam Jonache. mirabil tumultus ortus eer i castris philistinor. ita ut gla

XXVI

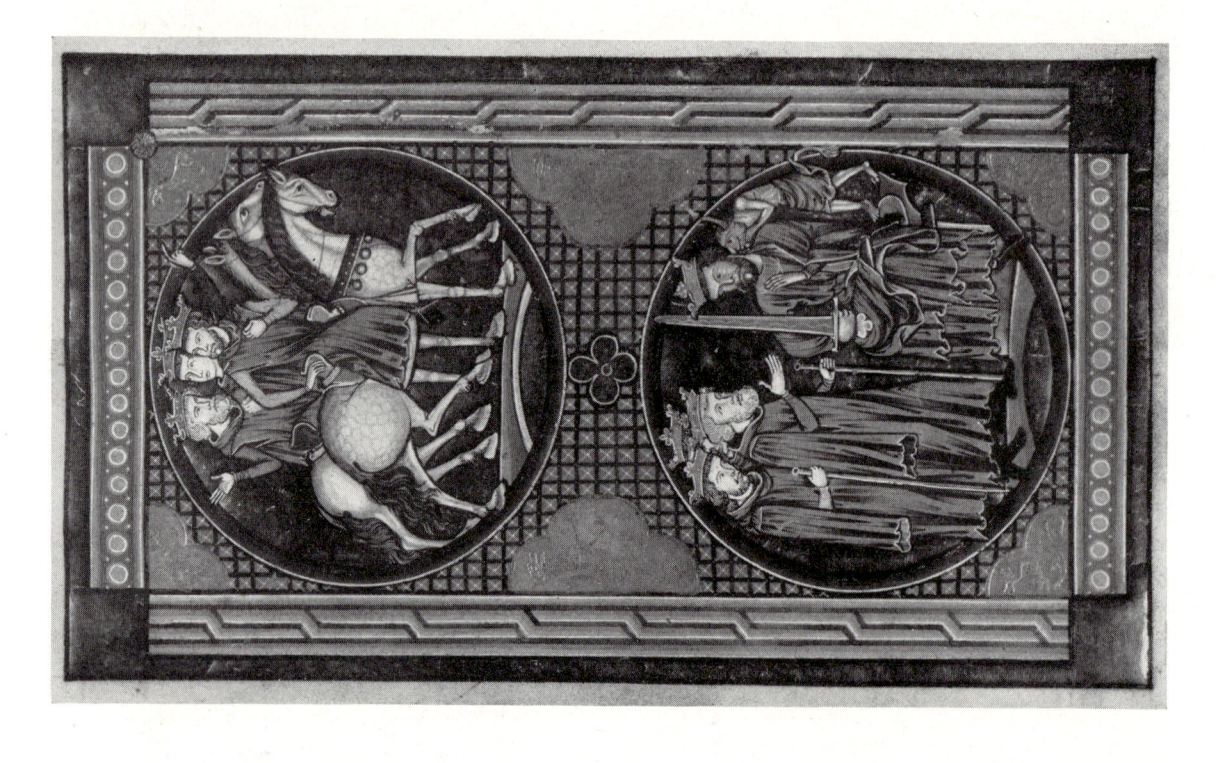

XXVII

59

58

XXVIII

47

At right, above: 51

At right, below: 54

XXIX

XXX

XXXI

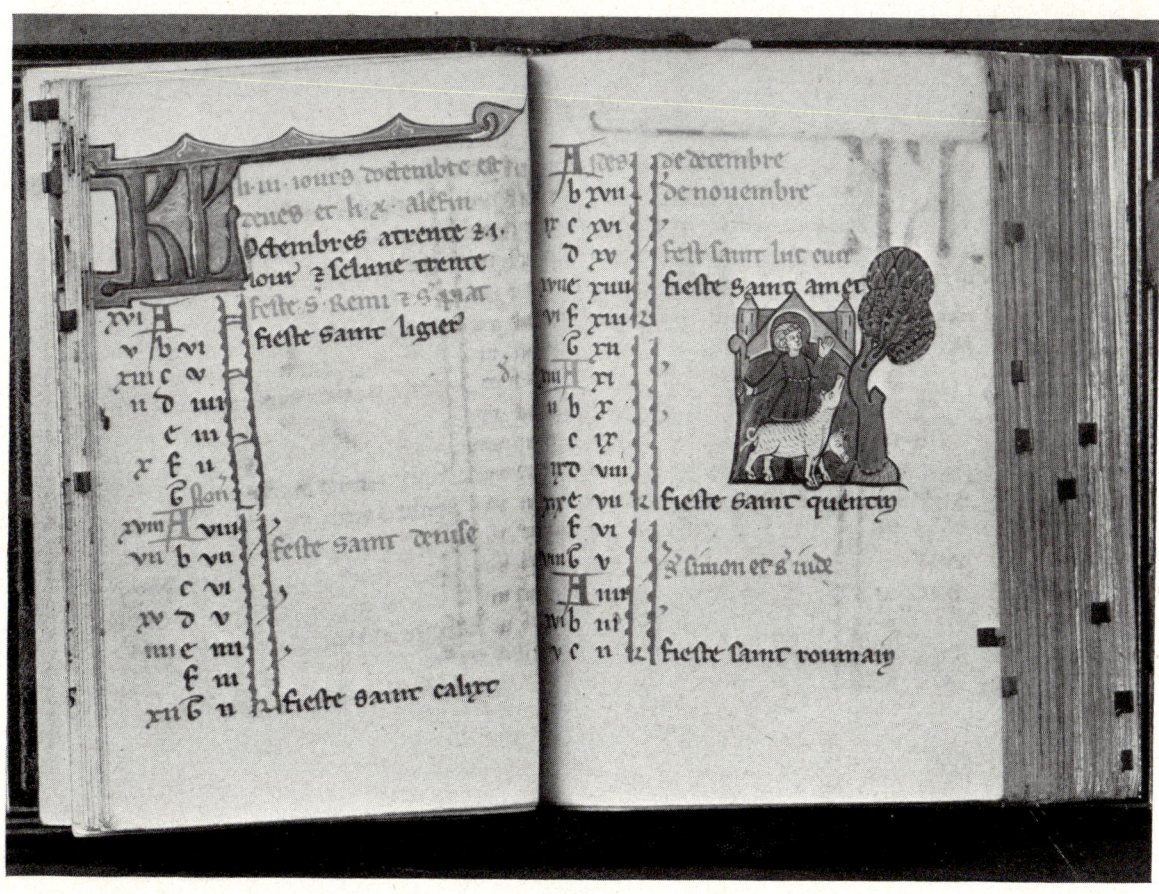

49

55

56

XXXII

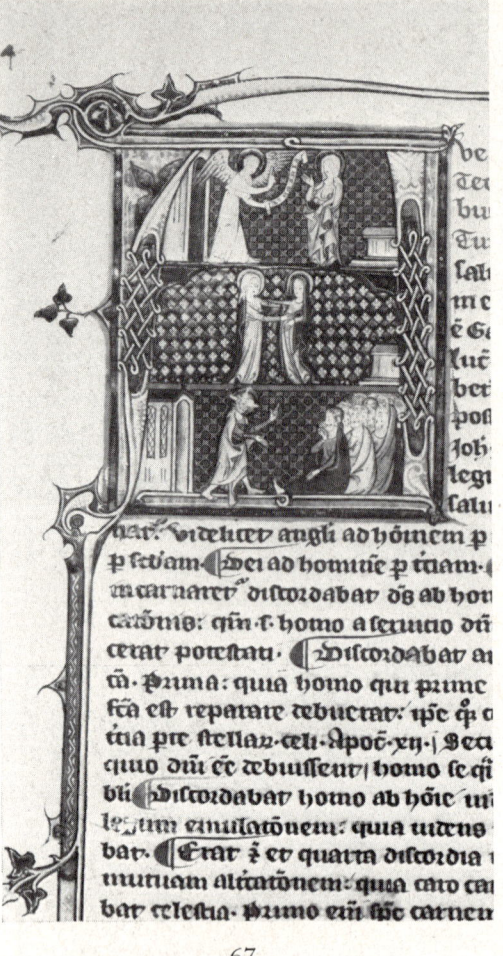

67

68

64

XXXIII

suions
le crate
ce crati
ate ter
noraus
non m
et orgu
de celi a
tous. e
lauce. e
ces pm
ur les h
le dieu
dire des

70

XXXIV

XXXV

At left: 81 *At right:* 80

XXXVI

XXXVII

84

85

XXXVIII

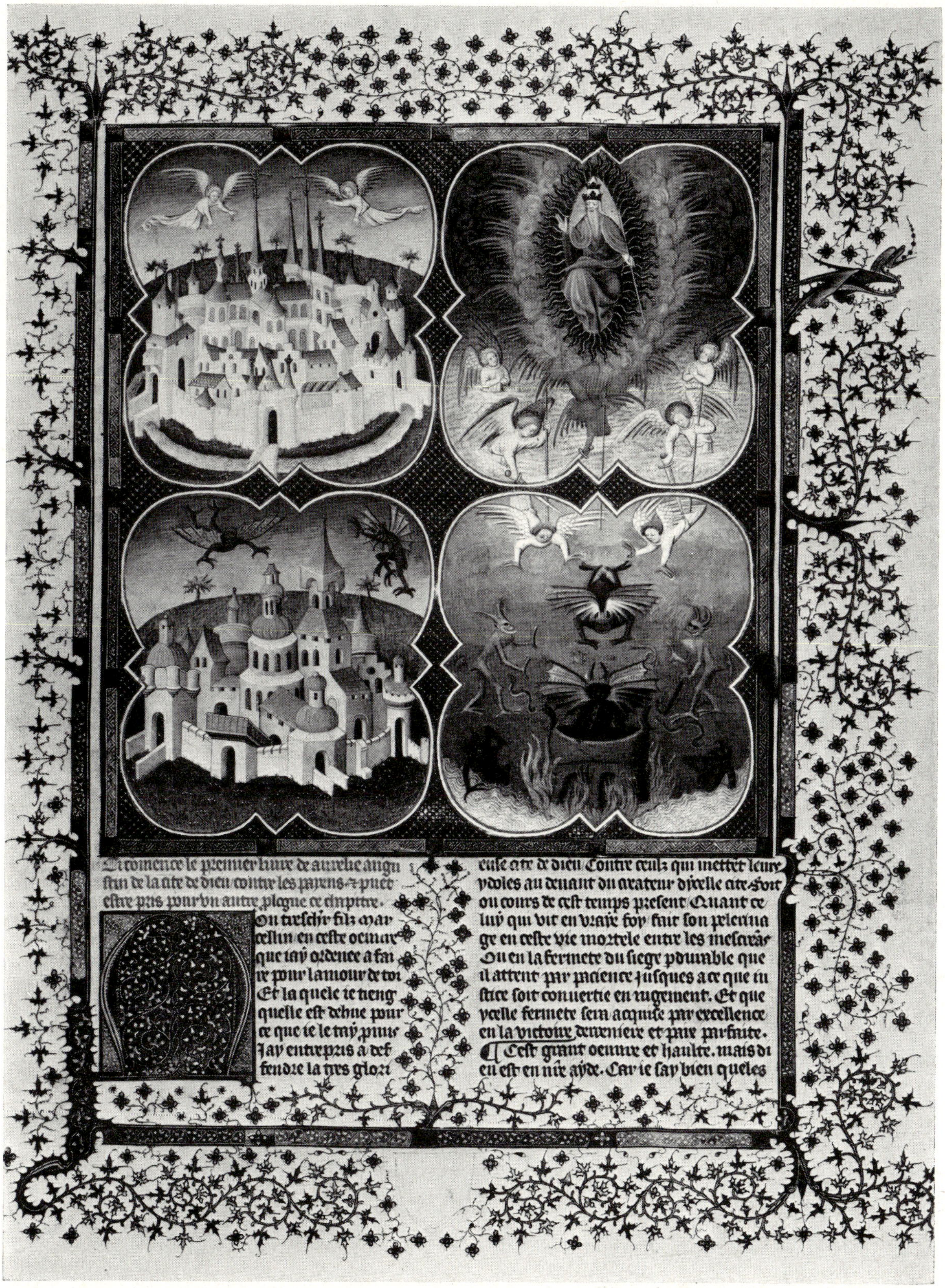
commence le premier liure de aurelie augu
stin de la cite de dieu contre les payens · et peut
estre pris pour vn autre prologue ce chapitre ·
On tresch[ie]r filz mar
cellin en ceste oeuure
que iay ordenee a fai
re pour lamour de toi
Et la quele ie tieng
quelle est deue pour
ce que ie le tay promis
Jay entrepris a def
fendre la tres glori
euse cite de dieu contre ceulz qui mettet leurs
ydoles au deuant du createur dycelle cite · Soit
ou cours de cest temps present quant ce
luy qui vit en vraie foy fait son pelerina
ge en ceste vie mortele entre les mescreans
Ou en la fermete du siege pdurable que
il attent par pacience iusques a ce que iu
stice soit conuertie en iugement · Et que
ycelle fermete sera acquise par excellence
en la victoire derreniere et paix parfaite ·
Cest grant oeuure et haulte · mais di
eu est en nre ayde · Car ie say bien queles

XL

XLI

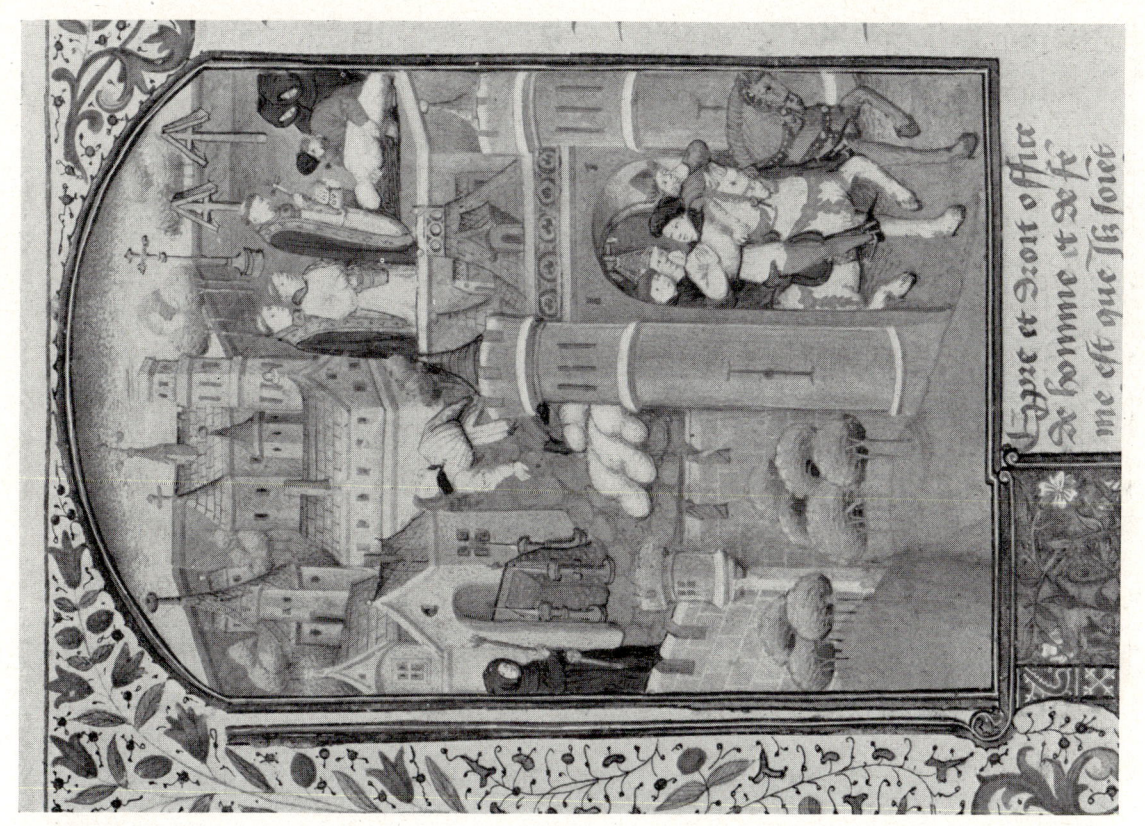

XLII

XLIII

96

XLIV

93

135

XLV

106

XLVI

110
At right, above: 111
At right, below: 109

XLVII

116

At right, above: 107
At right, below: 104

XLVIII

103a

XLIX

128

L

119

121

LI

LII

LIII

137

138

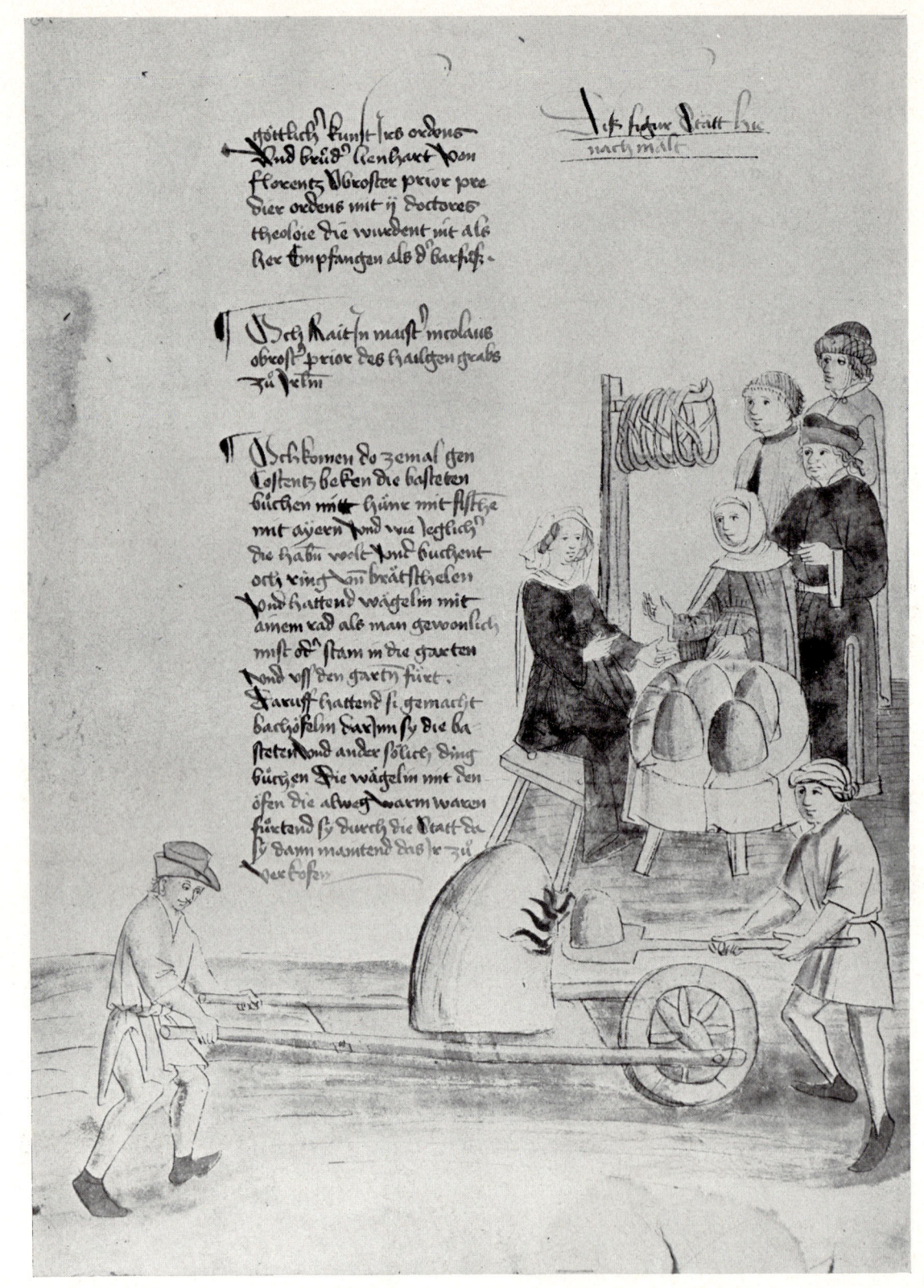

LIV

göttlich kunst des ordens
vnd bruder lienhart von
florentz obroster prior pre
dier ordens mit ij doctores
theoloie die wurdent mit als
her empfangen als d'barfuß.

Och rait in maiſt nicolaus
obroſt prior des hailgen grabs
zu ſelm

Och komen do zemal gen
Coſtentz becken die baſteten
buchen mit hünr mit fiſtze
mit aieren vnd wie jeglich
die haben wolt vnd buchent
och ring an brätſchelen
vnd hattend wägelim mit
ainem rad als man gewonlich
miſt od' ſtain in die garten
vnd uß den garten fürt.
Daruff hattend ſi gemacht
bachöfelin darjnn ſy die ba
ſteten vnd ander ſölich; ding
burgen Die wägelim mit den
öfen die alweg warm waren
fürtend ſy durch die ſtatt da
ſy dann mamtend das ſi zu
verkofen

Des ſchane ſtatt hie
nach malt

147

d' engl wante si ab sa | mit rechter red auff tun den mund
ditz was main eng da | Si sprach zu dem manne was slahes
an ain dürrn witer was | auch ze dem dritten male nu
d' was gezaymet als ich ez las | do sprach d' man pey name nu
die eslin treib für sich d' man | anust vo maine henden nu
d' engl slug si wid an | Schir han v'lorn das lebn
vn wart si also sere | wär mir in dy hant icht gebn
das si mit abe chere | Ein swert das war so slug ich
dem manne sein fuez zerstiez | auff disem weg zetod dich
Got durich senau wund hiez | do wurdn ane laugn
dy eslin and sehn stund | auch Balaames augn

in consilio impiorum: & in uia pec
catorum non stetit: & in cathedra pe
stilentie non sedit.
Sed in lege domini uoluntas eius:
& in lege eius meditabit die ac nocte.
Et erit tanquam lignum qd plan
tatum est secus decursus aquaru:

154

LVIII

LIX

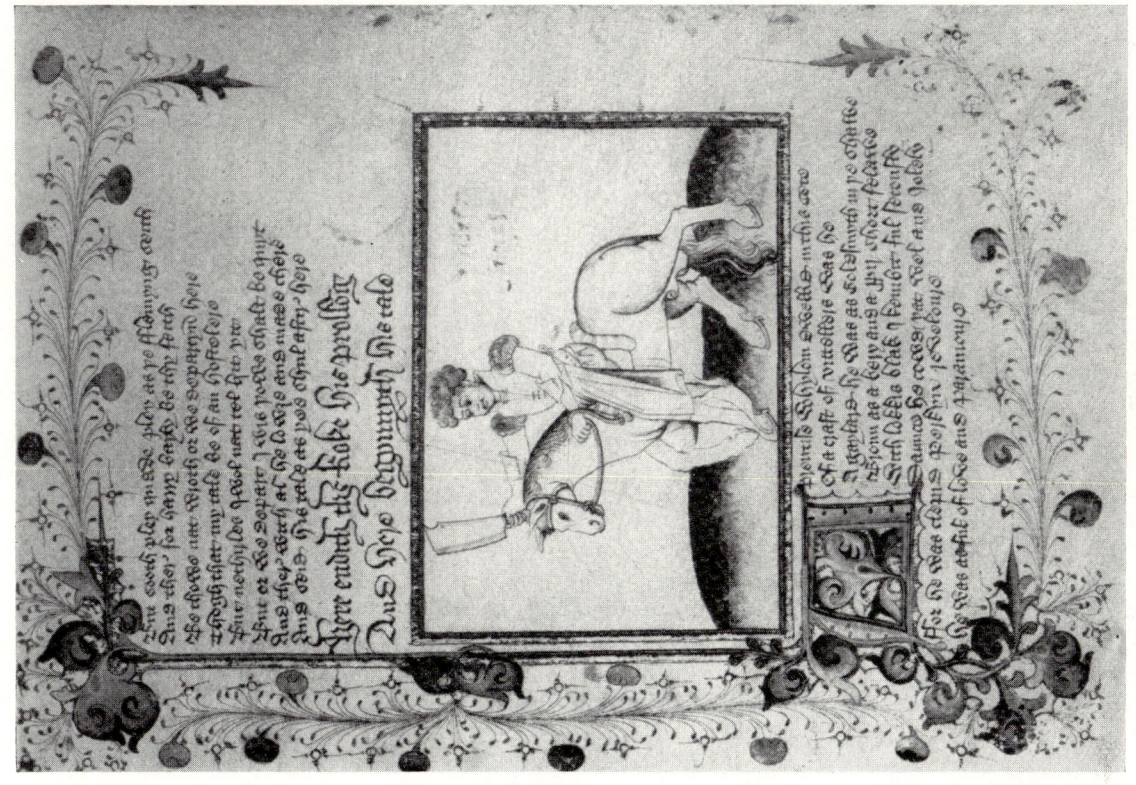

LX

156

159

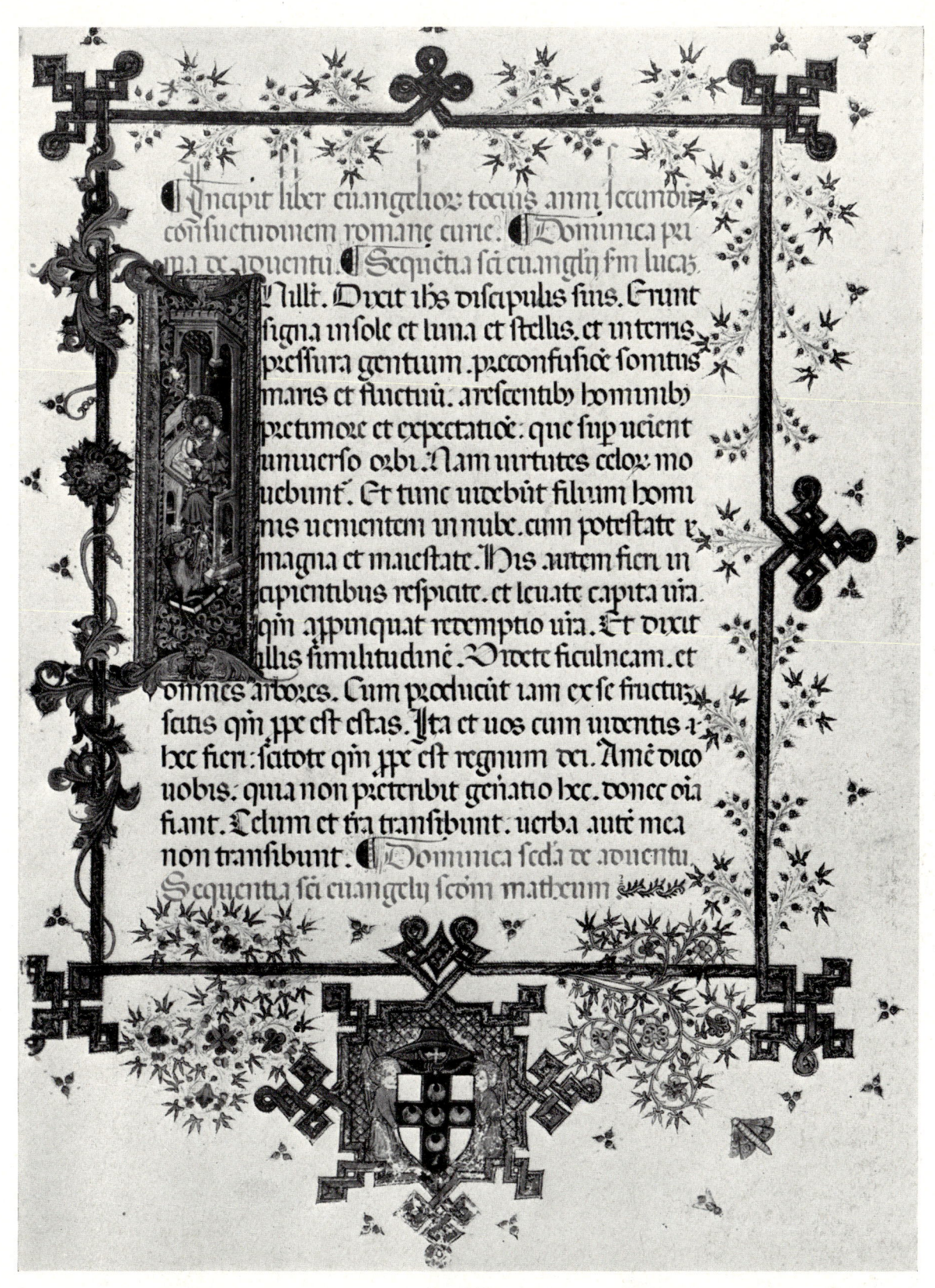

Incipit liber euangelior̃: tocius anni secundũ
consuetudinem romanę curie. Dominica pri
ma de aduentu. Sequentia sci euangelij sm lucã.

In illo. Dixit ihs discipulis suis. Erunt
signa in sole et luna et stellis. et in terris
pressura gentium. pre confusione sonitus
maris et fluctuũ. arescentibꝫ hominibꝫ
pre timore et expectatione: que sup uenient
universo orbi. Nam virtutes celor̃ mo
uebunt. Et tunc videbunt filium homi
nis uenientem in nube. cum potestate &
magna et maiestate. His autem fieri in
cipientibus respicite. et leuate capita ura.
qm appinquat redemptio ura. Et dixit
illis similitudinẽ. Videte ficulneam. et
omnes arbores. Cum producit iam ex se fructũ
scitis qm ppe est estas. Ita et vos cum videritis
hec fieri: scitote qm ppe est regnum dei. Amẽ dico
vobis. quia non preteribit generatio hec. donec oia
fiant. Celum et tr̃a transibunt. verba autẽ mea
non transibunt. Dominica secda de aduentu.
Sequentia sci euangelij secm matheum

LXII

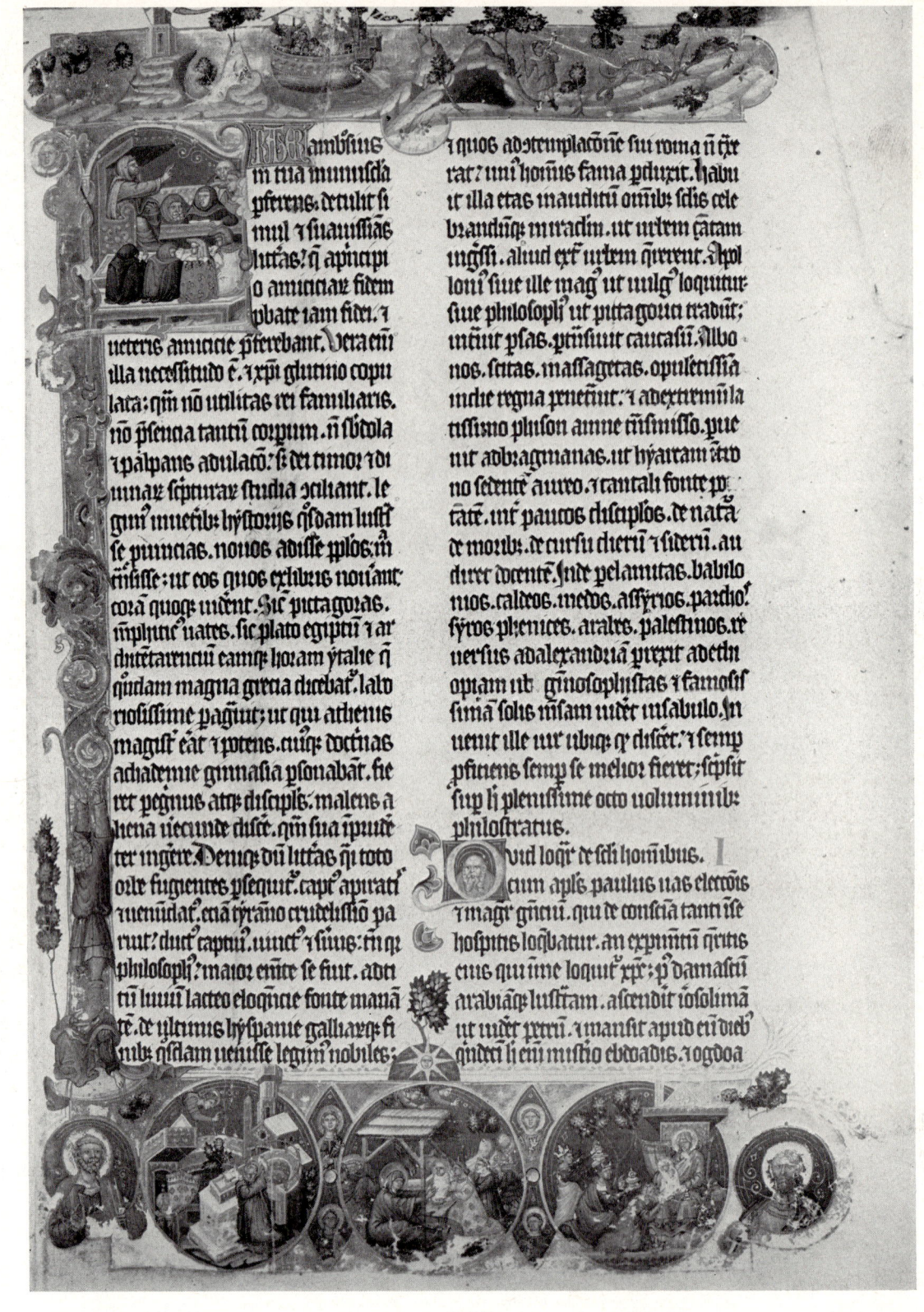

LXIII

162

LXIV

161

163

LXV

164

165

LXVI

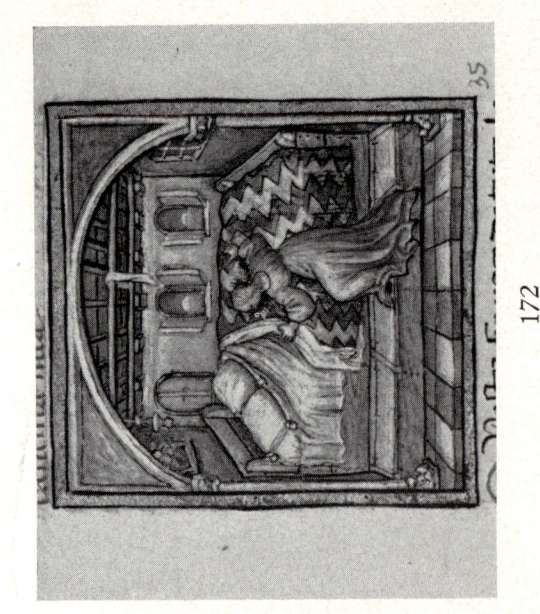

172

171

169

LXVII

175

179

LXVIII

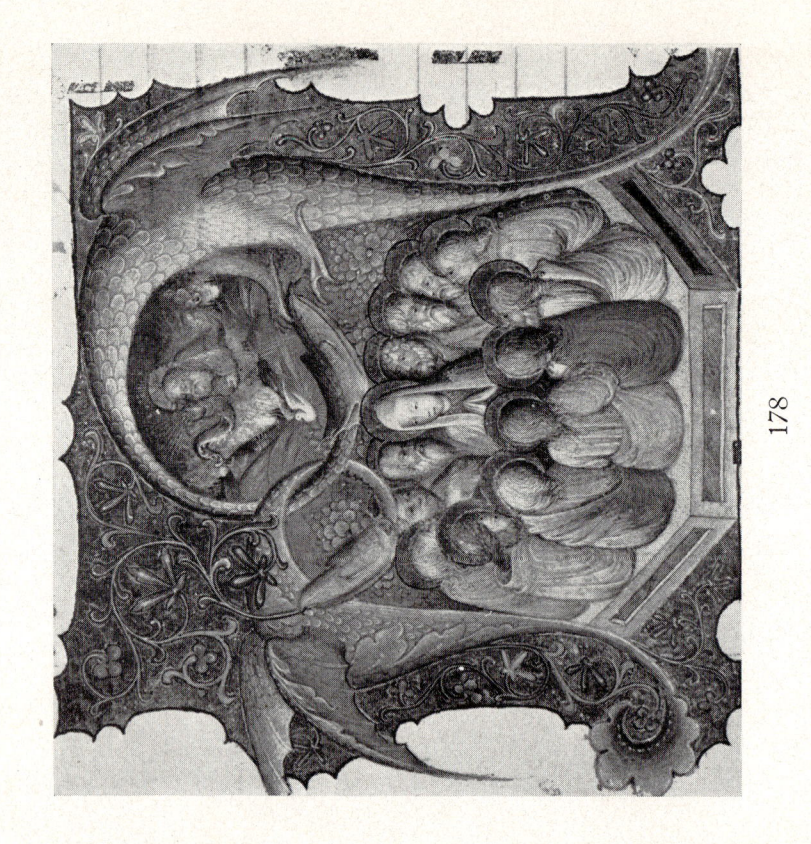

178

180

TITI·LIVII·PATAVINI·DE·SECVNDO·BELLO·PVN·CO
LIBER PRIMVS INCIPIT

IN PARTE OPERIS MEI LICET
prefari mihi quod in principio sume
totius professi sunt pleriq; rerum scrip
tores bellum maxime memorabile
omnium que unq; gesta sunt me scri
pturum. quod Annibale duce Car
thaginenses cu populo Romano ges
sere. Nam neq; ualidiores opibus ul
le inter se ciuitates gentesq; cotule
runt arma. neq; his ipsis tantum unq;
uirium aut roboris fuit. & haud ig
taf belli artes inter se. sed expertas primo punico coserbant bello Et
adeo uaria belli fortuna ancepsq; Mars fuit ut propius periculo fue
rint qui uicerunt. Odiis etiam prope maioribz certarunt q uirib;
Romanis indignantib; quod uictoribus uicti ultro inferrent arma
Penisq; quod superbe auareq; crederent imperitatum uictis ee. fama
etiam est Annibalem annorum ferme nouem pueriliter blandiente
patri Hamilcari. ut duceretur in Hispaniam. cum pfecto Africo bel
lo exercitum eo traiecturus sacrificaret altaribz admotum tactis
sacris iuriurando adactum se. cum primum posset hostem fore po
puli Romani. Angebant ingentis spiritus uirum Sicilia Sardinia
q; amisse. Nam & Siciliam nimis celeri desperatione concessam
& Sardiniam inter motum Africe fraude Romanorum stipendio et
superimposito interceptam. His anxius curisque ita se Africo bello quod
fuit sub recentem Romanam pacem per quinq; annos ita deinde
nouem annis in Hispania augendo punico imperio gessit ut ap
pareret maius eum q quod gereret agitare i aio bellum & si diu
tius uixisset Hamilcare duce Penos arma Italie illaturos fuisse q
Annibalis ductu intulerunt. Mors Hamilcaris peroportuna &
pueritia Annibalis distulerunt bellum. Medius Hasdrubal inter
patrem & filium octo ferme annos impium obtinuit. Flore etatis
ut ferunt primo Hamilcari conciliatus. Gener inde ob aliam
indolem profecto animi adscitus & quia genere erat factionis

192

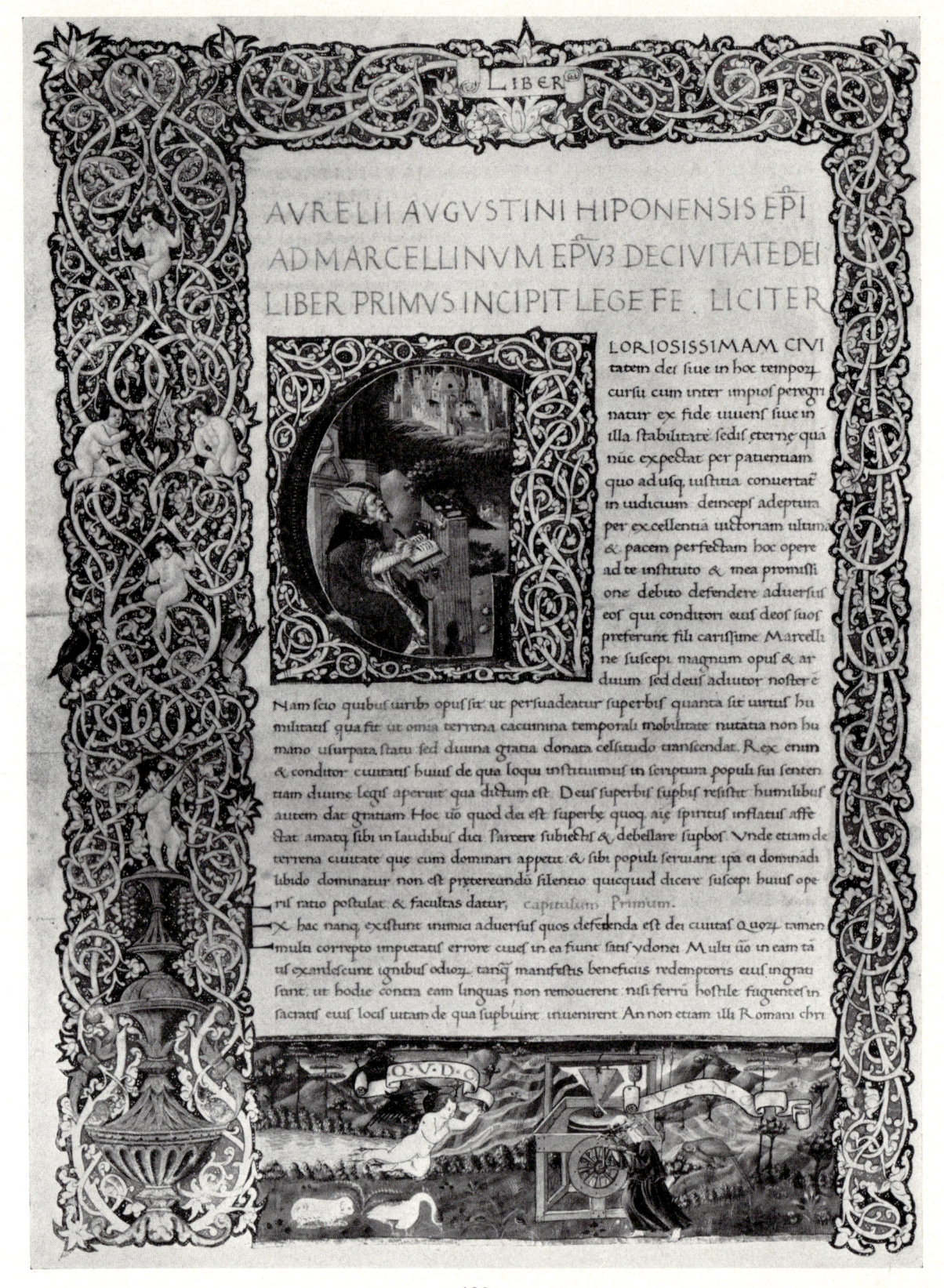

LIBER

AVRELII AVGVSTINI HIPONENSIS EPI
AD MARCELLINVM EPV3 DECIVITATEDEI
LIBER PRIMVS INCIPIT LEGE FE . LICITER

LORIOSISSIMAM CIVI
tatem dei siue in hoc tempor
cursu cum inter impios peregri
natur ex fide uiuens siue in
illa stabilitate sedis eterne quā
nūc expectat per patientiam
quo adusq, iustitia conuertat
in iudicium deinceps adeptum
per excellentia uictoriam ultima
& pacem perfectam hoc opere
ad te instituto & mea promissi
one debito defendere aduersus
eos qui conditori eius deos suos
preferunt fili carissime Marcelli
ne suscepi magnum opus & ar
duum sed deus adiutor noster e
Nam scio quibus uirib; opus sit ut persuadeatur superbis quanta sit uirtus hu
militatis qua fit ut omia terrena cacumina temporali mobilitate nutatia non hu
mano usurpata statu sed diuina gratia donata celsitudo transcendat. Rex enim
& conditor ciuitatis huius de qua loqui instituimus in scriptura populi sui senten
tiam diuine legis aperuit qua dictum est. Deus superbis superbis resistit humilibus
autem dat gratiam Hoc uo quod dei est superbę quoq; aie spiritus inflatus affe
ctat amatq; sibi in laudibus dici. Parcere subiectis & debellare superbos. Vnde etiam de
terrena ciuitate que cum dominari appetit & sibi populi seruiant ipa ei dominādi
libido dominatur non est prytereundū silentio quicquid dicere suscepi huius ope
ris ratio postulat & facultas datur, capitulum Primum.
X hac namq; existunt inimici aduersus quos defendenda est dei ciuitas Q uor; tamen
multi correpto impietatis errore cuius in ea fiunt satis ydonei Multi uo in eam tā
tis exardescunt ignibus odior; tanq; manifestis beneficiis redemptoris eius ingrati
sunt. ut hodie contra eam linguas non remouerent nisi ferrū hostile fugientes in
sacratis eius locis uitam de qua superbuint. inuenirent. An non etiam illi Romani chri

VALERII·MAX·LIB·II·

DE INSTITVTIS ANTIQVIS·CAP·I· IVES ET PRAEPOTENS·

Dnaturæ regnum scrutatus initiam stilum tam nostræ urbis quam gentium ceterarum: priscis ac memorabilibus institutis. Opus est enim cognosci huiuscemodi: ut æ quam sub optimo principe felicem agimus quæ nam fuerint elementa: ut eor quoque respectus aliquid presentibus moribus prosit; Apud antiquos non solum publice sed etiam priuatim nihil gerebatur nisi auspicio prius sumpto: quo ex more nuptiis etiam nunc auspices interponuntur. Qui quam auspicia petere desierint: ipso tamen nomine ueteris consuetudinis uestigia usurpantur; Femine cum iuris cubatibus sedentes cenitabant: quæ consuetudo ex hominum conuictu ad diuina penetrauit. Nam Ioui epulo ipse in lectulum: Iuno & Minerua in Sellas ad cænam inuitabatur. Quod genus seueritatis ætas nostra diligentius in capitolio quam in suis domibus conseruat: uidelicet quia magis ad rem pertinet dearum q̃ mulierum disciplina contineri; Quæ uno contente matrimonio fuerant corona pudicitiæ honorabantur. Existimabant enim eum precipue matrone sincera fide incorruptum esse animum qui post depositæ uirginitatis cubile in publicum egredi nesciret: multorum matrimoniorum experientia quasi legitime eius intemperantiæ signum esse credentes. Repudium inter uxorem & uirum a condita urbe usque ad centesimum & quinquagesimum annum nullum intercessit. Primus autem Spurius Curbilius uxorem sterilitatis causa dimisit

LXXII

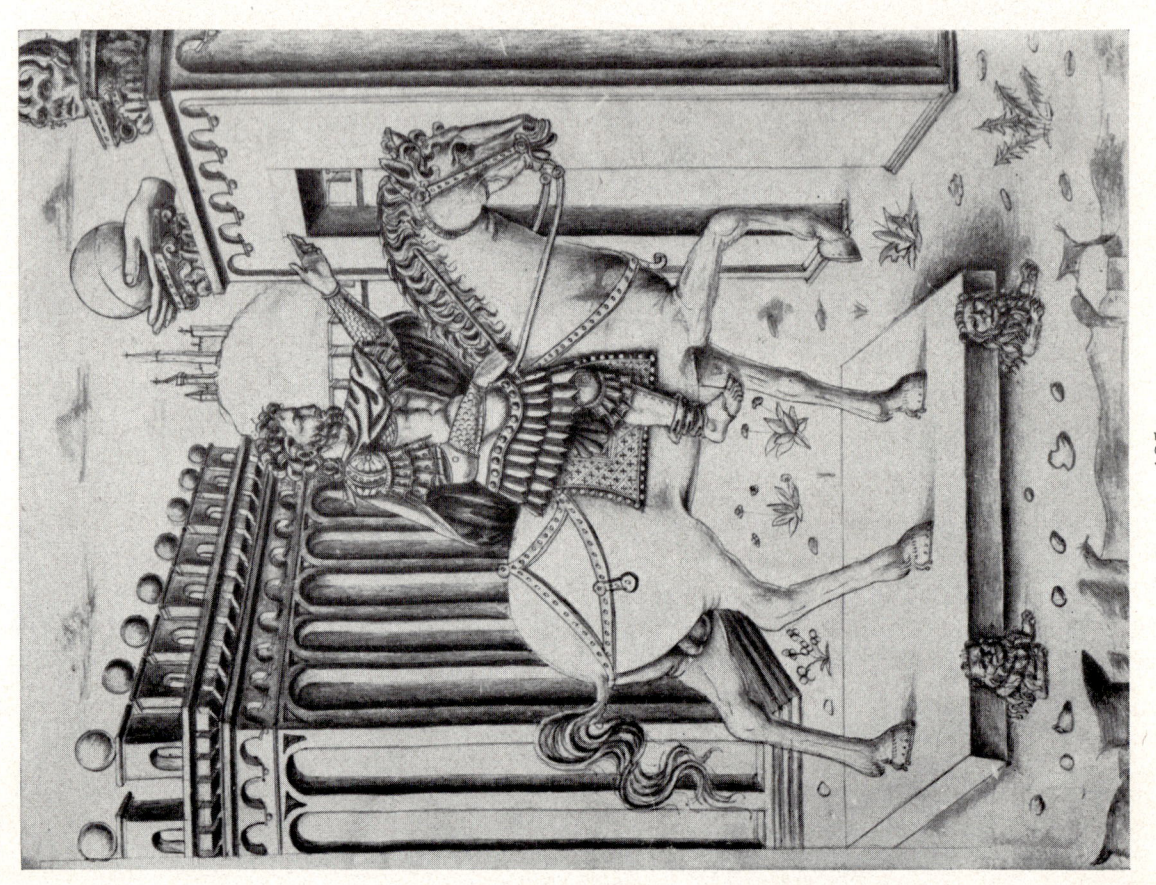

184

185

LXXIII

*Aquarius habet pedem in hyemali circulo fixos. manum autem sinistram usq̄ ad capricorni por-
rigens, tergum dextra iubet pegasi prope con-
tingens. spectat ad exortus, qui cum ita sit figu-
ratus, necesse est, cum corpore prope resupina-
to uideri. Effusio aquae peruenit ad eum pisces
qui solitarius figuratur: de quo posterius dicemus.
Sed aquarius & occidit & exoritur capite prius q̄ reliquis membris. Hic habet in capite

oritur ante diuersus. Sed habet stellam in naso una
Infra ceruicem unam : in pectore duas : interfia
pede unam : in priore eodem alteram : interfta
pillio habet stellas septem . in uentre septem : in t. v
cauda duas. & ita est omnino stellarum numerus
uigintiunus.

papulo
t xxvi

—

Capricornus ad occasum spectans & totus in zodi-
aco circulo deformatur: cauda & toto corpore medius diuiditur ab hyemali circulo suppositus aqua-
rij manu sinistra. Occidit autem praecipiti & ex-

diuiditur Ante pedes eius est quaedam corona stellis effecta: de qua prius diximus. Hic praeceps occidit: Exoritur directus. Habet autem in capite
stellas duas : in arcu duas : in sagitta unam : in dex
tro cubito unam : in manu priore unam : in uentre
unam : inter scapillis duas . in cauda unam : in priore genu unam : in pede unam : in inferiore genu unam : in poplite unam. Omnino est stellarum
quindecim Corona autem centauri est stellarum
septem.

scrupulo

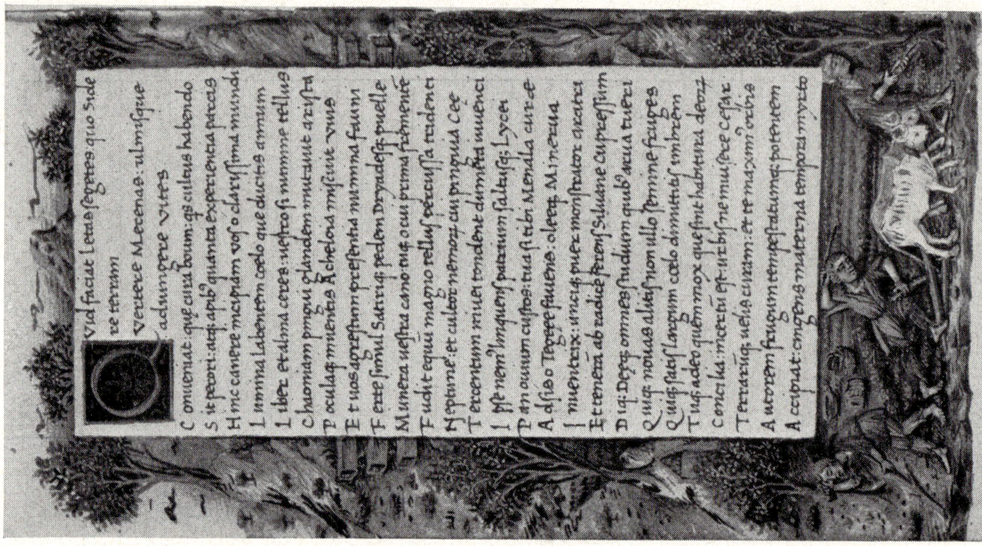

LXXIV

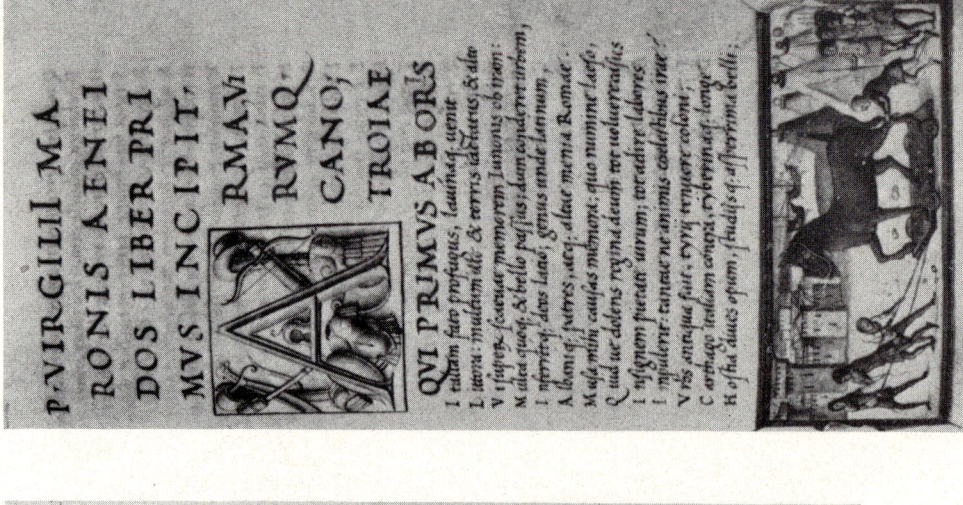

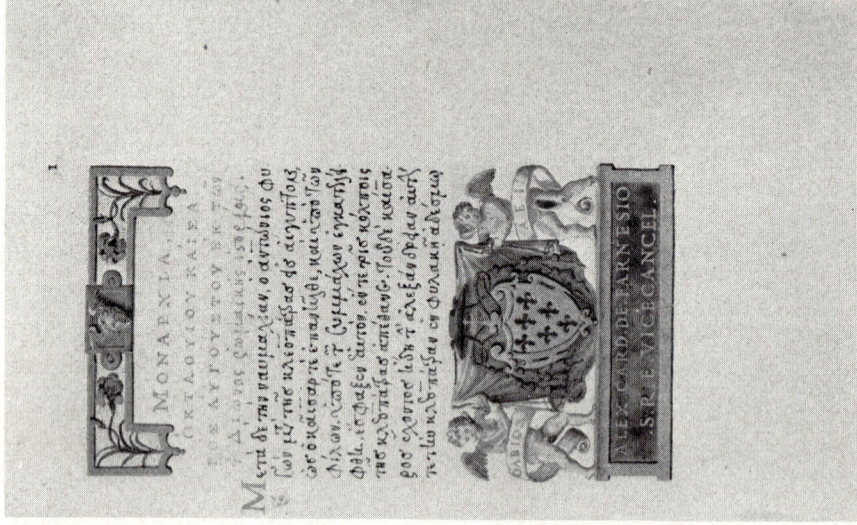

ξε̅

Μ λεσθαι·
Λεγει παλιν ἐξελθὼν ἐις τὸ γ πδίοτι
οἰκίω. οὐδεὶ ἔξω, ὅτι πᾶ-
σι λεγων σαφῶς καὶ διάρρην λαβόντες
αὐτοὶ δὲ οὐ χρήσιμοι, μᾶλλον παρω̈τοῦν
τοῦ ἀγαθοῦ. οὐδέποτε αὐτῶν δρα-
λυσωσι, λεγων, χρήσιμος ἔση
τοῖς διαβεβωσι, νυκτος αὐτοῖς
ὡς γεγονὼς ζύσβρων οἰδε ἔργλεκ
ἀπὸ διασοωσανων θυσων, κ τοῖς ψαῖν
ἐκείνους ἰδ' εἰσάραι· σωθηναι
ἡμᾶς οὐκ ἔχει.

Ὁ μισθοσόπος, ὅτι σταπιμώλισε
τοῖς πονηροῖς ἐνθιδώσαις, ὁ τοῖς
χρηστοῖς ἀπὸ καρποτητασιω·

ξς̄

ΞΖ̅ παραωθε·
Ἐγδρωπος ἄφρων ἐυἰσκαια
χορον ἰδώ, ἐχειν κλωνὼν βατ δ' βρην
καὶ δὴ κηρὺς λαμε ὡς τῆς φραπ, τὸ
ἤ θεσφορρα εὐφονος ξιη. καὶ ἀλ-
τιπροφως ὡσ στανω, ἀνιωθείν κ.
ἀναβα σοι αὐτοῦ ἰδοὺ ξαντας, κα κα-
μυοσοτὶ ἰδοὺ ξαντας, λίθοις ἐξ
σωι τὸν πλουσιον. ὁ ὑστω και δ' ας
ὁ μισθοσόπος. ὁ ζωστιμουντος
ρηωσεων ὅτι εἰς εἰ τὰς χρελαστρωσθ-
ψαι ἐιγα λιδου. ὅταν ἰάσι λα τε
ἡ Ιδας ἀφιαιρτιν οὐδανοι ἀφίει
εἰσω·

LXXVI

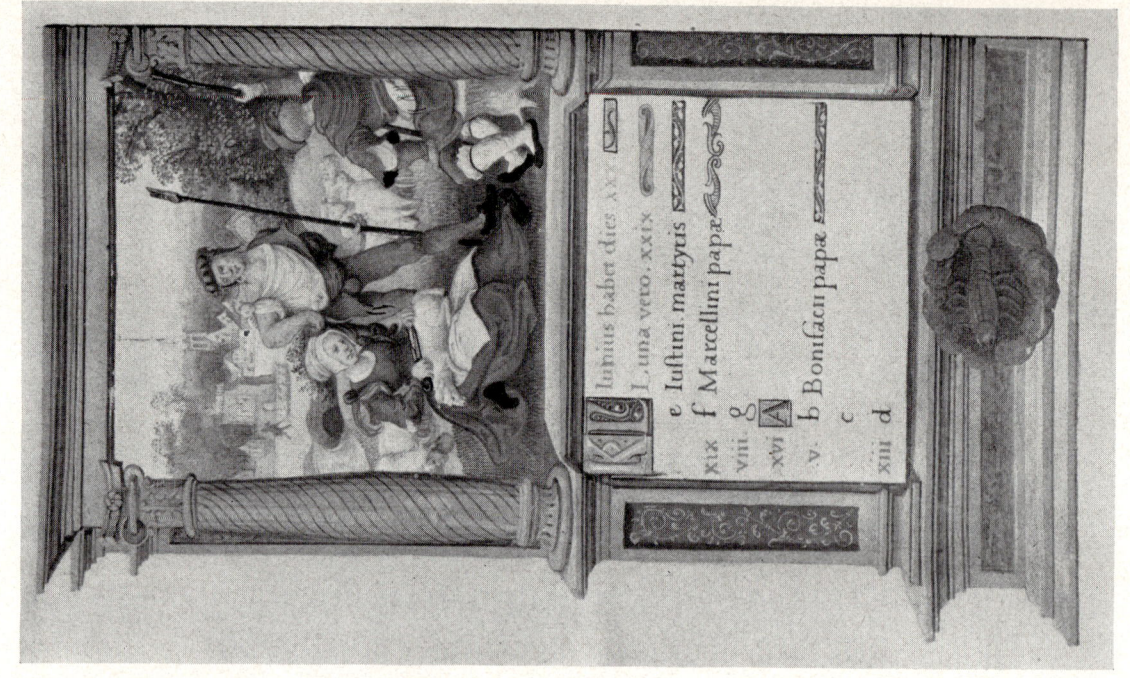

221

222

LXXVII

204

LXXVIII

206
At right, above: 214
At right, below: 203

LXXIX

212

LXXX

228